THEODOR HERZL

Theodor Herzl

The Charismatic Leader

❖❖❖

DEREK PENSLAR

Yale

UNIVERSITY

PRESS

New Haven and London

Yale University Press books may be purchased in quantity for educational,
business, or promotional use. For information, please e-mail sales.press@yale.edu
(U.S. office) or sales@yaleup.co.uk (U.K. office).

Set in Janson Oldstyle type by Integrated Publishing Solutions.
Printed in the United States of America.

Library of Congress Control Number: 2019944801
ISBN 978-0-300-18040-4 (hardcover : alk. paper)

A catalogue record for this book is available from the British Library.

This paper meets the requirements of ANSI/NISO Z39.48-1992
(Permanence of Paper).

10 9 8 7 6 5 4 3 2 1

Frontispiece: Theodor, Julie, and Jeanette Herzl with colleagues and their spouses
at Altaussee, 1902 (Austrian Archives / Imagno / picturedesk.com)

CONTENTS

_____

THEODOR HERZL

Introduction

THE LIFE OF Theodor Herzl (1860–1904) was as puzzling as it was brief. How did this cosmopolitan and assimilated European Jew become the leader of the Zionist movement? How could he be both an artist and a statesman, a rationalist and an aesthete, a stern moralist yet possessed of deep, and at times dark, passions? And why did scores of thousands of Jews, many of them from traditional, observant backgrounds, embrace Herzl as their leader? This book seeks to answer these questions.

Herzl's life illustrates that political leadership depends upon, and responds to, its following. This book examines Herzl's persona, but it also illustrates how he was perceived by others, and how others' perceptions shaped his sense of self. I shun a "great man" theory of history precisely because such an approach does not reveal the secrets of Herzl's greatness.

Mine is the latest in a long line of Herzl biographies. Some have depicted him as a larger-than-life figure, a prophet and martyr to his people, or as a major figure in the history of Jewish political thought. Others have taken a decidedly critical tone, focusing on Herzl's psychological torment, dysfunctional family, and rivalries with other Zionists.[1] I have learned a great deal from these books, but my approach is different. It avoids both hagiography and deconstruction. I see Herzl not as a great thinker but as a great leader, and I read his Zionist writings as manifestos, not treatises—calls to action, not rumination. Herzl was profoundly troubled, and those troubles help explain why he turned to Zionism, yet Herzl's inner demons do not explain how and why he was able to appeal to the masses and transform the Jewish world. Herzl was different things to different people, a screen onto which Jews projected their yearnings and aspirations. Herzl's status as an assimilated Jew who returned to his people, and as simultaneously an insider and outsider within European and Jewish society alike, enhanced his appeal to the Jewish masses. Last but not least, he was possessed of an electrifying charisma.

The early Zionist movement was particularly dependent upon charismatic leadership because it was small, weak, and scattered, without mechanisms of patronage or means of coercion. Herzl had nothing to offer his followers but hope and nothing to maintain their support but trust. Herzl's charisma was formidable, and he was well aware of his powers. But charisma is culturally specific. Had Herzl been dropped into a different era or continent he might not have been charismatic or prepossessing at all. Under different circumstances, Herzl might have been nothing more than a fanatical demi-intellectual, whiling away his days in cafés, scribbling feverishly in a diary.

Despite this book's attention to cultural context, I also emphasize Herzl's powerful will and his talent for self-fashioning. Herzl's provocative, flamboyant, and at times outrageous political speech and acts were carefully orchestrated. In this sense Herzl can be compared with another great leader of Jewish origin, Benjamin Disraeli, whose claim to be the natural leader of the English gentry was even more baseless and staggeringly audacious than Herzl's pretention to be a self-appointed guardian of the Jewish people.

This book centers around three interwoven themes: Herzl's inner life, his relationship with the Zionist movement, and his position in the world as a professional journalist and amateur statesman.

The first theme requires addressing head-on Herzl's psychological instability. Herzl suffered periodic bouts of depression and notable mood swings. He was self-absorbed and plagued by doubt and insecurity. Aloof and guarded, Herzl made few friends, and he never formed a healthy romantic relationship. His marriage was miserable, he was an absent father, and his three children all suffered from mental illness. Herzl's hagiographers have skirted around or glossed over these issues, and Herzl's critics have reveled in them, but it is not my intention to do either. Rather, I want to show how Herzl's psychological anguish nourished his political passion. Herzl desperately needed a project to fill his life with meaning and keep the blackness of depression at bay. Zionism was that project, which contained, sustained, and inspired him. Possessed of a prodigious work ethic, Herzl poured every ounce of his formidable energy into Zionist activity, which drained him physically and mentally, and contributed to his premature death.

In his book *A First-Rate Madness*, the psychiatrist Nassir Ghaemi writes that many of the greatest political leaders of modern times have suffered from mental illness. Analyzing the likes of Abraham Lincoln, Winston Churchill, Mohandas Gandhi, and Martin Luther King, Jr., Ghaemi depicts their struggles with anxiety and depression, even to the point of suicide attempts (as in the case of Gandhi and King). Although severe depression is debilitating, in its milder forms it can instill a sense of realism and capacities for resilience and empathy. These

3

leaders also had a penchant for hyperthymia, an exuberance that falls short of manic psychosis and can generate productive energy, creativity, and charismatic appeal.

I am not a psychotherapist, and in this book I do not attempt to diagnose Herzl from beyond the grave. I try to understand Herzl through his own eyes, relying on his own words and those of people who knew him. But without definitively claiming that Herzl suffered from what today would be called a mood or personality disorder, it is well documented (mostly by Herzl himself) that he often veered between depression and giddy excitement. Moreover, Ghaemi's main point appears to fit Herzl very well: "Our greatest crisis leaders toil in sadness when society is happy. . . . Sometimes they're up, sometimes they're down, but they're never quite well. Yet when calamity occurs, if they are in a position to act, they lift up the rest of us, they can give us the courage we may have temporarily lost, the fortitude that steadies us."[2]

In both his depressive tendencies and capacity for greatness, Herzl strongly resembled another modern leader, Winston Churchill. In a classic essay titled "Churchill's Black Dog," Anthony Storr notes that had Churchill "been a stable and equable man, he could never have inspired the nation." Churchill's triumphant moment in 1940, like Herzl's in 1896, occurred only because "all his life, he had conducted a battle with his own despair that made it possible to convey to others that despair can be overcome." Both men catapulted between self-deprecation and self-aggrandizement: Churchill was writing very much in a Herzlian mode when he claimed that "we are all worms. But I do believe that I am a glow-worm."[3]

For people like Herzl and Churchill, the aspiration to political leadership stems from something deeper than ambition for power or material gain. Rather, the belief in one's heroic mission is an expression of deep-seated psychic needs. Yet the would-be hero cannot achieve greatness without a following. This observation brings me to the second theme of the book: that the Zionist movement needed Herzl as much as Herzl needed it, and that Herzl's charisma both emanated from within him and was constructed from without.

In popular parlance, "charisma" is associated with charm, magnetism, and sex appeal, but according to the sociologist Max Weber, true charismatics are by definition political or religious leaders, not performers, and they attract followers, not fans. Weber defines charisma as "a certain quality of individual personality by virtue of which [the charismatic leader] is considered extraordinary and treated as endowed with supernatural, superhuman, or at least specifically exceptional powers or qualities."[4] Charismatic authority asserts itself only in times of collective distress and in environments where traditional or bureaucratic-statist power structures are weak or nonexistent. The charismatic leader does not simply respond to peoples' expectations but elevates them, inspiring them to hope for what they had considered impossible. The charismatic allays the anxiety of the fearful, raises the self-worth of the oppressed, and channels their rage into purposeful collective activity.

Herzl perfectly fit the mold of a charismatic leader. The Zionist movement arose at a time when traditional rabbinic authority was in crisis and the modern state had failed to protect the physical security and psychological well-being of great swathes of European Jewry. Herzl emerged from outside the traditional centers of Jewish power: the rabbinate and the Jewish financial elite. He claimed authority to act as an agent on behalf of the entire Jewish people and created the Zionist Organization with himself as its self-appointed head, not subject to recall. He captured and represented Jews' longings through the convening of annual Zionist Congresses, which Herzl's lieutenant, the celebrated writer Max Nordau, passionately depicted as "the autonomous parliament of the Jewish Risorgimento" and "the authorized, legitimate, representative of the Jewish people."[5]

Herzl's charisma manifested itself in his stately carriage, his baritone voice and elegant German, and, most important, his beauty. In a 1937 essay titled "What Did Herzl Look Like?" Samuel Bettelheim describes Herzl's visage as combining aspects of an English lord and east European rabbi "in his Jerusalemite glory." The First Zionist Congress, writes Bettelheim, would have had little import had there not sat in the Congress president's chair a man who was no less than "a miracle . . . as if King Solomon had arisen from his grave, because he could no longer bear the suffering of his people and its humiliation."[6] Many an observer was fascinated by Herzl's "Assyrian" beard, which bestowed upon him the look of ancient Semitic royalty. The artist Ephraim Lilien depicted Herzl as Moses, that prince of Egypt who rejoined and redeemed his people, and also as the biblical figures Jacob, Aaron, Joshua, David, Solomon, and Hezekiah. But Bettelheim, like most who recorded their impressions of Herzl, was especially drawn to Herzl's eyes: "large and circular," darkly tinted yet endowed with a "mysterious light" that captivated world leaders and common folk alike. "Herzl's eyes were of enormous expressive power. Often in speech he lost himself in infinite distance, as if he saw things that were insensible to us, and in the next moment fixed his forceful gaze upon his interlocutor." It was a gaze filled with "nobility, power, spirit, genius and goodness. He never displayed indecisiveness or resignation: the greater the obstacle or danger, the sharper was his eagle's gaze."[7]

There are two types of charismatic political leaders—those whose warmth and charm make their followers feel important and esteemed, and those who are cool and distant from others yet inspire adulation and veneration, which in turn generate solidarity and hope. Herzl was the second type. As the Bohemian Zionist activist Berthold Feiwel put it, "In our earliest youth he [Herzl] signified all beauty and greatness. We, the young, had been yearning for a prophet, a leader. We created him with our longing."[8] His position as a secular, assimilated, Western Jew, alien to the world of traditional Jewish practice and culture, enhanced his charismatic appeal to eastern European Jews who could never have accepted one of their own as he would have been so utterly familiar. He was seen as a latter-day Moses, a prince raised in the court of the Pharaoh who was called to return to his people and lead them out of bondage. Veteran Zionist activists from eastern Europe were irked by Herzl's Judaic ignorance and autocratic style, yet it was Herzl, not they, who captured the attention of scores of thousands of eastern European Jews, dazzled them with his very strangeness, and replenished their self-esteem.

Herzl's charismatic powers had their limits. By the time of his death, less than 1 percent of world Jewry was officially affiliated with the Zionist Organization, and Herzlian Zionism provoked considerable opposition. Most Orthodox Jews dismissed it as blasphemous. Jewish socialists called it utopian, preferring what they thought to be the far more realistic scenario of a revolution that would put an end to economic oppression and to the antisemitism that it nurtured. Assimilated Jews, who claimed to be firmly rooted in their homelands, found Herzl ridiculous and even embarrassing. Yet his message of Jewish national liberation, enunciated with mesmerizing oratory or couched in finely polished prose, struck a chord with many Jews, and it is not difficult to understand why.

It is more of a challenge to explain how Herzl managed to become a figure in the international arena who, over the space of a few years, managed to gain access to the German kaiser, the Ottoman sultan, the kings of Italy and Bulgaria, the British foreign and colonial secretaries, the Russian interior and finance ministers, and the pope. This leads to the book's third theme: Herzl's presence on the world stage and his geopolitical ideas.

Herzl's charisma was only one factor behind his access to world leaders. Herzl charmed the German ambassador to Vienna, Philipp zu Eulenburg, but most leaders were not so much captivated by Herzl as they were interested in the practical benefits he could bring them. To the Ottoman sultan Herzl offered promises of vast sums of Jewish banking capital that could restructure the empire's swollen sovereign debt. To the German kaiser and Russian government Herzl promised to get rid of their unwanted Jews and the revolutionary movements with which Jews were closely identified. To the British government Herzl offered Jews as loyal colonial servants in a British protectorate over Palestine, a nearby territory, or even British East Africa. All of these promises were based in fantasies about Jewish power, fantasies in which Herzl himself appeared to believe.

Whether or not the stories Herzl spun were grounded in reality, he was in an excellent position to get them heard, because he was one of Europe's most prominent journalists. Between 1891 and 1895, Herzl was the Paris correspondent of central Europe's most prestigious newspaper, *Die Neue Freie Presse*, and he was the newspaper's literary editor from 1895 until his death in 1904. In an era when newspapers were the most common means by which the political elite presented itself to the public, attentive and influential journalists were valuable commodities. Herzl was on good terms with two of Austria's prime ministers, who kept him abreast of the empire's nationality conflicts and sought his assistance in dampening them. At the outset of his Zionist career, Herzl gave a flattering interview to the Ottoman grand vizier, whom Herzl allowed to downplay his government's atrocities against the Armenians.

Thanks to his profession and his wide-ranging reading, Herzl was intimately familiar with the geopolitical machinations of the European powers. Much as he loved to play at diplomacy, however, he did not play it very well. Time and time again, Herzl was manipulated or rebuffed, as his interlocutors concluded that Herzl could not deliver what he promised, or that a mass migration of Jews to Palestine would not work to their benefit. Herzl himself was capable of duplicity and opportunism, as he attempted simultaneously to win the protection of a European Great Power over Palestine while appealing for Ottoman support in the name of preventing the empire's dissolution.

Herzl took pride in Europe's conquest of Africa and Asia, and he believed that the Jews had a civilizing mission in Palestine. Herzl's attitudes about Palestine's Arabs, and about indigenous peoples in general, were complex and contradictory: shot through with paternalistic and colonialist sensibilities, at times haughty and harsh, yet also empathetic and humanitarian. Herzl occasionally indulged in fantasies of gunboat diplomacy, but at its heart Herzl's Zionism was about the creation of a model community that, as depicted in his novel *Altneuland* (Old-Newland), welcomed natives as equals and had no military. As much as Herzl strove to evacuate Europe's persecuted Jews to safety, he wanted to move them to a land that would possess all of Europe's cultural riches but none of its hatreds or inequities. It would be admired and respected by its Middle Eastern neighbors and by the European countries that had previously scorned their Jews.

A word about the sources upon which this book is based: For a biographer, a glut of sources is both a blessing and a curse. In addition to hundreds of journalistic pieces published in his own lifetime, Herzl kept a diary from 1882 to 1885, and some six thousand letters written by Herzl over the course of his life have survived. (The diary and letters were published in a seven-volume German edition between 1983 and 1996.) The source most commonly cited by Herzl's biographers has been what Herzl called his "Zionist diaries," which were composed between the time of his turn to Zionism in 1895 and his death in 1904. The Zionist diaries are an essential yet problematic source. On the one hand, the diaries appear to offer expressions of Herzl's innermost feelings, but on the other hand, the diaries are filled with invented dialogue and drafts or copies of political statements. At the beginning of the diaries, Herzl wrote that he hoped they would be published as a testimony to "what I had to put up with, who have been the enemies of my plan, and, on the other hand, who stood by me." As I read the diaries, I kept in mind Georges Gusdorf's observation that autobiographers are "not engaged in an objective and disinterested pursuit but in a work of personal justification." Like an autobiography, Herzl's diary purports to offer a faithful account of a person's life while giving that life structure and a morally meaningful narrative arc. "The truth of the facts," writes Gusdorf, "is subordinate to the truth of the man."[9] In biography, unlike autobiography, the bar is somewhat higher, as the biographer must strive to ascertain both the truth of the facts and the truth of the person. I hope to show in the pages that follow that humans, even great leaders, create their own truth not out of thin air but in response to their inner selves, environment, and interactions with others.

1

Becoming Theodor Herzl

To ONE WHO BELIEVES in destiny, the names given to Theodor Herzl at birth seem to have determined that he would be a great leader. Herzl's given name, Theodor, and its Hungarian equivalent, Tivadar, mean "gift from God" (*theos*, "God" + *doron*, "gift"). In time, many of Herzl's followers, and even Herzl himself, would come to see him in messianic terms. On the other hand, Herzl's Hebrew name, Benjamin Zev, refers to the youngest child of the biblical patriarch Jacob, who in his deathbed blessing of his children in the biblical book of Genesis likens Benjamin to a "ravenous wolf [*zev*]." In Jewish tradition, the name Zev connotes strength and courage, not destructive power. But Herzl's opponents, from his day to our own, would depict him as a threat to what they cherished most—be it Jewish sacred law, or the Jews' integration into their home countries, or the triumph of universalism over particularism, or the rights of the Palestinians in their struggle against Israel.

Despite the legends that grew up about him in his own lifetime and after his death, Herzl was all too human. He was intelligent and talented, but he also suffered from psychological turmoil, for which he compensated with outward displays of energy, wit, and charm. Herzl possessed great beauty and extraordinary charisma, yet his rise to greatness was the result of happenstance more than design. For the first thirty years of his life, Herzl was a rather ordinary and typical representative of the central European Jewish upper-middle class.

Herzl came into the world at an auspicious time for central Europe and its Jews. He was born on 2 May 1860, in the Hungarian city of Pest, across the Danube from Buda. Just a dozen years before his birth, Hungary, like much of Europe, had been convulsed by revolutions that combined nationalism with liberalism, proclaiming that the rights of the individual could only be realized within independent and united nation-states. The same movements that aspired to create modern Italy, Germany, and Hungary also championed the rights of people to live, work, and think as they pleased. An important component of these revolutions was emancipation of the Jews, whose choice of residence and occupation had for centuries been severely restricted. The revolutions failed, but nonetheless liberalism and the cause of Jewish rights continued to advance. When Herzl was seven, the Hapsburg Empire became a constitutional union in which the kingdoms of Austria and Hungary had equal status. In this new entity, known as Austria-Hungary or the Dual Monarchy, Jews were fully emancipated. In 1873, Buda and Pest merged to form the metropolis of Budapest, home to almost two hundred thousand people, of whom 16 percent were Jews. The city's population grew rapidly, but its Jewish population shot up at an even faster rate, and Budapest's Jews enjoyed expanding access to higher education and professions such as law and medicine.

The story of Herzl's family ancestors is one of movement from the Hapsburg Empire's periphery to its center, from poverty to affluence, and from strict to attenuated religious observance. The roots of Herzl's family lie in Bohemia, Moravia, and Silesia. In the eighteenth century, the ancestors of Herzl's paternal grandfather, Simon Loeb Herzl, moved to a region that would shift over time between Turkish, Austrian, and eventually Serbian control. Simon hailed from Semlin, a town across the Sava River from Belgrade. Simon's son Jakob left Semlin at the age of seventeen, and by the time he was twenty-three he was an established businessman in Budapest with sufficient wealth and promise to win the hand of Jeanette Diamant, the daughter of Hermann Diamant, a wealthy textile merchant from Pest. Jakob went into banking, in which he enjoyed considerable success, only to lose a good deal of his fortune in the stock market crash of 1873. Despite this reversal, Jakob and Jeanette remained well-off and raised their children Pauline and Theodor in comfort.

Theodor Herzl liked to tell a rather different story of his family background. He related to his first biographer, Reuven Brainin, that on his father's side he was descended from one of a pair of Spanish Jews who were compelled by the Inquisition to convert to Christianity and become monks. They rose high in their order yet secretly remained loyal to the faith of their fathers. Assigned to travel on monastic business to Innsbruck, they escaped the clutches of the Church and returned to the Jewish fold. The story says a good deal about Herzl as an individual—his capacity for self-fashioning, and his own successes in the Gentile world, translated here from the newspaper to the monastery. But the story is also deeply indicative of Herzl's milieu, that of upwardly mobile Ashkenazic Jews in the second half of the nineteenth century. Although most central European Jews did not go so far as to fabricate a family tree, they venerated medieval Sephardic Jewry as a model of success, integration, and refinement. Hearkening to the distant Sephardic past was a means of deflecting attention from their immediate ancestors, who were Yiddish-speaking craftsmen, peddlers, and livestock traders from the backwaters of eastern Europe.

Jakob Herzl was a stolid, somewhat stiff, yet kindhearted man who adored Jeanette and his children. Jakob was in awe of Jeanette, who was far better educated than he, and who was steeped in Germanic culture. As was so often the case in bourgeois, especially Jewish, families of that time and place, Jakob left the management of the household and the upbringing of the children to their mother. Ambitious and strong willed, Jeanette ensured that the children would be impeccably educated and groomed. When Theodor was five and Pauline six, Jeanette hired a private tutor to devote a full year to preparing the children for the rigors of primary school. Over the course of Theodor's life, Jeanette would stand over his shoulder as a powerful, even domineering, presence.

Herzl's first home was next to the Dohany Street synagogue, an imposing neo-Moorish structure that had been completed the year before Herzl's birth. Later in life, Herzl referred to having attended that synagogue with his father. But the level of Herzl's childhood exposure to Judaism remains something of a mystery. Between the ages of six and ten Herzl attended a Jewish school, where he studied Hebrew and religion alongside math, science, and modern languages. It is likely that Herzl's parents sent him to the school more for its academic reputation than for its Judaic focus. Jeanette had inherited her father's stringent anticlericalism, although her uncle Samuel Bilitz emigrated to Jerusalem, most likely out of religious devotion. As a child in Semlin, Jakob had a traditional Jewish upbringing, but as an adult Jakob's religious observance was perfunctory, inspired by filial piety, not vibrant faith. Jakob's father Simon presents a more interesting case. Unlike his two brothers, who converted to Christianity, Simon remained strictly Orthodox.

What's more, Simon was inspired by the Semlin community's rabbi, the proto-Zionist luminary Yehuda Alkalai. Alkalai believed that the messianic age was at hand, but that for it to unfold the Jews must take active steps to return en masse to Eretz Israel. Since Simon regularly visited the Herzl household and died when Herzl was nineteen, it stands to reason that Simon would have told his grandson about Alkalai and the Return to Zion, yet in his voluminous life writings Herzl barely mentions his grandfather, let alone his proto-Zionist ideas.

Nor does Herzl mention having had a bar mitzvah. There are archival records of invitations for a "confirmation" ceremony to be held at the Herzl family home on 10 May 1873. At that time Budapest was suffering a cholera outbreak, which would have led people to shun congregating in public spaces. Jakob's financial misfortunes may have also played a role in transforming the bar mitzvah from a synagogue service to a family party. Nonetheless, Herzl's paternal uncle Max wrote in 1910 that on the occasion of his bar mitzvah Herzl chanted haftarah (a reading from the biblical prophets) in the Dohany Street synagogue and gave a speech. Given Herzl's love of drama, it is likely that had such a thing happened, Herzl would have at some later date referred to what would have been a debut public performance. Had he delivered the customary commentary on the Torah and prophetic readings for that week, Herzl would probably have faced considerable challenges composing it. The Torah portion, Tazria-Metzora (in Leviticus), goes into minute detail about skin diseases and ritual impurity, and that portion's haftarah, taken from the second book of Kings, tells the story of an Aramean warrior who is afflicted with a skin ailment but is miraculously cured after immersing himself in the Jordan River in the presence of the prophet Elisha. Not only would Herzl have had to deal with one of the Torah's more arcane sections, he would have been under considerable pressure to please his mother, who was a rationalist and skeptic, and would have regarded these biblical stories as atavistic superstition.

Herzl's diaries from his adulthood are rich in detail and filled with revealing personal admissions, so the silence about religious influences or knowledge is telling. At the outset of his Zionist career, Herzl encountered criticism of his pamphlet *The Jewish State* from Vienna's chief rabbi, Moritz Güdemann, who supplied rabbinic texts abjuring an organized return of Jews to the land of Israel. Herzl could offer only the weak rejoinder "that it would be possible to find at least an equal number in favor of Zionism. To be sure, I am too ignorant to supply them."[1] Herzl told Reuven Brainin that he first heard about the Exodus as a schoolboy but then later read about it in a book of Jewish legends that he received as a bar mitzvah gift. It was this version, not the biblical one, that Herzl found riveting and compelling. He blended together in his mind aspects of the Exodus story with that of the Messiah and felt compelled to write a poem about it, but he was afraid to tell his schoolmates about his fervid thoughts lest they taunt him as what Herzl called a "man of dreams." Sometime after that, Herzl relates, he dreamed that he beheld the Messiah, venerable and majestic, who took Herzl up in his arms into the heavens, where they encountered Moses (who, in Herzl's description, bore a striking resemblance to Michelangelo's famous statue of the prophet). The Messiah then said to Moses, "for this child I have prayed!"

One wonders, if Herzl truly had this dream, how he could have recalled it so clearly across a span of thirty years, and if as a child he was in fact familiar with biblical phrases such as "a man of dreams" (Joseph, as described by his jealous brothers) or "for this child I have prayed" (from the encounter between Hannah and the priest Eli before the birth of Hannah's son, the prophet Samuel). We have already seen that Herzl had a penchant for creating stories about himself. And since Herzl was derided by his critics as a man possessed by lunatic dreams, and hailed by his followers as the one for whom they had prayed, Herzl may have been engaging in conscious fabrication. Or maybe not. Over time, memory fades, but it can also sharpen and reconfigure experience. Herzl himself, whose life was devoted to acting out a dream, may not have easily distinguished between an event and its embellishment. What's more, great leaders and liberators enthralled the young Herzl. As a teenager, Herzl wrote essays praising Muhammad, the Florentine demagogue Girolamo Savonarola, Martin Luther, and Napoleon, each of whom, in his own way, was a revolutionary. Herzl's dream of his encounter with Moses and the Messiah has been cited by Orthodox-Jewish Zionists as proof of Herzl's deep-seated religiosity, but perhaps it is more indicative of a rebellious spirit and a yearning for achievement that were formed early in life.

At thirteen, Herzl wrote an essay titled "Social Relations of Ancient Peoples," in which he described the function of religion in purely socioeconomic and psychological terms. In ancient societies, he wrote, "civil positions were closely tied to their relationship with religion. The members of one religion persecuted the believers of another religion and did not allow them to hold civil service jobs."[2] Religion, the precocious youngster reckoned, offered rationalizations for social exclusion, but, he noted, it also provided individuals and groups with the strength to overcome adversity.

Herzl's first essays, which may have been written for school assignments or for pleasure, were carefully composed, in both Hungarian and German, with multiple drafts and substantial textual variations. Young Herzl also experimented with genres as varied as literary criticism, satire, translations, and poetry. Even if one discounts claims of continuity between the content of these precocious sallies and Herzl's adult intellectual development, the diligence, polish, and range that Herzl brought to bear on his writing certainly portended Herzl's future literary success and his astonishing fluency as a Zionist spokesman.

Not surprisingly, Herzl absorbed information like a sponge, although his academic strengths and performance were far from uniform. In 1870, he completed the first round of his formal education and moved to a technically oriented school known as a *förealtanoda*. Herzl was a mediocre student in science and technology, and he was terrible at drawing and design. After enduring two unhappy years at the school he spent a year receiving instruction at home, while remaining enrolled and submitting assignments to his teachers. Herzl returned to the school in the fall of 1873, only to miss much of the spring term for unknown reasons. In the middle of the 1874–75 academic year, Jakob and Jeanette pulled the suffering lad out of the school altogether and, after another period of home tutoring, moved him to a language- and humanities-oriented institution, the Evangelical Humanistic High Gymnasium of the Augustinian Confession of Pest. (Despite the school's name, its student body was largely Jewish.) Herzl's marks improved, particularly in Hungarian, German, Latin, and algebra. He also did very well in Greek, history, and geography. While in high school, Herzl improved his French to near fluency and gained a command of Italian and English. Herzl's marks began to slide, however, as he got increasingly involved in literary activity and journalism. At seventeen, he published an essay in the *Pester Lloyd*, a prestigious German-language newspaper, and he went on to publish several book reviews in another newspaper, the *Pester Journal*.

Already in his early teens Herzl displayed a taste for leadership as well as journalism. When just shy of fourteen, he established a literary society whose members consisted of his sister, his cousin, and a few friends. Herzl grandly called it "WIR" (WE), proclaimed himself to be its president, and composed its lengthy and detailed bylaws. In this instance and more generally, Herzl's attitude toward his peers was cordial yet slightly condescending; he appeared poised and in command, yet also aloof and guarded. We get a glimpse into what lay underneath Herzl's distant pose from his play *Die Ritter vom Gemeinplatz* (The Chevaliers of Platitudes), which Herzl began to write during the summer after completing high school. The play's hero is a man of great integrity and courage who controls his passions, displaying what Herzl called "icy calm" under the most difficult of conditions. Striving to control one's emotions in this manner is common among adolescents, who seethe with feelings and physical desires. The yearning of a hormonally ravaged youth to be in control, to not feel lest he be rejected or hurt, accounts for the popularity of modern fictional characters ranging from Sherlock Holmes to Mr. Spock. It certainly helps us understand young Herzl, who in his later teens encountered two devastating emotional blows: an unrequited schoolboy crush on a girl who later died, and the death of his beloved sister Pauline.

In a diary that Herzl kept in his twenties, he writes of his love as a teenager of one Madeleine Herz. Herzl writes that he dared not speak to her but instead worshipped her from afar: "I hid my love from its object with greater fear than that of a poacher who hides a slain deer from the hunter's watchful eyes."[3] (This is indeed an odd metaphor for love, which becomes a source of guilt and shame if Herzl is the poacher, Madeleine is the hunter, and his feelings for her are the slain animal.) What must have made Herzl's love for Madeleine even more painful is that the Herz and Herzl families knew each other and met on social occasions. Herzl and Madeleine met in 1875, shortly after he moved to the Evangelical Humanistic High School. They were both fifteen. She was blond-haired, blue-eyed, and enchanting. At a family event, Herzl held Madeleine's two-year-old niece, Magda, in his arms. Madeleine and

Pauline were in contact when Herzl's first journalistic piece was published in the *Pester Lloyd*. Madeleine moved to Vienna in 1878, the same year that the Herzls also moved to the imperial capital, but we do not know if they continued to see each other. The unconsummated relationship intensified Herzl's romantic, poetic, and melancholy nature, and Herzl lost her altogether when, tragically, Madeleine died in 1880 at the age of twenty. Six years later, Herzl wrote that the encounter with Madeleine "was the first and only time in my life that I was truly in love . . . from that time on, only stupid, self-delusional, little feelings, without any real momentum. Never since have I felt my heart beat so anxiously and fast."[4]

Herzl was even more deeply affected by the loss of Pauline, who died of typhoid fever in February of 1878. Pauline's death devastated Herzl, as revealed in a hastily written essay in 1882:

> The first true great grief of my life. . . . [At the funeral] my father, mother and I slowly walked behind the slow-moving hearse. In it lay my dead sister, whose mouth I would never again seal with a brotherly kiss to make up after a mock quarrel. I vaguely felt how hard that was going to be, but the people by the wayside stopped to watch us, and somehow that seemed to comfort me a little as I led my father by the arm. He stumbled along, all but doubled over, and he has remained so ever since. . . . Eight days later we left town, settled in a large city which I had always been longing for. . . . There my mother at last found the tears she had so long kept back. My father and I finally succeeded in changing her sighs into sobs, her sobs into incessant crying that went on for years. What did my father do with his tears in the meantime? . . . But now that even my mother has calmed down somewhat, it is my turn. Now my tears are flowing, and I am mourning my sister, who certainly deserved to be mourned.[5]

In an autobiographical sketch written in 1898, Herzl focused entirely on his mother's grief as the reason for his family's sudden move from Budapest to Vienna shortly after Pauline's funeral. Now a public figure, and an aspiring world leader, his "icy calm" persona concealed the grief that he had expressed sixteen years previously. But the grief never completely passed, and his memory blended together the memory of Pauline and that of Madeleine, and hence familial and erotic love. Herzl mistakenly recalled Madeleine's death as taking place in February of 1878, the same time as Pauline's, but in fact she died on 16 November 1880, as per her death notice in the following day's issue of the *Neue Freie Presse.*[6]

Before Pauline's death, Herzl's family had already been planning on moving to Vienna for the sake of the children's educational and career prospects. Pauline was a budding actress, and the Magyar theater offered fewer opportunities than Vienna provided. Similarly, Herzl could better pursue his literary ambitions in Vienna. He also planned to study law in university, and the law faculty in Budapest was already suffused with antisemitism, whereas that was not the case in Vienna. Pauline's demise, however, transformed a rational strategy into an emotional outburst, and Jeanette insisted that the family leave Budapest at the first opportunity. The Herzls settled in a comfortable home in the Praterstrasse, in Vienna's Second District, east of the inner city, and home to some eighty thousand Jews. Gustav Mahler lived just a few doors away, and both Arthur Schnitzler and Sigmund Freud had grown up nearby.

Because Herzl had been torn from Budapest before completing high school, he had to finish his studies independently and return to Budapest three months after the move to take his final examinations, which he barely passed. Under the circumstances, his poor performance was understandable. Yet, as an omen of Herzl's future refusal to admit failure, and of his ability to endure grueling workloads and maintain his cool under adverse conditions, Herzl did much better on the national matriculation examination, the *matura*, a seven-day battery of written and oral tests. Based on his performance he was admitted to the faculty of law at the University of Vienna for the 1878–79 academic year.

Despite the tragedy that brought him to Vienna, Herzl was thrilled to be in the cultural capital of German-speaking Europe, and when he enrolled in university he had much more than scholarship on his mind. He was an aspiring playwright and journalist, and his publications to date had all been in German. Surprisingly, although Herzl listed German as his mother tongue in his first semester at university, in the following term he switched it to Hungarian and kept it that way for two years before returning to German. As a child, Herzl's very first letters to his parents had been written in both German and Hungarian, but by his teens he wrote to them only in German, and it is highly likely that he spoke to them mostly, if not exclusively, in that language. Herzl spoke Hungarian at school, but there is little reason to believe he would have considered it his mother tongue. It is probable, therefore, that there were purely instrumental or bureaucratic reasons for Herzl's decision to list Hungarian as his mother tongue over the bulk of his university career.

As soon as he got to university, Herzl publicly and consistently identified with German nationalism. Upon visiting Budapest in 1881, Herzl wrote that he had become alienated from the city and its language. Budapest appeared small and provincial; "over the time of my absence Hungary has become much more Hungarian." Herzl mocked Germanophone Jews who were determined to Magyarize, swap German names for Hungarian ones, and break their teeth on the language. "Here," notes Herzl wryly, "I have consistently spoken not a word of Hungarian."[7] There is, however, evidence suggesting that Herzl remained deeply bound to the Hungarian language. In his youth, Herzl addressed his parents in writing as Mama and

Papa, but in adulthood he switched to the Hungarian diminutives *mamakam* and *papakam*.

At university, Herzl read widely in legal history and philosophy. He took four courses from Lorenz von Stein, a moderate conservative who may have influenced Herzl's later thinking about the ravages of industrialization and the need to steer a middle path between unrestrained capitalism and revolutionary socialism. Herzl also took courses from another social reformer, Anton Menger. Tellingly, Herzl's "youth diary" ends with a cluster of aphorisms taken from Stein's lectures, referencing Plato and leaving behind the humdrum reality of social practice for more ethereal pursuits: "At the basis of all that is perceived is an idea, and this is what I seek."[8] This rather anodyne statement testifies to Stein's debt to idealist philosophy and especially to Hegel, with whom he had studied. But for Herzl, ideas were akin to dreams; they were not abstract truths instantiated by human action so much as myths that drive men to do unprecedented, unheard of, and miraculous things. While he was at university, this aspect of Herzl's persona was still undeveloped, but it was present nonetheless.

Herzl faced the prospect of having his studies interrupted by a spell of military service. At the time, each half of the empire had its own national guard, the Austrian *Landwehr* and the Hungarian *honvéd*, as well as a common imperial armed force. As a Hungarian national, Herzl could not be conscripted into the *Landwehr*, but in November of 1879 he was called to appear before the 20th infantry regiment of the common army. Herzl put himself forward to be a "one-year volunteer," a privilege that was reserved for young men who had completed secondary school, and which usually involved a year of light duties, although in 1878 the army had seen real action during the occupation of Bosnia-Herzegovina, with thousands of casualties. The one-year position was preferable to a regular, much longer, term of service, and whereas ordinary draftees could be promoted only through the ranks for meritorious service, one-year volunteers could be considered immediately upon completion of their term for a prestigious reserve officer's commission. Unlike Prussia, where Jewish one-year volunteers rarely received commissions, in the Dual Monarchy they were common, and in 1900 Jews—who made up about 5 percent of the empire's population—made up almost a fifth of the army's reserve officer corps.

In January of 1880, the draft board declared Herzl unfit on unspecified medical grounds, and the decision was confirmed ten days later by a supervisory board. Undeterred, at the end of the year Herzl tried his luck again with a different infantry regiment, only to be again found unfit.[9] At that time, being rejected from the army on medical grounds was the norm, not the exception. In Austria-Hungary in 1875, almost two-thirds of called-up young men were turned away due to disease, injury, or stunted growth due to malnutrition. Some recruits, eager to avoid the draft, induced tachycardia by fasting or excessive caffeine consumption or even mutilated their hands. But Herzl was eager to serve and was a well-nourished, middle-class male, with no obvious illnesses. By the standards of his time and place, he was taller than average (5'8" versus the median height of 5'5"). Since there was apparently nothing visibly wrong with him, the most likely explanation for his rejection is that the medical examination picked up a heart murmur. (At the age of thirty-six, Herzl was diagnosed with what he described vaguely as a "heart ailment.")

Why did Herzl try so hard to be conscripted? We have no direct evidence to answer that question, but clues emerge from Herzl's experiences at university, where he developed an attachment to German nationalism, which he identified with manliness and strength of character. Early in his studies, Herzl joined a student union known as the *Akademische Lesehalle* (Academic

Reading Hall). The *Lesehalle* provided access to a large private library and to a variety of social clubs. It was not a political organization per se, but it was impossible at that time for student organizations in Austria to be immune to the nationality conflicts that were beginning to threaten the stability of the Dual Monarchy. At the University of Vienna, one student union supported Austria-Hungary as a dynastic, multinational empire, and another preached the supremacy of Austria's ethnic Germans and advocated close ties with the recently united German Empire. The *Lesehalle* stood somewhat between these two, but over the course of Herzl's first two years it moved decidedly in the direction of German nationalism. Herzl did not object. Quite the contrary: when in the fall of 1880 Herzl decided to join a fraternity, he avoided the ones with large numbers of Jews and non-Germans and put himself forward for admission to an unequivocally German-nationalist fraternity, Albia. Once provisionally accepted, Herzl immersed himself in fencing classes to prepare for the all-important rite of initiation, a duel that would only end when blood had been drawn. In the brief duel, fought on 11 May 1881, Herzl and his opponent both drew blood, and a photograph taken shortly afterwards showed Herzl with a sticking-plaster on his left cheek.

Herzl would have had the pleasure of dueling in any fraternity, but he identified with Albia's Germanophilia. Herzl did not particularly care about the political cause of ethnic Germans in Austria, but he intensely admired the Prussian nobility, which to him was the epitome of virility, discipline, and control over the passions. The Prussian chancellor, Otto von Bismarck, was his hero. We have already seen how as a teenager Herzl struggled to restrain his feelings. This conflict persisted into his late adolescence and early adulthood. Herzl berated himself for what he called an "unhealthy" surfeit of feeling. Those emotions included fear and anxiety, which Herzl considered ignoble, and he accused himself of cowardice when, in 1885, he extracted himself from a duel in order to attend to his father, who had fallen gravely ill.

Herzl was contending with a European political atmosphere that, from the 1870s on, grew increasingly antisemitic. Antisemites routinely depicted Jewish men as physically weak, lacking bravery and resolve, and prone to nervous disorders. Many central European Jews who were eager for social acceptance were willing to blame themselves for the animus directed against them. Herzl was one of them, and Albia represented the means to overcome Jewishness in what Herzl considered an honorable fashion.

It is a sign of both Herzl's attempts to escape from being Jewish and the futility of that effort that the sobriquet he chose while in Albia was Tancred—the name of an Italo-Norman Crusader warrior who became known as the Prince of the Galilee. Adopting the name of a noble Gentile who conquered Palestine is all the more significant when one considers that Herzl may have been aware of Benjamin Disraeli's 1847 novel of that name, which tells the story of a young British aristocrat who journeys to Palestine and who supports the restoration of the Jews to their ancient homeland. Underneath Herzl's idolization of warriors like Bismarck and Tancred was a devotion to, even an obsession with, personal honor. Striving to be a man of honor, Herzl did not mind the anti-Jewish barbs that saturated Albia's beery, German chauvinist air as long as he was accorded respect and the chance to prove his worth. As Albia became increasingly and virulently antisemitic, however, Herzl felt that he had been robbed of the opportunity to distinguish himself from other Jews, and in 1883 he submitted his resignation.

In the year before completing his doctorate in law in 1883, Herzl began to keep a diary in which he recorded his knowledge and concerns about the Jews. Eugen Dühring's splenetic 1881 book, *The Jewish Question as a Racial, Moral and Cultural Question*, infuriated him. Herzl himself was capable of describing Jews in unflattering terms; when his first play, *Tabarin,* premiered in New York City in 1885 and a celebration was held in his honor at the home of one of his father's colleagues in Berlin, Herzl described the attendees to his parents as "thirty or forty little, ugly Jews and Jewesses. Not a very comforting sight."[10] This startling barb may well have been meant as a joke—the sort of self-mockery that members of an ethnic or racial community feel comfortable engaging in among their own kind, but against which they would take offense if it came from outside their group.

With his peers, Herzl affected a witty, wry, and somewhat detached manner. He labored to appear nonchalant. Yet in fact he was tightly wound and plagued by bursts of melancholy. His first recorded depressive episode came in September of 1879, when, paraphrasing Goethe's play *Egmont,* Herzl described himself as "crying out to the heavens, up one moment, down the next, despondent unto death."[11] Four years later, in the wake of his resignation from Albia, the unhappy end of a love affair, and rejections of his first plays, Herzl claimed he was "overcome by the hopelessness of my existence. . . . Yet I need success. I thrive only on success."[12] That success could only come from the theater, not from the practice of law. After completing his university degree, Herzl dutifully worked in Vienna and Salzburg as a state attorney, but he found the work tedious and unsatisfying.

Years later, Herzl would write that he was happy in Salzburg and would have continued to work in law but for antisemitism, which would have limited his career prospects. That motivation was never mentioned in Herzl's extensive correspondence from the time with a friend from university, Heinrich Kana, with whom Herzl formed, for the first time in his life, an intimate and unguarded relationship outside the circle of his immediate family. "I am open (foolish and vain) with only one, sole person, and that is you," Herzl confided to Kana, although Herzl's frank admissions were never completely free from mannerism and studied wit: "It seems that you have still not found the key to my character, perhaps because I make a show of presenting myself as wide open. I do not always speak the truth, not even often. Yet I am a sincere animal. (And if I often lie, I never do so if there is no apparent advantage in it.)"[13]

Kana's friendship helped sustain Herzl, as did unconditional love from his doting parents, who supported Herzl while he was a struggling playwright and paid for long jaunts throughout Europe. In his mid-twenties, Herzl insisted that his parents write to him every day, yet Herzl was not willing to return even half the favor. In response to a request to write every other day, Herzl declared to his parents that he would not write to them on a regular basis: "Believe me, it is for the best."[14] But when he needed their attention, he wrote daily, as when he visited Berlin toward the end of 1885 to try to gain a foothold in journalism and theater in the imperial capital.

Herzl was a self-centered and overwrought young man, but he possessed a surprising inner strength. Although he was not a particularly diligent student, once he left university and set about trying to break into theater, he displayed a prodigious work ethic. Herzl became a workaholic, composing plays and essays at a furious rate and complaining to his parents about a chronic lack of sleep. By March of 1887 Herzl had reached the point where his "wild and exhausting" working habits had brought him to the brink of nervous collapse. But he did not collapse; instead, he restored himself through travel. For Herzl, travel was both a stimulus and a balm. It inspired some of his finest writing, but it also gave him opportunities to slow down, reflect, and drop the mask of insouciance that was such a heavy burden. Herzl was a lonely man, yet he was also resolutely capable of being alone. "When one is alone so much, for such uninterrupted periods," he wrote his parents, "one naturally has time and opportunity to reflect. Indeed, today I am a more serious and thoughtful person than ever before. I understand more about life, understand it more thoroughly, than previously."[15]

One important aspect of life that Herzl never understood was how to relate to women. He was trapped in the all-too-common bourgeois stereotype that divided women into two types: those who were virginal and pure, and those possessed of "easy virtue," suitable to be objects of the basest sexual desires. While in university and shortly after graduating, Herzl had some dalliances with prostitutes and a shop girl. In June of 1880 he contracted gonorrhea, and in a letter to Kana, he referred to its painful symptoms as well as the standard treatment (zinc sulfate). Zinc sulfate was not medically efficacious, but Herzl appears not to have suffered long-term complications such as infertility. (He later fathered three children.)

Herzl continued to have affairs, but he developed profound anxiety about the sexual act. In a letter to Kana in 1882, Herzl offered a particularly graphic comparison between writing a novel and prolonged intercourse: "The first two-three chapters were fun for him, but now [the author] realizes the all too demanding damsel wants to go on being screwed to Chapter Twelve. The poor though grateful boy's strength threatens to give out, but he spurs and whips himself on to constantly new deeds, so as to help his muse reach the ecstatic seizure she lusts for." Herzl concludes: "I'll tell you this much—from experience on both ends—both a love affair and a novel can wear you down."[16] Herzl would eventually write a novel—a work that would be his greatest solace as his Zionist diplomatic efforts went awry—but evidence from his diaries and correspondence suggests that he gave up on erotic love, marital or otherwise, and contented himself with fantasies of unattainable young women, and even of barely pubescent girls.

In 1882, while visiting Budapest on the anniversary of Pauline's death, Herzl developed a strong attraction to his sixteen-year-old cousin. The timing of the visit and Herzl's arousal may not have been coincidental. Herzl's confusion of brotherly and erotic love was more clearly on display when, while on a train in the Swiss Alps in August of 1883, he noticed a young French woman who reminded him of his sister:

> Her light-brown complexion shone in just the same pearly way, so modest and clever were her eyes, now forever closed, that looked upon the world, which was so much better than today. And just so she lifted a white veil on her lovely face. The white veil deeply touched me. . . . [Her] young husband threw me a dirty look, because I was incessantly gazing at his wife. What I would have given for such a foolish fellow to be my brother-in-law! She would live. I would have compelled him to treat her right. . . . For naught is my heart suited like no other for the feelings of an uncle. Others enjoy this happiness in full measure and don't understand it at all.[17]

The woman's resemblance to Pauline dampened Herzl's romantic ardor. Avatars of Madeleine Herz, however, had a more variable effect on him. Sometimes it was relatively innocent, as with a "little blond, clever-eyed" girl whom Herzl met on a train in Bavaria, and who caused him to see "the poetry of travel . . . through the eyes of a child. For this little page in my book of memories is dedicated to you, O petite, charming traveler. I wager—he to whom you will someday belong, will be happy, you fair, tender child. Today I understood for the first time how one may fall in love with a child."[18]

There was somewhat less innocence in the encounter between Herzl and a little girl aboard a Rhine river boat in August of 1885: "How she so tenderly directed the pencil with her delicate, light-tan gloved little hands, how she, no less daintily, brought it from time to time to her red mouth, in order to moisten the tip, so that for a second her shimmering white little teeth were visible; how the grey veil flapped about her rosy face in the morning wind, how her blue eyes shone thought-fully; it was all so lovely to regard, that I was drawn to her with that strong and warm affection that I evince for all my female fellow travelers—the pretty ones, that is." The girl was travel-ing with her father, whom Herzl described as "grumpy and fat." Some time after all three disembarked, Herzl wrote in his diary that he searched for her for a long while to "restore to her the little book from which still wafts the half-evaporated scent of that day. Now I will publish it. Perhaps she will get in touch."[19]

Five months later, this desire to maintain contact with the object of his affections assumed the form of an obsession when, at a children's ball in Budapest, Herzl spied Magda Herz, Mad-eleine's niece, whom he had held in his arms as a toddler and who was now thirteen. (Herzl was twenty-six.) "Still short her little dress, the sweet body is undeveloped—but such a fine, distinguished, lovely face. The golden, golden hair! And the coiffure of a grown-up. . . . Later, when her hair fell loose and she stood before a lamp, I saw a halo around her small face." Herzl grew fiercely jealous of boys who danced with her—so much so that "I went out of my head completely. I had to force myself not to tell her, as to an adult, that I love her." Herzl dreamed of her. In the following days he sought her out, find-ing her at an outdoor ice-skating rink and gazing at her from afar. Five days later he went back to the rink and did not find her, but he wrote on the back of his admission ticket, "I shall keep this ticket for the days to come. Perhaps one day I shall be able to show the beloved this little sign of hidden affec-tion." Herzl resolved to marry her, to wait the three years until she was of age. Herzl was aware that his thoughts were not lucid, but they filled him with "immense happiness." Herzl fretted that he could not marry without being a financial suc-cess: "I need success. Success for this golden bird." But then he began to doubt that his beloved's unique, ethereal charm would survive the transition to sexual maturity: "When she is fully developed, she will perhaps be just another marriageable daughter."[20]

Herzl did not wait for Magda. Instead, barely a month after these events, Herzl directed his erotic energy toward Julie Naschauer, the daughter of a wealthy businessman whose family had known the Herzls since their move to Vienna in 1878. By 1886, Julie was a fully grown young woman of eighteen: pretty, blond-haired, blue-eyed, and beguiling. While visiting the Naschauer home, with her parents close by, the couple exchanged kisses that sent Herzl into rapture. Along with Herzl's desire for a sexually mature woman, however, came an outpouring of feelings of disgust, self-hatred, and what Herzl called a "wild nausea" that drove him to thoughts of suicide. At least some of Herzl's anguish stemmed from feelings of inadequacy, as he had yet to establish himself as a playwright, but Herzl also appeared to be undone by the strength of his passion, which he had long striven to suppress.

Feigning indifference to Julie, Herzl cut off contact with her and threw himself into his work, churning out journalistic pieces for newspapers in Berlin, Budapest, and Vienna throughout the rest of 1886, until he developed excruciating headaches and desperately needed a change of both pace and scenery. As was his wont, Herzl traveled, this time to Italy, where he spent six weeks in the spring of 1887. On his journeys, Herzl produced travel sketches that impressed the editors of the *Wiener Allgemeine Tageblatt*, for which he had already published several pieces, and on 15 April he became its literary editor. This was a great coup, and Herzl's first real job since leaving Salzburg, but after three months he was fired. The reasons for his dismissal are not clear, and it could simply be that this man of only twenty-seven, who had never had a real job outside of his brief stint as a junior state attorney, was not accustomed to the breakneck pace of a major newspaper's editorial offices. However short-lived, this job, coupled with some crucial theatrical successes,

gave Herzl a boost of confidence. Herzl now felt ready to re-
connect with Julie. Whatever ambivalence he may have felt
about her, or about women in general, Herzl was under parental
and societal pressure to marry, and Julie appeared to be a good
match. He proposed, she accepted, and they wed on 25 June
1889. Herzl had indeed married up; Julie's dowry was 75,000
guldens, equivalent to $1,250,000 today.

We have no surviving records of the wedding, and there is
some mystery about Julie herself. Her maternal grandmother's
family may not have been Jewish. We know about her personality and character only from Theodor and other observers, as her
letters either were destroyed or did not survive World War II.
There is also confusion about the birth date of their first child,
a girl who was, not surprisingly, named Pauline. Most biographies and Zionist and Israeli websites list the birth date as 29
March 1890. Yet a letter by Herzl, dated 5 March, barely eight
months after the wedding, states that Julie had just given birth,
and that Herzl was glad that a planned business trip to Prague
on the seventh had been postponed. When Herzl returned from
Prague, he found that "fortunately, mother and child [were] in
the best of health."[21]

The pushing back of the birth date may have been a simple
error, as it appears in Alex Bein's pioneering and still widely
consulted biography of Herzl, and many others have replicated
the date ever since. It is also possible that Bein or others fabri-
cated the date, motivated by concern that the birth came four
weeks short of a full term, and could be interpreted as evidence that Theodor and Julie had engaged in premarital sex.
The baby's birth did, however, come as a shock to Herzl, so it
is likely that Pauline was conceived during the Herzls' honey-
moon and was born after thirty-six weeks, somewhat but not
dangerously premature.

The guardians of Herzl's memory had much more to worry
about, however, than Pauline's birth date. Julie was no less psy-

chologically troubled than Theodor, and perhaps more so. According to accounts by Herzl and contemporaries who knew the family, she was mercurial and given to fits of rage; spent money extravagantly on furnishings, entertainment, and clothing; and frequently (and theatrically) threatened suicide. According to Herzl's correspondence, less than three months after Pauline's birth, the couple had a terrible row, and Herzl left home. This was not the first altercation: "I will consider," Herzl wrote to his parents, "whether I should come back once again to Julie or if I will split from her—which is unfortunately only a question of time." In another letter to his parents, Herzl attributed at least part of the problem to his own artistic temperament: "The testiness, the sensitivity to every impression, which are an advantage to a writer, are a flaw among [ordinary] people. Perhaps my way of living is the wrong one. Perhaps the woman by my side, in that she does not have the devotion and self-denial of a mother, is more to pity than to accuse."[22]

Although Herzl was expressing neediness and immaturity, he did so honestly. And no less honestly, he contemplated the unpalatable options of divorce or life with Julie: "Just as I would not conceal from you that I have no faith in the durability of our marriage, nor would I conceal that its dissolution would hurt horridly." Summing up their relationship, Herzl wrote, "I like her, but I cannot live with her." "We don't get along with each other. When two animals in a cage consistently go at each other, so do compassion and common sense demand that they be separated before they have ripped each other to shreds."[23]

The couple reconciled, largely for Pauline's sake, and Julie conceived again, but they quickly fell back to fighting. Herzl did not want to divorce Julie while she was with child, but this time he was determined not to stay with her for the children's sake. Sending a list of complaints and demands to his father-in-law, Herzl highlighted Julie's "loveless, hurtful conduct toward my parents."[24] Herzl declaimed that his daughter was either a wicked person or an outright hysteric and that he had saved her from numerous attempts to hang or poison herself. Herzl blamed Julie's parents for having reared a crass, spoiled, and empty-headed daughter. Behind this jab at her parents lay Herzl's long-simmering resentment toward the Naschauers for their wealth, which was much greater than that of Herzl's parents. Herzl was furious with Julie for her rudeness to his mother, but he was not exactly respectful of his father-in-law, and behind his back called him "crafty and sycophantic." Herzl's mean-spirited comments evoke the time when Herzl was infatuated with Magda Herz and wrote angrily that girls like her only marry "rich, crude stock-exchange speculators."

Hans's birth, on 10 June 1891, gave the couple a slight reprieve, as Herzl was overjoyed to have a son: "We somewhat dreamy and ambitious men see in such a little fellow the certain promise that in this continuation of our self, everything will be fulfilled, which our own shabby beginning did not bring forth."[25] But Herzl's heart soon hardened again, and he schemed to gain custody of at least one of the children in a divorce. In late June, Herzl wrote Julie a long letter in a condescending and bitter tone. He claimed to have had forebodings about the marriage even before it took place, but said his sense of honor prevented him from backing out. Declaring that they never had, nor ever would have, anything in common, and threatening Julie with the wrath of his lawyer, Herzl demanded that she consent to a divorce, with Pauline left in her custody and Hans placed in Herzl's care.

As Herzl's relationship with Julie went through its cycle of long freezes and brief thaws, the one constant in Herzl's life was his parents, and it was precisely because of the depth of his attachment to them that he would not abide staying with Julie: "1) Because at no price in the world would I return to the confused life, in which it is impossible to work, which has been my marriage. 2) I would be disavowing, insulting, and setting you aside with the utmost ingratitude—you, my good, upright, dear parents—if I were to do this. I say this as the second reason, but you know that for me it is the first and primary one."[26]

At the beginning of his miserable marriage, Herzl could take refuge in his friends. He did not commiserate with them so much as delve into their problems so as to momentarily set his own aside. In his first letter to Heinrich Kana after Pauline's birth, Herzl strove to cheer up his friend, who had moved to Berlin and was in a deep depression about his own stalled journalistic career. "Don't fall into the mistake," wrote Herzl, "that so often has been mine: that the eyes of the entire world are directed towards me. The whole world has something entirely different to do. And [you] lack worldly wisdom, my dear Heinrich. You even more than I. But one must have this, forcefully make it one's own, otherwise one cannot bear life. Once more: Be sensible!"[27] Tragically, the advice did not take hold. In early February of 1891, Kana committed suicide.

When Herzl received news of his friend's death, he abandoned Julie, who was five months pregnant with Hans, and decamped for Italy and France, returning to Vienna only during the final weeks of the pregnancy, and then fled south again two months after Hans was born. On this second trip, sojourning in enchanting places like Biarritz and San Sebastian, Herzl began work on a novel, based on Kana's life, tentatively titled *Samuel Kohn*. In a draft passage, Herzl writes of the main character on the final evening of his life as "feeling superior to everyone because of his imminent death." Walking on Berlin's main avenue, Unter den Linden, Kohn passes a unit of royal guards and considers that he could take any of them with him into death. This prospect fills Kohn with pride: "When the thought of doing something useful with his suicide occurred to him, he became a commander. He walked in such a proud and lordly manner that instinctively everyone got out of his way. This pleased him; he went home quietly and shot himself."[28]

Herzl never completed this novel, and although he clearly had suicide on his mind, so far as we know, he never attempted it. Even in this dark time, Herzl remained energetic, and he took pleasure from life. While in France and Spain, he rose early, took daily exercise, wrote every morning, and read in the afternoons. Even in the depths of melancholy Herzl kept to a fixed schedule and enjoyed uninterrupted solitude.

With Kana gone, Herzl's only other close friend was his schoolmate Oswald Boxer, who, like Kana, moved from Vienna to Berlin to take a crack at journalism. Unlike Kana, however, Boxer enjoyed professional success. Nonetheless, in May of 1891 Boxer sailed off to Rio de Janeiro at the behest of the German Central Committee for Russian Jews to seek opportunities for Jewish agricultural settlement in Brazil. He had been involved in the organization for some time and had declined a previous invitation to undertake the arduous journey. Kana's death may have pushed him to seek an adventure abroad, just as Herzl had gone off to Spain. Tragically, Boxer died of yellow fever on 26 January 1892. Herzl was now bereft of friends, and he and Julie wavered between long bouts of open warfare and fragile truces. Herzl responded to this accumulation of losses by reverting to the "icy calm" of his teenaged persona: "Life is not only a sorrow, but also a game over which the gods laugh in Homeric fashion. One must simply keep it at a proper distance."[29]

Work remained the center of Herzl's life. Since his adolescence, Herzl had craved success on the stage, and his greatest ambition was to see his plays performed at Vienna's prestigious Burgtheater. Suiting the fashion of the time, Herzl's plays were mostly drawing-room comedies, centered around the pursuit of love and marriage, stocked with farcical situations and stereotyped characters, and gently mocking of human foibles such as vanity and ambition. Herzl's studied detachment, however, robbed his scripts of warmth. The actor Ernst Hartmann wrote to Herzl in 1887, "You are obviously gifted, you have talent, inventiveness, everything that a playwright needs. But it seems to me that you ought to have a somewhat more respectful attitude toward humanity; you ought to look deeper into it."[30] Despite his plays' contrived plots and flat characters, a few of them did enjoy considerable success. Herzl's play *His Majesty* (1888) got largely positive reviews during its runs in Prague and Vienna. Early in the following year, Herzl collaborated with the Viennese journalist Hugo Wittmann, who was a popular writer for the prestigious *Neue Freie Presse* and who had a more sprightly sense of humor than Herzl. The result was a fluffy but charming comedy titled *Wild Love*. Writing under a pseudonym, lest his previous failures scotch his chances of success, Herzl submitted the play to the Burgtheater, and, to his giddy delight, it was accepted. Not only did the play receive strong reviews, it became a regular part of the theater's repertoire. Later in 1889 Herzl wrote a short comedy for the Burgtheater that was accepted with no need for recourse to a pseudonym.

Alas, Herzl's good luck did not hold out. A few months after his wedding, Herzl wrote a bleak and obviously autobiographical comedy about unhappy marriages that the Burgtheater turned down and that bombed when produced in Prague and Berlin. Over the next couple of years, Herzl wrote the libretto for an operetta that did very well, but two more collaborative efforts between Herzl and Wittmann also failed, and Herzl's play *The Prince of Geniusland* closed after one performance.

If Herzl had limited his writing to the theater, he would have disappeared into the footnotes of history. But he excelled at journalism, and it was in this field that he established an international reputation. Although Herzl had difficulty fathoming human emotions, and the complexity of real people's motivation escaped his linear mind, he was adept at sketching a tableau of a place and the interactions of people within it. He had a knack for vivid descriptions of people's appearance and actions. And the aloof, protective stance with which he approached the world, the wry and occasionally sardonic wit that barely concealed a churning melancholy, was perfectly suited to the journalistic genre of the feuilleton, which flourished throughout continental Europe at that time.

Refined by the great writer Heinrich Heine in the middle of the nineteenth century, the feuilleton was an observational essay or a piece of cultural or literary criticism, set in lively, accessible language and peppered with gentle humor. As the genre developed, the feuilleton came to embrace pretty much every topic under the sun, and it could take the form of short fiction as well as an essay, so long as the treatment had a certain lightness of being and was both entertaining and didactic. In fin-de-siècle Vienna, the middle classes, denied opportunities for serious political engagement by the Dual Monarchy's ossified political structure, steeped themselves in art, music, opera, and literature. In turn, the feuilleton's aesthetic dimension and its capacity for internal reflection were particularly valued. Herzl was a master of polished, elegant prose, and his tone, which was both worldly and a tad world-weary, struck just the right balance between irony and sentimentality.

Herzl did not respect his feuilletons. At the ripe old age of nineteen, Herzl wrote that he wished to renounce further attempts at the genre, which he considered superficial and inferior to his great love, the theater. Throughout his life, Herzl often looked upon writing feuilletons as a burden, something he had to do to feed his family. Herzl wrote more than three hundred of them, two-thirds of which were published between 1895, when he became literary editor of the *Neue Freie Presse*, and his death in 1904. When he was well into his Zionist career, Herzl told one of his acolytes that his feuilletons had no literary value. Herzl was being a bit hard on himself, but the fact is that the work was often formulaic and mannered, designed to appeal to, but not challenge, his middle-brow, central European readership. The feuilletons could, however, also be deeply re-vealing, as they employed recurring themes and characters that had a strongly autobiographical quality. The fact that Herzl tossed them off quickly meant that he had to draw on material readily at hand and which he found worthy of depiction—that is, himself. It takes little effort to detect intrusions of his per-sona through the delicate filigree of his sparkling prose.

In 1887, Herzl published his first collection of feuilletons, *News from Venus*. In Herzl's prudish age, the word "Venus" could immediately bring to mind carnal love, but the essays were anything but an endorsement of eros. Their unifying themes were the folly of romantic love and humanity's vast proclivity for hypocrisy. In the volume's title essay, three young men about Herzl's age speak of love, and one of them admits to having ad-mired a woman for a decade. He has just now conversed with her for the first time, only to find out that her voice is deep and manly. His ardor evaporates at once. One of his friends remarks, "People like you should never seek to discover the composition of the stars—as you would find out!" To which his crestfallen friend replies, "News from Venus!" In another story, a young nobleman professes his love to a woman, whom he strives to convince that his feelings are pure, and not mere "sophisticated love" (*weltmännische Liebe*, a euphemism for sexual attraction). At the end of the story, the nobleman muffs the woman's name, thus proving that he had just been playing a sexual game with her all the while.

A brewing misanthropy emerges in Herzl's story "The Mind Reader," about a clairvoyant who is privy to the devious thoughts swirling around in his interlocutors' heads:

> I believe that in the beginning everyone is good, or as I would put it, genuine. . . . Then something intervenes, it may be only the passage of time, and they become shams. Of love nothing remains but the tender glance, of friendship

nothing but the tender handshake. But I observe the change at once, however deceptively alike the two phenomena may be. . . . I have a nose for the decay of the genuine. . . . I see the transformation into the non-genuine going on all about me. . . . Put yourself in the condition of that unhappy man who can with the naked eye see the infusoria swimming about in the water when he drinks. He perishes between revulsion and thirst. In such a case am I.[31]

Criticism of stultifying social norms and the exposure of hypocrisy were staples of fin-de-siècle literature (for example, the psychologically fraught plays of Henrik Ibsen, or the thunderous polemics of Max Nordau's 1883 best seller, *The Conventional Lies of Our Civilization*). Herzl also felt a kinship with another warrior against hypocrisy, the eighteenth-century Irish satirist Jonathan Swift. The image of microscopic creatures in drinking water brings to mind the second chapter of Swift's *Gulliver's Travels*, in which Gulliver has a close-up encounter with the imperfections of a gigantic woman's skin. Herzl's second collection of feuilletons, *The Book of Folly* (1888), features an epigraph taken from another book by Swift, *A Tale of a Tub*: "This is the sublime and refined point of felicity, called the possession of being well-deceived, the serene, peaceful state of being a fool among knaves."

The fin-de-siècle Viennese feuilleton was a study in melancholy and irony, and Herzl was genuinely melancholy and ironic. When writing, he had to strike a pose, but it was the very same pose he had assumed for much of his life. Like most cynical people, however, Herzl had a sentimental streak, which suited the Viennese taste for both tart and sickly sweet. Nubile women were objects of desire and suspicion, but children were paragons of innocence and purity, and whereas a tale about the pursuit of Venus would likely provoke a smirk, the story of a child would evoke warm smiles and the occasional tear. In his story "The Rizzolini Family" (1887), Herzl pulls out all the stops, portraying a five-year-old boy who loses his loved ones, falls prey to violence, and finally dies.

In "The Son" (1890), which was written while Julie was pregnant with Hans, Herzl tells a tale of a man, on trial for embezzlement and fraud, who pleads guilty but seeks the court's compassion, as he committed these crimes out of love for his son. The defendant's pleas begin on a heartwarming note: "He is the reason I am sitting here today. When he was born, my life was fulfilled. . . . While still in the cradle, he cured me of all my sarcasm and flippancy. Children are our best teachers. He taught me true love of life!" But as the text goes on, the defendant's sensibilities grow bizarre and disturbing: "From the first day on I was totally in love with him, painfully, foolishly in love with him. I suffered, so to speak, from monomania regarding my son." Devoting every waking moment and every penny to his son (and presumably neglecting his wife and daughter, who are mentioned only briefly), the defendant sinks into debt, to the point that he decides to commit suicide. Equipped with a revolver in a room at his home, the man is readying himself when his son bursts in, grabs the revolver, and holds it to his own head, threatening to shoot himself unless his father vows to go on living. As a result of that vow, the man is now in court and faces a hefty prison term.[32]

The narration offers a pungent blend of sickly, unnaturally close love, neediness, narcissism, and no small amount of resentment, for were it not for the son's grand gesture, the narrator would be out of his misery. Nor is its sentimentality genuine, as just before the defendant begins to speak, we learn that he has carefully planned his remarks, with "an especially delicate first course, stirring appetizers for the epicure, saving the heavy stuff for the ending: . . . first, the sentimental slop, then the high-flown judicial prose; first, jerk their tears, then a quick jab of the dagger. An advertisement like this trial doesn't come very often." The defendant is precisely the fraud and con man he is accused of being. This twist salvages the story from being utterly maudlin, but it is also revealing about Herzl's emotional defensiveness as well as his own ambivalence about parenthood.

Herzl wrote "The Son" when he was thirty. He had failed to establish human connections and a sense of purpose through marriage, family, or friendship. For a man of his time, place, and class, there was one other possible source of engagement and fulfillment: religion. Yet Herzl's existential anxieties were not relieved by religious faith. He believed neither in an omniscient and omnipotent God nor in providence, and although he often dwelled on his own mortality, he never wrote about an afterlife other than his political legacy. In August of 1895, Herzl wrote in his diaries of a vague sense of God in terms that mashed together Spinozist pantheism, a Hegelian belief in the advancement of reason through history, and contemporary monism (a doctrine that preached the underlying materiality of all being). Herzl claimed that there was an underlying meaning to life, but that he neither could fathom it nor wished to.

Still, even if Herzl himself had no faith, he had room in his heart for the faithful. Visiting Lourdes in September 1891, Herzl wrote a feuilleton that displayed great reverence for Bernadette Soubirous (later, Saint Bernadette), the peasant girl who claimed to have multiple visions of the Virgin Mary. Herzl was similarly compassionate to those who flocked to the shrine in search of cures for devastating ailments, though he was agnostic about the shrine's curative powers. He tells of two pilgrims, both women, one of whom was apparently cured and experienced a rapturous state, while the other, no less pious or virtuous, emerged from the grotto as broken as before. Herzl saved his irony and derision for the Church, which, he claimed, grew rich from the suffering of others. He focused on the bishop of the shrine. As befits a playwright, and a man with a strongly theatrical personality, Herzl was struck by the grandeur of the bishop's persona and his impressive gestures while he celebrated the mass. But Herzl rejected the very essence of the shrine when he wrote that there is a "Beloved Lady in every dark wood, in all human despair. Everywhere a poor heart searches for reasons to press on, she appears in one way or another. For there are more than one, O Bishop of Meaux. Poetry, art, philosophy (the true kind), labor, hope are such beloved Ladies, steeped in pain."[33]

Herzl was proud of this feuilleton. He told his parents, "If I do not err, it is the best. It is serious. It's the first time that I've written something that moves me to tears."[34] He was aware, but also defiantly proud, that its criticisms of the Church could cause legal trouble for the *Frankfurter Zeitung*, which published the piece. Basking in the early autumnal glory of San Sebastian, Herzl felt ready to put mourning for Kana aside and to stop wallowing in misery about his marriage. He began to socialize in the evenings. He wrote to his parents, "Now a grander time will begin for me. As in interactions with others I believe I am attaining a mature serenity, so will my work also begin to show the real man."[35] Herzl had taken his own advice from the feuilleton at Lourdes. Labor was his "beloved lady," and its rewards were munificent. Less than a week after writing these sanguine words to his parents, the editors of the *Neue Freie Presse*, Eduard Bacher and Moriz Benedikt, invited Herzl to be the newspaper's Paris correspondent.

Herzl took up the post immediately on a four-month probationary basis, with a monthly salary of 1,000 francs, or about $5,000 in today's U.S. currency. Happily ensconced in a series of hotels, far from the annoyances of his family, Herzl felt that he had at last arrived. His flawless French endeared him to the country's political and literary elites, and Herzl now had abundant opportunity to deploy his ironic wit on a stage filled with sufficient corruption, hypocrisy, and greed for a thousand drawing-room comedies. Herzl was relieved of the burden of trying (and usually failing) to create three-dimensional characters. Humanity stood before him in all of its complexity, and he needed only to observe and record. It took Herzl a few months to make the transition from the precious, delicate feuilleton to hard-boiled political reportage, but once he did, he became a master of the genre.

Herzl began to miss his children, whom he had not seen since leaving home shortly after Hans's birth. Sharing every intimate detail with his parents, Herzl reckoned that he and Julie should, for the sake of the children, maintain their marriage, albeit a loveless one. (He determined that the two would have separate bedrooms.) In February of 1892 Julie, Pauline, and Hans came to visit him in Paris. The couple formally agreed to reconcile. Herzl and family returned to Vienna to prepare for the long-term move to Paris, and Herzl rented an apartment at 8 rue de Monceau, in one of Paris's most luxurious neighborhoods. The rent was equal to half of Herzl's salary, and Julie insisted on bringing a retinue of servants, but Julie's dowry made up for the deficit between a journalist's income and Julie's desired standard of living. In April, the entire Herzl family moved in.

Unfortunately for Julie, "entire" included Herzl's parents, who, at Herzl's insistence, moved in with them. Julie's presence in the Herzl household was to be merely a means by which the children could be kept under one roof and in the presence of both of their parents. Herzl was far more deeply tied to his own parents, especially his mother, than he was to Julie. He now had a prestigious and important job, and Julie faced the pleasant prospect of entertaining fascinating and famous people, but the fundamental incompatibility between husband and wife, and the poisonous dynamic between Julie and Herzl's mother Jeanette, ensured that the Herzl family would continue to be an unhappy one.

It was one thing to be unhappy in Vienna, and quite another to be unhappy in Paris. Paris was Europe's most vibrant and dynamic city at that time, "the capital of the nineteenth century," as the literary critic Walter Benjamin dubbed it. In Paris, Herzl would no longer vent his petty grievances and existential angst in doggerel stories and plays. He would, instead, immerse himself in affairs of state, social problems, and, eventually, the plight of the Jews.

2

---◆◆◆◆---

Our Man in Paris

FRANCE IN 1891 was in the midst of what would, in the cold light of the twentieth century, be nostalgically called *la belle époque*—the period from the last quarter of the nineteenth century until the outbreak of World War I. Today, we associate the Paris of that time largely with the arts, with the zenith of Impressionism and the birth of literary modernism, or with technological wonders such as the Eiffel Tower, which was showcased at the 1889 Paris World's Fair. But this was also a period of social turmoil. As in the rest of the Western world, industrialization created an urban proletariat and horrific working conditions in many enterprises, especially coal mining. Paris was a magnet for not only bohemian artists but also a growing underclass.

It had taken France a decade to stabilize politically after the disastrous Franco-Prussian War of 1870–71. France's republican government was split between moderates and radicals, and it was assailed by conservatives who wanted to bring back the monarchy and by anarchists who wanted to get rid of government altogether. The country was haunted by the memory of the Paris Commune of 1871, an experiment in revolutionary socialism that had been bloodily repressed by founders of the republic, and of two Bonapartist dictators, the last of whom, Louis-Napoleon, had fallen along with France in 1871. In the second half of the 1880s, General Georges Ernest Boulanger led a populist movement that almost succeeded in installing him as dictator, but due to rigorous governmental opposition, and his own poor leadership, in the elections of 1889 Boulangism was stopped in its tracks. This was the Paris to which Herzl came in the fall of 1891.

For four years, Herzl would watch parliamentary debates in the magnificent eighteenth-century Palais Bourbon, attend operas in the recently completed Palais Garnier, and stroll in the Tuileries Garden. He was not just another aspiring writer but rather a journalist employed by the most prestigious newspaper in Austria-Hungary. The *Neue Freie Presse* was read by the educated middle and ruling classes throughout the empire, and the impact of its cultural reportage was felt throughout German-speaking Europe. Its subscribers numbered only about thirty-five thousand—half in Vienna, a third elsewhere in the empire, and the rest abroad. But the newspaper had clout. In small communities in the eastern backwaters of the Austrian half of the empire, the small-town bourgeoisie would inscribe "Subscriber to the Neue Freie Presse" on their calling cards. At the other end of the power scale, newly installed Austrian prime ministers and directors of the prestigious Burgtheater would go straightaway to the newspaper's publishers and request their support.

The publishers who held such great power were Eduard Bacher (1846–1908) and Moriz Benedikt (1849–1920). Hailing from Bohemia and Moravia, respectively, they were, like Herzl, assimilated, German-speaking Jews with a commitment to economic and political liberalism. However, each was, in his own way, more successful and stable than Herzl. As a young man, Bacher displayed a genius for political reporting. At the age of thirty-three he became the *Neue Freie Presse*'s chief editor, and, a year later, its co-publisher. A reserved, modest, and phlegmatic man, Bacher had a gift for making friendships among the mighty and powerful. Benedikt had a more lively temperament and a creative spark. His literary ambitions, like Herzl's, shone early; as a high school student, he wrote a play about the death of the Roman rebel slave Spartacus. But unlike Herzl, Benedikt combined writing talent with a deep knowledge of business and economics. After joining the paper at twenty-three, within seven years he had become its co-publisher. Valued for his expertise by the Austrian Finance Ministry, in 1892 Benedikt helped design the empire's currency reform and adoption of the gold standard, and the 1907 revision of the Austrian-Hungarian compromise of 1867 bore a "Benedikt clause" dealing with monetary union.[1]

Bacher was only three years older than Benedikt, but he had a more avuncular character, and he dealt with Herzl more gently than did Benedikt. (In later years, Herzl would nickname Benedikt "Maledikt.") After 1895, Herzl and his editors would joust over Herzl's Zionist activity, which made both Bacher and Benedikt profoundly uncomfortable, and which they refused to so much as mention in their newspaper. But when Herzl started on the job, his editors' first concern was preparing this writer of lighthearted plays and feuilletons to be a hard-hitting and wide-ranging reporter. Herzl had scarcely arrived in Paris when he received a letter from Bacher with a long list of instructions: He was to read all of the Parisian dailies in the early morning so as to telegraph important information to Vienna in time to make the evening edition. His main task was "to personally attend the meetings of Parliament, which at times are turbulent." He was to report via telegraph on every meeting concerning affairs of state, foreign policy, or the future of the governing coalition. Finally, he was to keep in mind the political orientation of the newspaper, which sympathized with France's centrist republicans. At times the paper would take an editorial stand against one aspect or another of French policy, but Herzl was free "to be more friendly to France in a variety of ways."[2]

Herzl had some teething pains, albeit mild ones. In January of 1892, he was gently reprimanded by Bacher for flat, wooden reportage of a spectacular incident in the Chamber of Deputies, France's legislative assembly. A fight broke out on the parliament floor between Francis Laur, a Boulangist member of the chamber, and Ernest Constans, the minister of the interior and a member of the parliament's upper house, the Senate. Laur accused Constans of a variety of crimes and spewed insults at him. Constans responded by running across the floor to Laur and punching him in the face. Pandemonium ensued, with sporadic fighting and dueling in the palace's lobbies and corridors. After a couple of hours, the chamber was reconvened, Constans apologized, and, ignoring a fuming Laur's demands for retribution, the chamber went back to its business. Reports on such events, Bacher wrote to Herzl, "are gobbled up by the public and one can't give readers enough of them," so he urged Herzl to be more colorful and expansive, "at least in sessions that come to blows."[3]

The criticism was anything but harsh, yet Herzl was terrified that he was going to be sacked. In February of 1892, toward the end of his probationary period, an anxious Herzl wrote to Bacher that since he had not yet heard from the newspaper, he assumed he was to be dismissed due to a failure to perform up to expectations. Herzl began to make plans for his successor's hire and for his departure. Bacher calmly assured Herzl that they were extremely satisfied with his work and wanted him to

stay on. Sure enough, about two weeks later Bacher offered
Herzl a permanent position, with an increase in salary to 12,000
francs per year and an additional 100 francs per feuilleton. Herzl
asked for more, but Bacher politely held his ground. The terms
had already been agreed to by Herzl's father, Jakob, who was
involved in the negotiations from the start.[4] Jakob had also
been contacted by Bacher about the terms of Herzl's probationary hire while Herzl was traveling through Spain and
France in the fall of 1891, but given that by March of 1892 Herzl
could easily be reached in Paris by his own editors, one wonders why Herzl was still relying on his father to take charge of
his financial affairs.

Herzl quickly adapted to his new regimen—rising early,
gathering and writing material over the course of the day, and
shuttling to and from the telegraph office, at times hourly, in
the case of an urgent update. Herzl worked fourteen to sixteen
hours a day, with only one assistant, to satisfy Bacher's inces-
sant demand: "Even if there is no time for cooking, for God's
sake, supply the raw material!"[5] He kept up with this grueling
schedule until October of 1893, when, while traveling on business in southern France, he contracted a mysterious and severe
illness, which left him bedridden for seven weeks. It may have
been malaria, though there is evidence that it could have been
a general autoimmune disorder. Although he eventually recovered and went back to his breakneck work pace, it is possible
that this illness aggravated his heart defect, with lethal long-
term consequences.

From a social standpoint as well as a professional one, the
early Paris years were good ones for Herzl. Although he would
never find another soulmate like Kana, in 1892 he began to
form a friendship with the writer Max Nordau (1849–1923). As
with Benedikt and Bacher, Nordau was in many ways similar to
Herzl, but older, more secure, and more renowned. Like Herzl,
he was born and raised in Budapest, which he left in his teens.

Also like Herzl, he was completely at home in both German and French culture. Although raised as an Orthodox Jew, in his adolescence he left religious observance behind, became a physician, and developed an entirely materialistic, rationalistic worldview. Barrel-chested and given in later life to sport a massive, snowy white beard, Nordau was almost as physically impressive as Herzl, and he was a spellbinding orator.

A prolific journalist and playwright, Nordau achieved notoriety for his works of cultural criticism, especially *Degeneration* (1892). *Degeneration* was a blistering attack on artistic modernism in virtually every form, be it the aestheticized mythology of Richard Wagner, the decadence of Charles Baudelaire, the gritty naturalism of Émile Zola, or the psychological introspection of Henrik Ibsen. For Nordau, these were all "egomaniacs" who had abandoned the cardinal virtues of rationality and self-restraint. It is easy today to dismiss Nordau as possessed of staggeringly poor artistic judgment. But his social criticisms were, at times, prescient. In his earlier book *The Conventional Lies of Our Civilization* (1883), Nordau warned of a future society enslaved by frantic production and joyless consumption. At the end of *Degeneration*, Nordau vacillated between a technologically sparkling utopia and a darkling dystopia featuring a now all-too-familiar combination of public drug-peddling, random shootings, graphically violent popular entertainment, and a massive reduction of the human attention span.

Herzl himself admired a good deal of modern art, literature, and music, but his commitment, dating back to adolescence, to maintaining an aristocratic "icy calm" resonated with Nordau, and the spirit of Nordau's work, if not its specifics, appealed to Herzl. Unlike Herzl, Nordau married late (at the age of forty-nine) and very happily, although when he first met Herzl he was in the midst of a tempestuous, decade-long affair with an antisemitic Russian noblewoman named Olga Novikova. (The two had only occasional trysts but wrote to each other constantly.)

At first, Herzl and Nordau engaged in casual exchanges of opinions about each other's plays and enjoyed sniping at theater critics. But by the end of 1894, Herzl was frequenting Nordau's Paris home. (One evening, Herzl stopped by for an early supper, followed by Nordau's reading aloud the entirety of his newest play, an entertainment that took well over two hours.) Letters between the two men increasingly contained long, serious exchanges about literature and philosophy. Their letters do not mention familial matters or personal feelings. Their relationship is best described as a literary friendship, one that was based on mutual interests and appreciation. It is no coincidence that in 1895, when Herzl turned to Zionism, Nordau was one of his first supporters and remained his most steadfast ally.

Herzl developed a more intimate friendship with the celebrated Viennese playwright Arthur Schnitzler (1862–1931). The two men had known each other while Herzl was living in Vienna, but Herzl claimed to have found Schnitzler "unlikable" and "arrogant." Herzl was envious of the aspiring young writer, and Herzl was aware of the ignobility of his feelings: "When I see a talent like yours blossom, I take joy, as if I had never been a littérateur, that is . . . mean-spirited, impatient, envious, spiteful . . . in such a way, my dear, I would have very much liked to write."[6] A year after taking on the position in Paris, Herzl wrote that in the past he might have overtaken Schnitzler but that he had given up his literary ambitions and now "I sit like a rock in the road and let others run me over."[7] Protesting a tad too much, Herzl vowed not to write any more plays, claiming that he had reconciled himself to being only a journalist and no longer needed "to elicit applause from an opening night audience in Vienna or Berlin or some other city."[8] Despite these obvious outbursts of insecurity and competitiveness, Herzl became genuinely fond of Schnitzler, and in the summer of 1894 they went on a holiday together, along with the writers Hugo von Hofmannsthal and Richard Beer-Hofmann, in the Austrian spa town of Altaussee. By early 1895 the two men were writing openly about the warmth and sympathy that they felt for each other. "I have a great need for a good friendship," Herzl wrote baldly, complaining that he had no close friends in Paris: "I don't know if I am too distrustful or too shy or if my eyes are too sharp . . . one is too stupid, another is untrustworthy, a third turns me off."[9] Within a few years, both Herzl's and Schnitzler's spikiness would cause the friendship to cool, leaving Nordau Herzl's closest confidant.

Herzl's family life continued to be turbulent. The birth of a third child, Trude, in 1893 offered only a temporary respite in the continuous battles between Julie and Jeanette on the one hand, and Herzl and Julie on the other. Herzl gained a sense of enhanced power in his marriage when his father-in-law died in January of 1895, leaving Herzl in full control of Julie's dowry and inheritance. There were also signs in his writing that Herzl was developing a somewhat more mature attitude toward romantic relationships than had been the case in his early plays and feuilletons. In the spring of 1894, Herzl wrote an odd little play called *The Glossary*, in which one Philippus von Montaperto in thirteenth-century Bologna wins back his straying wife by reciting an ancient Roman marriage code. The play was not free from conventional comedic themes such as the pursuit of love or man's capacity for hypocrisy and self-delusion, but it also explored the transformative power of speech and the social necessity of the law. The Burgtheater rejected the play, and Herzl did not try to get it performed elsewhere. It is difficult to say if he acted out of sulky frustration or mature reflection, but Herzl decided the play would be more effective as a printed text for the reading public, and with Nordau's support, he prevailed upon Bacher and Benedikt to serialize it in the *Neue Freie Presse*. When they refused, he had it published privately.

Despite the relative seriousness of *The Glossary*'s subject matter, a chasm divided Herzl's lighthearted plays and feuilletons, on the one hand, and the gritty subject matter of his political reportage from Paris's Palais Bourbon, on the other. Herzl enjoyed having a ringside seat as France's Third Republic lurched from one crisis to another. Herzl provided in-depth coverage of the decline of the Boulangist movement and the outbreak in 1892 of a scandal surrounding the bankruptcy of the Panama Canal Company. In the wake of that scandal, Herzl wrote to Hugo Wittmann, his colleague at the *Neue Freie Presse*, that journalism was giving him political training. This comment is illuminating given that at this time Herzl was thinking seriously about antisemitism and about his own potential role as a leader in the campaign against it. Yet it would be misleading to analyze Herzl's time in Paris solely in terms of his worries about the Jews and his embrace of Zionism in June of 1895. Out of some three hundred articles and feuilletons that Herzl telegraphed to his newspaper over the years 1891–95, only about a dozen dealt directly with antisemitism. During his time in Paris Herzl received an education about mass politics, demagoguery, high finance, and social radicalism, all of which would inform not only his Zionism but also his general view of the world and of human nature.

Herzl covered the Panama scandal and trials intensively, writing more than forty articles about them. The Panama Canal Company had been founded in 1876 by the legendary diplomat-*cum*-entrepreneur Ferdinand de Lesseps. (Lesseps was the brainchild behind the Suez Canal, which had been completed in 1869.) Unlike the Suez Canal project, however, the Panama Canal ran into enormous difficulties. The technical challenges of building a sea-level canal across the Isthmus of Panama were vast, and tropical diseases decimated the canal's construction crews. As cost overruns mounted and the company faced bankruptcy, Lesseps and confederates bribed members of the French parliament to allow the company to continue to function. When the scandal broke and the company went bust, hundreds of thousands of French citizens lost their life savings as the company's shares became worthless paper. Some five hundred parliamentarians were accused of corruption, and over a hundred were convicted, along with Lesseps and the distinguished engineer Gustave Eiffel. The scandal assumed a strongly antisemitic tone when public attention focused on the alleged role of two Jews in distributing the payoffs: the banker Jacob Adolphe Reinach and Cornelius Herz, a technological entrepreneur who had founded several companies to bring electric power to France.

The Panama scandal played a major role in the intensification of French antisemitism. Among other things, it served as a springboard for the rise to fame of Édouard Drumont, whose 1886 book *La France juive* would become a best seller, and who in 1892 founded a daily antisemitic newspaper, *La libre parole*. The newspaper gained popularity by publishing the names of parliamentarians linked with the Panama affair, but it indulged in a wide range of slurs against Jews, including a claim that the French army's Jewish officers got promotions and choice assignments through bribery and string-pulling. In June of 1892 these articles led a headstrong Jewish cavalry lieutenant named André Crémieu-Foa to challenge first Drumont, and then Drumont's colleague Paul de Lamase, to duels. There followed a sword fight between Lamase's chief second, the Marquis de Morès, and a Jewish artillery captain, Armand Mayer, who was the nephew of a prominent French rabbi. Mayer was a fencing master at France's prestigious École Polytechnique, but his right arm had recently been injured, and, a few seconds into the duel, Morès ran him through.

Herzl was close to all of these events. He covered Mayer's death and funeral for his newspaper. Herzl read Drumont's *La France juive* and on one occasion met Drumont socially in the home of the author Alphonse Daudet, himself a self-declared antisemite. Despite what appeared to be a poisonous atmosphere for Jews, antisemitism in France concerned Herzl without consuming him. Whereas he always feared bearing the brunt of antisemitic abuse in Germany or Austria, in France "I pass through the crowd unrecognized."[10] At the end of August, Herzl wrote in the *Neue Freie Presse* that antisemitism in France was relatively benign, even "kindly," as it did not indulge in a blanket condemnation of Jews as responsible for the corruption and cruelty of capitalist society. Instead, Herzl wrote, French antisemitism was a variety of xenophobia: "In the land of the Franks Jews are mainly accused of being from Frankfurt." Jews who behave with honor and who display nobility of character, like the late Captain Mayer, were beloved: as Herzl noted, Parisians turned out in droves to watch the captain's coffin weave through Montmartre's rue de Douai. And none other than Mayer's murderer, the Marquis de Morès, called his victim "a man of honor." "A Jew," wrote Herzl without a speck of irony, "can, without being immodest, ask for no more."[11] The duel strictly adhered to codes of honor, and it was the captain's responsibility to inform his opponent of his injury, especially as the swords that Morès chose were unusually heavy.

The emancipation of the Jews, wrote Herzl, had come in an era of increasing social prosperity. For this reason, as a whole the French people find antisemitism alien, even incomprehensible. Herzl linked antisemitism with Boulangism, both of them being protest movements that would inevitably fade because of the "kernel of healthy reason and love of justice in the French people." Thus, in France "the movement will pass, although most likely not without excesses and isolated catastrophes." In the months following the publication of this article, as the antisemitic rhetoric in France grew more prevalent and more heated, Herzl became less sanguine. He noted the presence of antisemitism among the French left as well as on the right, and he condemned the demagoguery of the French socialist leader Paul Lafargue, who accused "Jews and entrepreneurs" of carrying out a "bloodbath" against the French people. Indeed, Herzl was deeply worried about the French left, but for reasons that went beyond some of their leaders' animus against the Jews.[12]

During Herzl's years in Paris, France was rocked by anarchist violence. In 1892, François Koenigstein, who adopted his mother's maiden name, Ravachol, as his nom de guerre, was accused of a series of radically inspired murders. In 1893, Auguste Vaillant hurled a bomb into the French Chamber of Deputies, and in the following year Sante Geronimo Caserio stabbed to death the French president Sadi Carnot. Herzl covered all of their trials. Before any of the trials took place, Herzl issued a blanket condemnation of anarchism: "Whoever becomes emotional about the anarchists is a traitor to the state. Whoever judges them with mercy might be a good person but a bad citizen."[13] Writing about Vaillant, Herzl declared that the most "ugly and frightening feature in his generally not unpleasant face was the eyes, sunk deep under thick brows, their dark glance piercing." At Ravachol's trial, however, Herzl could not stop himself from admiring the terrorist's clarity of purpose, courage, honesty, and confidence. Herzl even described Ravachol as expounding a "great idea" possessed of a certain "voluptuousness." In addition to reporting on these trials, Herzl attended socialist meetings, noting the effects of the speakers on the masses, whose uplifted spirits transcended their individuality, "like a great beast, just beginning to stretch its limbs, half unaware of its own power."[14] Herzl himself was a man of impeccably bourgeois values, terrified of social insurrection, and that very fear made him search for a means to kill the beast before it devoured him and his kind.

Herzl read the work of influential leftist theorists such as the anarchist Pierre-Joseph Proudhon and the socialist Ferdinand Lassalle. He reported on the coal miners' strike in Carmaux in 1892 and was familiar with the inhumane working conditions in the mines. Humanitarian concern for the plight of the laboring classes, combined with anxiety about their potential for violence, led him to develop an elaborate plan for public works employment, which in July of 1893 he shared with Baron Johann von Chlumecký, an Austrian liberal politician who had held cabinet portfolios in agriculture and commerce. Like many bourgeois social reformers of the time, Herzl hoped to provide the poor with something more than the "inadequate alms" provided by church or municipal charities. Herzl shared the widespread sentiment of the era that large cities had made the working classes ill, anxious, and enraged, and that they would be healed through outdoor labor in agriculture or land improvement. This would be a form of state socialism, in which the public purse would be opened to obtain a public benefit: "If nothing else were accomplished than an internal colonization, an improvement of the soil by the dangerous and helpless urban proletariat, much would already have been done."[15]

Herzl's proposal to Chlumecký took up two long letters and, in a fashion reminiscent of his later writings on Zionism, went into considerable detail about how the project would be planned and implemented. (For example, he envisioned the state railroads being mobilized to provide free or discounted fares for those en route to work relief projects.) This proposal formed the basis for his lead article in the *Neue Freie Presse* in August, and two years later he sent a copy of that article, along with a description of his Zionist plans, to the German chancellor Otto von Bismarck in order to convince him that he was not a socialist.

Herzl's thinking about the threat posed by the radical left was forged in Paris, but his attempts to solve the "Social Problem" were aimed at Austria-Hungary, where antisemitism was rampant and Jews were routinely blamed for the ills of capitalist society and the failings of governments to respond to people's basic needs. In 1878, the Christian Social Party, which combined antisemitism with critiques of secularism and free-market capitalism, had been founded in Germany. In the 1880s, the Christian Social movement spread to Austria, and the Austrian Christian Social Party was founded in 1891. The sparkplugs of Viennese Christian Socialism were the journalist Karl von Vogelsang and the charismatic city councilman Karl Lueger, who brazenly and repeatedly accused the Jews of dominating banking and the press, and who had nothing but contempt for the complacent liberalism of the *Neue Freie Presse*. Although Lueger's Viennese party, known from 1888 as the United Christians, was the most obvious source of concern for Herzl, antisemitism from Austrian liberals was also galling, and he was deeply hurt when the Austrian liberal student union passed a measure denying Jews the right to satisfaction in duels.

Observing these developments, Herzl wrote in 1890 that "the Jewish Question is neither national nor religious but is rather social. It is a formerly navigable arm of the great stream, which is called the Social Question. But great streams cannot be artificially separated, and when the snow melts on a spring day, the floods dig, tunnel, and rip their own way."[16] At the end of 1892, while sitting in Paris and anxiously following debates in the Austrian parliament about the Jews' alleged domination of banking and business, Herzl restated his comment from 1890, but did so even more baldly: the Jewish Question "is no longer—and it has not been for a long time—a theological matter. It has nothing to do with religion or conscience. . . . What is more, everyone knows it. The times are past for men to slaughter each other on a question of the [Lord's] Supper. Today it is not a question of the Supper, but of the dinner, of our daily bread."[17] Antisemitism, Herzl believed, no longer had to do with hatred of Jews as killers or rejecters of Christ. It was bound up with the Jews' historic concentration in commerce and the money trade and their more recent entry into law and journalism, where they competed with increasingly frustrated and angry Christians.

From late 1892 through 1894, Herzl led a double life. He

produced a stream of political and cultural reportage about France for the *Neue Freie Presse*, but he devoted increasing amounts of time and energy to the "Jewish Question," for which he formulated multiple and contradictory solutions. Some focused on political transformations within Germany and Austria-Hungary. Much as Herzl feared the masses, he suggested that his newspaper support universal male suffrage in Austria-Hungary so that "the Liberals could regain the ground they had lost among the people and the intelligent elements in the working class."[18] In Germany, there was already universal male suffrage for elections to the imperial parliament (the Reichstag), so that tactic would not work. Perhaps for this reason, in April of 1893, shortly before parliamentary elections, Herzl called for Germany's Jews to embrace socialism outright. (In the previous imperial election in 1890, the Social Democrats had won 20 percent of the vote—more than any other party— but due to the way districts were drawn, they received less than 10 percent of the Reichstag's seats.)

Herzl was willing to see Germany's Jews leap into the arms of Social Democracy, but when it came to his own native Austria-Hungary he would only brandish the threat of political radicalism, warning that if push came to shove, the Dual Monarchy's Jews might have no choice but to become socialists. Herzl preferred an entirely different solution to the problem of antisemitism in Austria-Hungary, involving not the reconfiguration of society so much as the reconfiguration of the Jews themselves. Austria's Jews, he wrote in January of 1893, must undergo complete assimilation, up to and including intermarriage and baptism. At the same time, they must win the respect of Gentiles by fighting for their honor: "Half a dozen duels will do a great deal to improve the position of Jews in society."[19] The bravery and selflessness that Herzl associated with dueling would compensate for what Herzl believed was a ghetto heritage that rendered Jews timid and obsequious, on the one hand,

and on the other, embarrassingly eager for success and recognition. The result, Herzl thought, was a penchant among Jews for vulgarity, materialism, shallowness, and shady dealings. Thus, Herzl advocated for the establishment of a newspaper that would take up the crusade against antisemitism but would have no Jewish staff members and would be unstinting in detailing the misdeeds of Jews.

Herzl wanted Jews to lose their collective identity, however it may be defined. Yet he also considered Jews, as he wrote in a lengthy letter to Baron Friedrich Leitenberger, president of the Vienna Defense Association Against Antisemitism, to be "living perpetually in enemy territory."[20] How could they assimilate into a consistently and eternally hostile environment? This paradoxical situation called for a paradoxical solution, which Herzl found in an orchestrated mass conversion of Austrian Jews to Catholicism. He raised this idea with his editor Benedikt toward the end of 1892 and again with Baron Leitenberger in January of 1893. Herzl coolly explained that the conversion would be conditional upon the pope declaring a campaign against antisemitism. The Christian world would see an end to the Jews, but in return it would have to put an end to hating them. Herzl fantasized that the conversion ceremony would be held in St. Stephen's Cathedral in the heart of Vienna and be presided over by the pope himself.

What appears at first glance to be an assimilationist fantasy turns out to have been something more ambiguous. Herzl explained that he himself would not convert, though his son Hans would. (Herzl made no mention of his daughters.) Filial piety and a sense of personal honor would prevent Herzl from abandoning the Jews while they were still a persecuted people. He would be a willing martyr for his people, a pariah whose actions would expiate the sins of the vulgar parvenus whom Herzl found so loathsome.

Benedikt and Leitenberger were taken aback by Herzl's

scheme and curtly dismissed it. Herzl returned to the goal of assimilation, which he discussed in the summer of 1894 with Lud-
wig Speidel, a colleague from the *Neue Freie Presse*, at Speidel's
summer home in the spa town of Baden, near Vienna. Herzl
reflected that antisemitism was a natural consequence of emancipation, claiming that Jews had retained particular traits that
Gentiles found threatening. But he spoke hopefully of antisemitism as instilling strength into the Jewish character and
believed it would lead Jews to undergo a process of "Darwinian
mimicry" that would lead to their successful assimilation. Maintaining the association between moral virtue, courage, and virility that he had made when writing about Captain Mayer,
Herzl spoke glowingly of the Jews' capacity to fight for their
country: "We were men who knew how to face war and how to
defend the state; had we not started out with such gifts, how
could we have survived two thousand years of unrelenting persecution?"[21] Despite praising the martial valor of ancient Israel,
at this time Herzl had no interest in solving the Jewish Problem through the reestablishment of the ancient Jewish homeland. In fall 1893, he had considered visiting "the new Zion
colonies" along with Jewish communities throughout eastern
Europe and the Near East, but only to document "the unde-
served misfortune of the Jews and to show that they are human
beings whom people revile without knowing them."[22] A year
later, he wrote, "if the Jews really 'returned home' one day,
they would discover on the next day that they do not belong
together. For centuries they have been rooted in new homelands, nationalized and separated from each other, preserved in
a particularity of character only by the omnipresent pressure
on them."[23]

Herzl was running out of possible solutions to a problem
that was not just about the Jews as a collective but also affected
him personally. In the carriage on the return from Speidel's
home, Herzl later wrote, two officer cadets passing by saw Herzl's

"Jewish nose and beard" and called him a "filthy Jew" (*Sau-jude*). Shortly thereafter Herzl returned to Paris, but his time there was approaching its end, as he was set to move back to Vienna in the following year to become the *Neue Freie Presse*'s literary editor. (Herzl's family returned earlier, allegedly so that Julie could be with her dying father, and Herzl moved into a hotel.) This was the mise-en-scène in mid-October, when Herzl had a burst of inspiration and in less than three weeks dashed off his most serious play, *The New Ghetto*. The opposite of a light drawing-room comedy, *The New Ghetto* was a tragic melodrama, and it was even more explicitly autobiographical than his previous plays and feuilletons.

The lead character, Jacob Samuel, is an earnest young attorney who, although staunchly bourgeois, sympathizes with the working classes. Jacob also has a guilty conscience: he once backed out of a duel with a blackguard cavalry officer, Count von Schramm, because Jacob needed to tend to his seriously ill father. (As we saw earlier, in his youth Herzl canceled a duel to care for his father, whose name, save for a minor difference in spelling, was the same as that of the lead character.) Jacob is married to a frivolous woman who, like Julie, is from a wealthy family. At this point the plot becomes more fictional, although it incorporates elements from Herzl's long-held fantasies. Jacob's brother-in-law, Fritz Rheinberg, is a sleazy stock exchange speculator, and Jacob loses the friendship of an upright Gentile because of this unsavory family connection. Von Schramm is a dissolute aristocrat who co-owns a coal mine that has been badly neglected and whose workers are poorly treated. Von Schramm reenters Jacob's life, not to fight him but to work with him and Rheinberg on incorporating the mine and selling shares at a tidy profit. The miners go on strike, a terrible accident kills many of them, and the value of the mine's shares collapse, ruining von Schramm. Although Jacob's role in the sordid affair had been limited to drawing up documents, von Schramm insults and strikes him. This time, Jacob does not leave his honor impugned; he challenges von Schramm to a duel, in which von Schramm shoots him dead. In the final draft of the play, Herzl has Jacob declaim as he expires, "Jews, my brothers—they will not let you live again, until you learn how to die. . . . I want to get out! Out of the ghetto!" At Schnitzler's advice, the words "until you learn how to die" were then taken out, but the withdrawn phrase powerfully communicates the essence of Herzl's message.[24]

According to Herzl's alter ego Jacob, the Jews have been emancipated yet remain in an invisible ghetto, imposed not only by antisemites but also by the Jews' own moral limitations. Like Herzl in his youth, Jacob exhibits shame over what he perceives as weakness and cowardice and aspires to be manly, altruistic, and self-disciplined. The Jews' worst qualities are embodied in stock exchange speculators, who lack honor and a moral compass. The Jewish women in the play are crass and pretentious, bedecked with jewels. Another unsympathetic character in the play is a rabbi who refuses to condemn social injustice and plays the stock market himself.

We can see in the play's stereotyped Jewish characters and wooden plot an unbalanced, neurotic Jewish self-criticism of the sort that at times in fin-de-siècle central Europe sank to the level of self-hatred. Schnitzler thought the play had much merit but criticized it for depicting Jews in too negative and harsh a light. Intriguingly, however, there is one likable character in the play, a stock exchange Jew named Wasserstein, who is vulgar and shabby but also unaffected, good-natured, and generous of spirit. He is not manly, but he is authentic. And this is the crux of the play—that Jews must seek honor, even if it means dying in a duel, and display authenticity, even if at heart they are simple tradesmen. As Jacob's wife says, "if you become untrue to yourself, you must not complain if others become untrue to you." Only a few weeks before writing the play, Herzl had seen assimilation as both desirable and feasible. In the play, however, Jacob, caught between the Jews' own failings and the corrupt snobbery of antisemites like von Schramm, realizes that it is both impossible and dishonorable to assimilate into Christian society. Jews must learn how to, in Jacob's words, "bow without servility, and stand upright without defiance."[25]

Foreshadowing concepts later developed by the philosophers Hannah Arendt and Jean-Paul Sartre, Herzl believed that Jews can attain authenticity only by accepting that they are pariahs. Shortly after finishing the play, Herzl briefly rejoined his pariah people by attending synagogue for the first time in his adult life. At Paris's grand synagogue in the rue de la Victoire, Herzl "found the services festive and moving" and thought fondly of the Dohany Street synagogue of his youth. But what stands out is the community of misfortune with which Herzl now identified. As Herzl sat among the congregants, he saw their "family likeness": "bold, misshapen noses, furtive and cunning eyes."[26]

Herzl did not quite live up to his play's lofty message about openness and authenticity. He urged Schnitzler to submit the play to theaters under a pseudonym lest the play be rejected out of hand because of its author's Jewish origins. Herzl wrote that despite the passion that drove him to write the play, and that now impelled him to see it produced, he also longed "to hide, to go underground—be it out of pride, cowardice, or shame . . . in the special instance of this play I want to hide my genitals more than any other time."[27] Underneath the puckish reference to his circumcised penis lay genuine anxiety about having exposed his innermost self and broken the patina of icy calm that he had maintained since his youth.

The play got no takers; it was not produced until December of 1897, by which time Herzl had gained fame as a Zionist leader, and the play was seen as a confession of Jewish nationalism. The play had another quality, however, that should not be overlooked. It is not a coincidence that the first play in which Herzl dealt explicitly with the Jewish Question was also the first in which he directly engaged the Social Question. The tragedies of the Jews and the coal miners are linked. Both are deformed by external factors, not their inner nature. Jacob tells his Christian friend, "By force you hurled us onto a pile of money, and now you want it all at once to no longer stick to us. You kept us in slavery for a thousand years, and now, from one day to the next, we must become inwardly free?" Just as Jews are prisoners of the invisible ghetto, the miners are captives of the "black hole that will one day devour them." The children are already deep in the bowels of the earth, hauling carts of coal for a pittance, and when they get older they will cut the coal in darkness, constantly exposed to danger, yet "they must! Otherwise those above will go hungry." Both the Social and Jewish Questions cried out for answers, but Herzl did not yet have a comprehensive answer.

Herzl completed *The New Ghetto* on 8 November. Ten days before, *La libre parole* had broken the news of the arrest of Alfred Dreyfus, a Jewish artillery officer on the French General Staff who was accused of espionage on behalf of Germany. Other newspapers jumped on the story, and Herzl filed his first reports on Dreyfus shortly thereafter: "The ugly business of Alfred Dreyfus is the talk of the day. It is still not definitively known if Dreyfus is in fact guilty. But the fact that the arrest of Captain Dreyfus was publicly announced from the General Staff, and that the Minister of War today brought the matter to the governmental [cabinet] meeting, gives room to believe that Dreyfus in fact committed the shameful deed."[28] Herzl offered detailed coverage of Dreyfus's 19–22 December trial, but only on the 27th did he explicitly mention that Dreyfus was Jewish, and even then it was an aside, a reference to a comment that Dreyfus allegedly made to one of his guards that he was being persecuted on account of his faith. When Dreyfus was found guilty and condemned to life imprisonment on Devil's Island, Herzl's reports did not protest the verdict. Even Herzl's report on Dreyfus's public degradation on 5 January was clipped and to the point. Herzl may have had doubts about Dreyfus's guilt, but there was no public sign that the captain's arrest, trial, and conviction had shaken him.

Why is it, then, that in an 1899 essay Herzl would claim, "What made me a Zionist was the Dreyfus trial"?[29] Why did he write in the same essay that the trial had inspired him to write *The New Ghetto?* After all, Herzl finished the play more than a month before the trial. To be fair to Herzl's recollection, the pretrial publicity, which was extensive and vitriolic, might have had an impact on the script. But Herzl himself claimed that the idea for the play came into his head all at once and that "the whole thing was finished in my mind" before he even put pen to paper. As for the Dreyfus trial, it is certainly possible that Herzl's articles for the *Neue Freie Presse* were censored by his editors, or that he practiced self-censorship and concealed his true feelings. But Herzl's letters at the time do not mention Dreyfus, and Dreyfus's name first appears in Herzl's diary on 17 November, half a year after Herzl became a Zionist. When it does appear, Herzl refers only to the anguish caused him by the accusation that Dreyfus had committed treason. There is no reference to his presumed innocence or to antisemitic reactions to the arrest and trial. And in March of 1896, the Odessa-based Hebrew newspaper *Ha-Melitz* attributed Herzl's turn to Zionism to antisemitism in Vienna. There was no mention of Dreyfus.

Herzl's narrative was an act of self-invention, which appears not to have been conscious. It occurred precisely as the Dreyfus trial ballooned into the international scandal known as the Dreyfus affair. In November of 1897, Herzl wrote in his diary of "the Dreyfus affair which, strangely enough, is active again at this particular time—just as it was three years ago, at the time when I was writing the Ghetto."[30] In Herzl's mind, the Dreyfus trial and the writing of his play had been conflated. Two months after this diary entry, the celebrated writer Émile Zola penned a polemical article, "*J'Accuse . . . !,*" which claimed that Dreyfus was the innocent victim of a French military conspiracy. France became torn between Dreyfus's supporters and his opponents, and in the following year Dreyfus was retried by a military court, convicted again ("with extenuating circumstances," wrote the court), and then pardoned by the president of the republic. The legitimacy of Zionism stood to be enhanced if the movement's leader could claim to have foreseen the tragic import of the arrest, show trial, and brutal punishment of an army officer for no other reason than his Jewish faith. In a small but highly charged change of wording, in 1899 Herzl recalled the mob at Dreyfus's degradation shouting "Death to the Jews," when according to his 1895 report the crowd had called for "death to the traitor," and a group of reserve officers had shouted "down with Judas!" (The French newspapers at the time, as well as the *New York Times*, confirmed Herzl's original wording.)[31]

Dreyfus's conviction, or more likely the swell of antisemitic rhetoric and demonstrations that followed, may well have added to the welter of forces that were pushing Herzl toward something he could neither understand nor articulate. More important than Dreyfus, however, were the Viennese municipal elections in April and May of 1895. No party won a majority, but the antisemite Karl Lueger was elected mayor. Herzl was horrified even though Lueger did not immediately take the position, preferring to wait for the next set of elections, when he could cement his authority. (In elections later in 1895 and again in 1896, Lueger and his United Christian party won a clear majority, but the Austro-Hungarian emperor refused to confirm Lueger's appointment until April of 1897.)

The Dual Monarchy was beset by many other problems

besides antisemitism. Herzl, as we have seen, was concerned about the empire's social problems, and he was also well aware of the nationality conflicts that threatened to tear the country apart. But ultimately it was the antisemitism that nurtured and bolstered separatist nationalism that drove Herzl to distraction. Herzl fantasized about fighting a duel against Lueger or the viciously antisemitic and chauvinist Austro-German politician Georg von Schönerer. If he were to be killed, he mused, he would die a martyr to the cause of fighting antisemitism. If he killed his opponent, he would be brought to trial and captivate the court with so thrilling a speech on the Jewish Question that he would be released—and antisemitism would be dealt a mortal blow.

Add to these grand political factors the fact that Herzl was imminently returning to Vienna: to his doting parents, on the one hand, but to his dysfunctional family, on the other. His new job as the *Neue Freie Presse*'s literary editor was a prestigious position, but one in which he would be knee-deep in submissions from poetasters whom he disdained or from gifted writers whom he envied. He was exhausted and repelled by the chaotic and increasingly threatening political atmosphere of Paris, but now he faced the prospect of going back to writing frothy feuilletons for which he had little respect. And *The New Ghetto*, which he hoped would mobilize the Jews and discomfit the antisemites, had not attracted a producer. (In contrast to what he did with his play *The Glossary*, Herzl did not consider publishing *The New Ghetto*, whose dramaturgical power lay in its grand, public declamations.)

By May of 1895, Herzl was in the grip of an existential crisis. Instead of falling into depression, as had been his past pattern, he experienced a prolonged period of heightened energy that in June escalated into a frenzy. If a professional trained in twenty-first-century psychiatry had assessed Herzl at this time, she might well have determined that Herzl was experiencing a manic episode and that he suffered from bipolar disorder. I see little value, however, in an attempt at retrospective psychiatric diagnosis. Rather, I want to understand how Herzl experienced—and later remembered—the weeks in 1895 that forever changed his life.

Herzl left behind abundant documentation of this period in a diary that he began to keep "around Pentecost [2 June] 1895." At first, Herzl consigned his thoughts to slips of paper upon which he wrote "walking, standing, lying down, in the street; at table, at night when I started up from sleep." Ten months later, Herzl gave them to his father to copy verbatim into a bound volume. "I know now, and knew throughout the whole tempestuous period of production, that much of what I wrote was wild and fantastic. But I made no self-criticism of any sort, so as not to cripple the sweep of these inspirations."[32]

The ascent into "inspiration" began in the first half of April, when Herzl told the author Alphonse Daudet he wanted to write a book about the Jews. Daudet recommended he write a didactic novel like *Uncle Tom's Cabin,* but Herzl demurred, saying he would rather write a "man's book." The idea of a novel stayed with Herzl, however, and he revisited his idea from four years earlier of a tale about his late friend Kana, but this time around, Kana would be a secondary character. He would still kill himself, but whereas in the earlier version that act of self-immolation was a form of empowerment, this time around it would be tragic and pathetic. Meanwhile, the hero, who is clearly Herzl himself, "discovers, or rather founds, the Promised Land," and at the book's end sails off to "new shores, together with a staff of officers expert in exploration"; "He stands at the bow of the boat and stares fixedly into the distance where the Promised Land lies."[33]

Herzl himself did not understand how and why over the next few weeks the idea of a novel began to slide into a concrete plan to direct the mass emigration of Jews from lands of persecution to a secure territory. In early May he contacted Baron Maurice de Hirsch, a Jewish banker, railway entrepreneur, and philanthropist who since 1891 had sponsored programs to settle Russian Jews as farmers in the New World, especially Argentina. In a haughty tone, Herzl promised a "new Jewish policy" that would make Hirsch into something more than a mere philanthropist. Hirsch granted his request for an audience—Herzl was, after all, a highly regarded journalist, and certainly worth an hour of the magnate's time—and the two met on the morning of 2 June. In preparation for the meeting, Herzl feverishly prepared a "thick bundle" of notes and distilled them into twenty-two handwritten pages, which he sought to commit to memory. Lightly soiling a pair of new gloves ("so as not to show rich people too much deference"), Herzl left his hotel and journeyed to Hirsch's mansion in the august rue d'Elysée.[34]

Herzl's diary provides the only account of the meeting. Here, as throughout the diary's pages, when Herzl describes his interactions with others he sets the scene, creates dialogue replete with dramatic tension, and casts himself in the starring role. How reliable, then, can the diaries be? Herzl usually wrote in the diary when the events of the day were fresh in his memory. Where other sources are available, they usually corroborate the main points of the conversation. There is also a good deal of overlap between what Herzl wrote in his diaries and in his correspondence, much of which has survived, along with letters back to Herzl. Besides, even when the veracity of the diaries can be questioned, they are still valuable in helping us see how Herzl wanted to represent himself to himself and to posterity. Immediately following the meeting with Hirsch, Herzl began to see the products of his pen not as mere diary entries, notes, and letters, but as documents to be carefully preserved as his legacy.

According to Herzl's account, he harangued the baron about the inadequacy of his programs that settled Jews in the New

World by the thousands, when millions were in danger. At first, Herzl raised themes from *The New Ghetto* about restoring Jewish honor and self-esteem. "Whether the Jews stay put or whether they emigrate, the race must first be improved on the spot. It must be made strong for war, eager to work, and virtuous. Afterwards, let them emigrate, if necessary."[35] Herzl suggested that the baron fund handsome prizes in antisemitic countries for Jews who perform "deeds of great moral beauty, for courage, self-sacrifice, ethical conduct, great achievements in arts and science . . . in short, for anything great." When Hirsch insisted that emigration was the only solution, Herzl "almost shouted": "'Well, who told you that I don't want to emigrate?'" Herzl said he would lay his plan before the German emperor and raise from Europe's wealthiest Jews a loan of ten million marks—a staggering sum, equivalent to twice the German imperial navy's annual budget.

Immediately after he got home from the meeting, Herzl saw to his dismay that he had only gotten through six of the twenty-two pages of notes. So he wrote Hirsch a long letter that, more clearly, yet with an even higher emotional charge than their conversation, laid out his coalescing migration scheme: "Money, money, and more money; means of transportation; the provisioning of great multitudes . . . the maintenance of manly discipline; the organization of departments; emigration treaties with the heads of some states, transit treaties with others, formal guarantees from all of them." He now spoke in terms of a billion marks for "working capital" with which to build "houses, palaces, workers' dwellings, schools, theaters, museums, government buildings, prisons, hospitals, insane asylums." There would be centrally directed propaganda through print and images, the most important of which would be a flag: "With a flag one can lead men wherever one wants to, even into the Promised Land. For a flag men will live and die." In his accelerating fervor, Herzl sketched out what would be on one level a technical and administrative enterprise demanding the most rigorous, rational administration. But Herzl also called this venture an "imponderable," a manifestation of will and spirit, for "visions alone grip the souls of men." Any man who did not grasp this truth "will not be a leader of men, and no trace of him will remain." And Herzl, now calling himself "a man of politics," would be that leader. True, he admitted to Hirsch, he was a young man—only thirty-five—but at that age, he noted, Napoleon was crowned emperor.[36]

Herzl spent most of June in an agitated state, which waned late in the month but persisted until, not coincidentally, his departure from Paris to Vienna at the end of July. He scribbled the equivalent of 160 printed pages in his diary in June but only thirty in July. In early July, he wrote that he was unsure if he was writing a novel or engaged in serious political activity. Only by the end of the month did it become clear to him that he had created a coherent plan for mass Jewish migration, which he would attempt to implement. If it failed, he would resort to the option of writing fiction, telling "the Jews didactic fairy tales" that "shall put seeds into the earth." But, he warned darkly, "I fear that by the time the seeds sprout, everyone will have starved."[37]

The diary entries from June and July are enthralling and illuminating, yet also unnerving and disturbing. They combine flashes of paranoia and of prescient wisdom, megalomania and altruistic idealism, delusions of grandeur and canny self-awareness. Throughout most of June, Herzl unleashed dubiously rational aphorisms like buckshot, but on 14 June he wrote a far more coherent, lengthy document that he wanted Moritz Güdemann, the chief rabbi of Vienna, to read aloud to Albert Salomon Anselm von Rothschild, head of the Vienna branch of the Rothschild banking dynasty—which Herzl saw as the cornerstone of his gargantuan fund-raising enterprise. The "Address to the Family," as Herzl called it, in turn formed the base of his pamphlet *The Jewish State*, published in February of 1896. The process by which Herzl's Zionist program emerged was a kind of condensation, in which an effulgence of psychic energy gradually thickened and solidified.

In the June diary entries, Herzl imagined himself as a great statesman, dictating terms to Hirsch and other wealthy Jews whom he had always envied and despised. He wrote that he would be an all-powerful leader and command unquestioning obedience in the future Jewish state. Bankers' daughters would be given in marriage to "vigorous young men" for the good of the state and the "self-fertilization of the nation." A "well-run secret police" would ensure Herzl's security. The Jewish state would be ruled by a Herzlian dynasty; his father Jakob would be the first senator of the Jewish state, and his son Hans would be its doge. Herzl envisioned a coronation ceremony with cuirassiers, artillery, and infantry, "marching in gold-studded gala uniforms." "The doge himself will wear the garb of shame of a medieval ghetto Jew: the pointed hat, the yellow badge. . . . Only inside the temple we wrap a princely cloak about his shoulders and place the crown on his head." Herzl wept at the grandeur of his own vision and the prospect of crowning his own son as doge. "Love and kisses to my Father-King," Herzl wrote in a telegram to his son on the little boy's fourth birthday.[38]

One striking aspect of Herzl's thoughts at this time is that he had no clear sense of where the Jewish state would be: "No one ever thought of looking for the Promised Land where it actually is—and yet it lies so near. This is where it is—within ourselves." He appeared to favor moving the Jews to Latin America, "far from militarized and seedy Europe." In South America the Jews could gradually "get an army together unobserved, but will for a long time proceed cautiously, exploiting the enemies of the republics and preserving their friendship through presents, bribes, loans, etc." The time would come, however, when the Jewish army would stand on its own.[39]

The diary brims with ruminations about military matters, reflecting Herzl's own ongoing shame at not having done army service and his obsession with discipline and manliness. At times his invocation of the military is metaphorical, as when he speaks of "labour battalions along military lines" or Europe's overeducated and underemployed Jewish intellectuals who will "form the general staff and the cadres of the army which is to seek, discover, and take over the land."[40] But he describes the preparation and structure of the new state's Jewish armed forces in great detail, ranging from the English sports that the youth will play in order to ready them for the army to the "experienced warriors" who will face death in battle.

The military is only part of a vast bureaucracy that Herzl imagines putting into place to carry out the transfer of humans and capital, the dissolution of Jewish-owned properties, and the purchase and improvement of land in the new Jewish homeland. The bureaucracy will not only manage a mass immigration of Jews, it will also "expropriate gently the private property on the estates assigned to us. . . . We shall try to spirit the penniless population across the border by procuring employment for it in the transit countries, while denying it employment in our own country. The property owners will come over to our side. Both the process of expropriation and the removal of the poor must be carried out discreetly and circumspectly. The property owners may believe that they are cheating us, selling to us at more than [the land is] worth. But nothing will be sold back to them." Although natives will be expelled, the freedom and property rights of sojourning non-Jews will be protected, and foreign visitors will be received "with aristocratic benevolence and proud amiability."[41]

If there is a unifying theme to these ramblings, it is the inversion of antisemitic stereotypes and practices for the empowerment of the Jews. The Jews will organize their own departure to a Promised Land "where it is all right to have hooked noses, black or red beards, and bandy legs without being despised for these things alone." Pioneer laborers will wear yellow ribbons, which, like the doge's yellow badge, hearken back to the distinctive, discriminatory markings that Jews were required to wear in medieval Europe. In the pursuit of honor, Herzl demands that those who attempt suicide be placed in mental asylums, and that the wills of those who succeed at killing themselves be declared invalid. Suicide and anarchism are, somehow, linked; thus, Herzl believes that he must "seize suicide by the throat." Dueling will be allowed, but only with swords, not pistols. (Those who insist on dueling with pistols will instead be sent on "dangerous missions" ranging from receiving experimental vaccines to fighting the unnamed "national enemy.") Although on the one hand Herzl argues that compulsory conscription for Europe's Jews should be ended, he also insists that those Jews who remain in Europe serve gallantly in their countries' wars and, "if on opposite sides, shoot at one another." It is a "debt of honor."[42]

Herzl was aware that his rantings could appear "ludicrous, exaggerated, crazy." "Am I working it out?," he asked himself. "No! It is working itself out in me": "During these days I have more than once been afraid I was losing my mind. This is how tempestuously the trains of thought have raced through my soul. A lifetime will not suffice to carry it all out. But I shall leave behind a spiritual legacy. To whom? To all men. I believe I shall be named among the greatest benefactors of mankind. Or is this belief already megalomania? I must, above all, keep myself under control."[43] Although he fears that others will think him mad, "they are wrong. I know that two and two is four." In a letter to Güdemann, Herzl referred murkily to his plan, avoiding detail but saying that it was a solution to the Jewish Question, and that he would convince interlocutors of its feasibility: "Oh yes, even in my most exalted expositions I shall, here and there, have to mention casually, as though accidentally, that 2 × 2 is four, 2 × 3 is six, and 17 × 7 is 119. And I shall say that I quite distinctly remember what you or somebody else said to me, or must have thought about me, at some earlier point in my life—just so people will see that I still have my wits about me."[44]

Wandering through Paris's Tuileries Garden on 18 June, "overstrained with thought," Herzl latched on to the idea of laying out his plans to the German chancellor Otto von Bismarck, who is "big enough to understand me or cure me." The next day he sent the chancellor a lengthy, disjointed letter, repeating the mathematical mantra he had presented to Güdemann, and referring to himself as someone who might be sent to an asylum's "Department for Inventors of Dirigible Balloons." (Three days previously, the physician and journalist Friedrich Schiff had told Herzl he looked as if he had invented the dirigible, an object that is both lighter than air and steerable, and a symbol of a flight of fancy.) Bismarck did not reply to Herzl, leading him to fret, "Will he take me for a gentle fool or a raving one?"[45] Despite Bismarck's apparent rebuff, Herzl persisted in seeing himself as a visionary, a leader, and, most importantly, an inventor who is undergoing the "shock of discovery—when gold first flashes before the alchemist's eyes, when a steam engine begins to work, or a balloon suddenly shows itself to be dirigible."[46]

In late July, Herzl noted that he was now ready to sacrifice himself to the Jewish cause but must do nothing to harm his parents in their old age or his children's future. For that reason, he wrote, people must not consider him mad. (Herzl used the Yiddish word *meshugge*.) Besides, Herzl assured himself, "there is no madness in creative writing itself. The important thing is the idea which the big writing [*sic*] puts on paper; if it is sound and clear, the only ridiculous elements will be the doubters."[47] In his published writings, Herzl often reflected on the link between genius and insanity, as in an 1895 essay: "The imaginations of a madman are much more colorful, wild, majestic and frightful than those of Shakespeare, even of [the French novelist] Ponson du Terrail."[48] In a Zionist essay of 1897, Herzl invoked another French writer, Pierre-Jean de Béranger: "How long must an idea wait, like an unknown maid for her bridegroom! / Fools call her mad. The wise man tells her: 'Hide.' / But then, far from the crowd / a lunatic, who still believes in tomorrow / meets her and marries her, and she becomes fecund / for the happiness of all mankind."[49]

Herzl explores the social aspects of his plan in language that is enthusiastic and exuberant, yet sane. Herzl ponders that he may be "solving much more than the Jewish Question. Namely, very neatly, the Social Question!"[50] Precisely because he wants to create a new society on "virginal soil," he can introduce radical reforms and thereby solve the Social Problem and the Jewish Problem together. Herzl proposes policies such as state monopolies on liquor and tobacco, regulation of the insurance business and stock exchange, and, most important, a humane, seven-hour working day. For this reason, the Jewish state's flag would have seven stars.

In late July, Herzl retreated from his earlier militarism. Shunning Jewish chauvinism, Herzl called for a multinational confederation like Switzerland. Despite the arduous process of migration and establishment of the new state, the goal was to create the opposite of a Spartan, warlike society: "Another thing to be prevented is a policy of future conquest. New Judea shall reign only by spirit."[51] It would also be steeped in Western creature comforts. On the ship to the new land, the passengers would dress for dinner, and in the new land there would be all the comforts of home: "*Salzstangel* [salted breadsticks], coffee, beer, familiar meats." The capital city would be a European paradise surrounded by mountains and forests.

Despite his stray comment about leaving behind "militarized and seedy Europe," Herzl desperately wanted to remain a part of it. "At present I am not recognized as a German. But that will come once we are over there." The Jewish state would be admired by the whole world, and the Jews would be respected at last: "In the beginning, we will only work on ourselves and for ourselves, in all secrecy. But the Jewish state will become remarkable. The land of the seven-hour workday is not only the model for social experiments, not only the treasure-house of works of art, but it is also a land of miracles pertaining to all forms of culture. It will be a target of the civilized world, which will visit us, just as it visits Lourdes, Mecca, and Sadagora."[52] Lourdes in France, Mecca in today's Saudi Arabia, and Sadigura (Sadagora) in today's Ukraine (formerly in Hapsburg Bukovina) are sites of Christian, Muslim, and Jewish religious pilgrimage. Herzl had a particular attraction to Lourdes and Sadigura as places where miracles were thought to happen. Herzl envisioned a Jewish state that would be no less miraculous. The Marian apparitions associated with Lourdes, along with the deeds of Yisrael Friedman, the Hasidic rabbi (in German, *Wunderrebbe*) of Sadigura, would give way to the new Jewish *Wunderland*, which would become a site of secular pilgrimage.

Herzl did not believe that God worked wonders at Lourdes or that Rabbi Yisrael Friedman of Sadigura communed with the divine. But he appreciated the transformative torque generated by people's belief in the miraculous. For this reason, Herzl wrote that the "Wonder Rabbi of Sadagora [is] to be brought over and installed as something like the bishop of a province." Having him in the Zionist camp would "win over the entire clergy": "Do I need to illustrate the phenomenon of masses and the ways of attracting them to any desired spot by discussing religious pilgrimages, too? . . . Let me just mention in passing what the pilgrimage to Mecca means in the Mohammedan world, Lourdes and the Holy Mantle at Treves to the Catholics, and so many other places from which people return home comforted by their faith. So, over there we will build a more

beautiful Sadagora for the Wonder Rabbi. After all, our clergy-
men will be the first to understand us and go with us."[53]

Herzl hoped to appeal to Jewish religious passion but would
not allow it to compel observance or dictate affairs of state.
"We shall let everyone find salvation over there in his own
way," he noted briskly. In the "Address to the Family," he writes,
"Faith unites us, science makes us free. . . . We shall restrict
[the clergy] to their temples, just as we shall restrict our professional soldiers to their barracks." Herzl saw the role of religion
in the future Jewish state as circumscribed yet essential, just as
the essence of Jewish peoplehood lay in a religion that Herzl
himself barely observed. It is a fundamental paradox that, as
Herzl noted, "The only thing by which we still recognize our
kinship is the faith of our fathers."[54]

The paradox was even deeper than that: although in June
Herzl wrote about Jewishness deriving from religion, a month
later he claimed that Jewishness had "nothing to do with religion" and that all Jews "are of the same race."[55] Four months
after that, he appeared to contradict himself yet again when
he met the Anglo-Jewish author Israel Zangwill, whom Herzl
described as a "long-nosed, Negroid type, with very woolly
deep-black hair." A racial definition of Jewishness, Herzl wrote,
makes no sense "if I so much as look at him and at myself. . . .
We are an historical unit, a nation with anthropological diver-
sities. This also suffices for the Jewish State. No nation has uni-
formity of race."[56] However difficult it was for Herzl to define
what it meant to be Jewish, he was consistent in believing it to
center around ideas, feelings, and aspirations rather than material or biological factors.

The embrace of Jewishness via Zionism was Herzl's miracle, his salvation, what he would later call "the sabbath of my
life." Antisemitism in Austria catalyzed it, but ironically it was
the art of a notorious German antisemite that gave Herzl inspiration and solace during those exhausting weeks in June. In the

late spring the Paris Opera was performing Richard Wagner's opera *Tannhäuser.* Herzl devoted a feuilleton to it in May, and in June he repeatedly attended performances of the opera, which, he wrote, soothed him. Why did this opera cool Herzl's fevered mind, and why was he so attached to the opera that he had music from it played at the Second Zionist Congress in 1898?

Tannhäuser tells the story of a gifted but arrogant minstrel who has left his band of troubadours for the goddess Venus, who keeps him in a grotto beneath a mountain called the Venusberg. Tannhäuser grows miserable in erotic captivity and longs for a return to earthly life, where he can repent of his sins and return to the spiritual love of the chaste Elisabeth, the niece of the count who hosts the troubadour band. Unable to overcome his pride and his past, Tannhäuser sings the praises of physical passion in the presence of Elisabeth and his peers, who banish him from their midst. Now truly penitent, Tannhäuser seeks forgiveness from the pope but is rebuffed. In despair, he calls for Venus to take him back to her lair, but he is reminded of Elisabeth (now dead), who redeems him from beyond the grave. Venus vanishes and Tannhäuser dies, his soul saved for all eternity.

Herzl's attraction to the opera has been read aesthetically, as an appreciation of its lush and stirring music, or politically, as an allegory on escape from the ghetto (the grotto of Venus) or the impossibility of assimilation (Tannhäuser's futile entreaties to the pope). It makes at least as much sense, however, to read his engagement with the opera autobiographically. Herzl was both proud of and insecure about his literary talents, and he was supremely ambitious. More important, Herzl was searching for an escape from his unhappy marriage and stunted erotic life. Already in 1887, a year after meeting Julie and being thrown into panic by his passionate attraction to her, Herzl had published his first volume of feuilletons, *News from Venus*, in which the goddess of love stood for self-deceit and hypocrisy. Eight years later, Herzl found in Zionism his Elisabeth—a source of spiritual rescue, and a cause to which he could sacrifice himself completely, driving him, like Tannhäuser, to a premature death.[57]

Elated yet exhausted by his metamorphosis, Herzl now looked upon Julie with a sense of distance, and even tenderness, for he had found a calling that would transcend the pettiness and melodrama of his family life. On 19 June, he wrote to Julie that he was engaged in a great project—one that he likened to childbirth—but that must be kept secret. In July, he was still toying with writing a novel, but it was clearly secondary to his crystallizing, increasingly ambitious plans for mass Jewish migration. Herzl's scheme to solve the Jewish Question was thrilling and captivating, even if often unhinged, but his ideas turned trite and schmaltzy when he thought about the novel. He considered a revenge fantasy in which Baron Hirsch's money unwittingly goes to help the Zionist cause, yet both Hirsch and the hero (a stand-in for Herzl) withdraw from all public activity just as the state is about to be recognized, forcing them to reconcile. Characters in the novel would include a blond-haired, blue-eyed male hero; his beloved, "a Spanish Jewess, slender, dark-haired, high-bred," a "clever swindler," and a virtuous girl who dies young.[58] (Her name is Pauline.) It is as if all of Herzl's creativity and imagination had been channeled into his Zionist vision, leaving nothing for literature.

During his final weeks in Paris, Herzl tentatively began to look for allies. On 6 July, he and Nordau talked about the Jewish Question over a beer. "Never before had I been in such perfect touch with Nordau. Each took the words right out of the other's mouth. I never had such a strong feeling that we belonged together." Yet Herzl did not dare to share his scheme with Nordau until four months later. Herzl continued to pepper Rabbi Güdemann with letters, asking for a meeting without offering specifics about what he had in mind. Güdemann was cautious, skeptical, and not a little worried about Herzl's sanity. Herzl was undeterred. On 25 July, he wrote, "to stand by idly and watch when a house is on fire is certainly more insane than to rush up with a modern fire engine. And that is what I want to do." Two days later Herzl returned to Vienna. He noted in his diary: "And today I am leaving Paris! One book of my life is ending. A new one is beginning. Of what kind?"[59]

3

The Organizational Genius

WHEN HERZL RETURNED to Vienna in July of 1895, he was thirty-five and in his prime. At some point over his years in Paris, he had shaved off the mutton chops of his youth and grown a full beard, which grew more massive and luxuriant over time. The beard bestowed upon Herzl an air of ancient Semitic glory as well as preternatural gravity. It came to symbolize his zeal, dedication, and bonds with the Jewish past and the Jewish people.[1]

In a tête-à-tête in Paris in November of 1895, Herzl revealed his Zionist vision to Nordau, who had succeeded Herzl as Paris correspondent for the *Neue Freie Presse*. Nordau was but one of many individuals to whom Herzl turned in a feverish search for allies. Herzl's years of hawking his plays had accustomed him to networking and public relations, and his sparkling prose, which had previously described the lives of others, was now placed in the service of his own political vision. Between late 1895 and early 1898, Herzl's charismatic and organizational genius came into full flower, as he created a new international Zionist organization, convened its first Congress, and set out to win the world's attention and approval for his fantastic scheme.

Herzl believed in the power of words. As a playwright, he was accustomed to reading his works aloud, in their entirety, to prospective backers and directors. Treating his draft address to the Rothschild family like a script, in the second half of 1895 Herzl performed two-hour readings of the address in meetings with luminaries such as the chief rabbis of France and of Vienna, the co-founder of the Paris-based Alliance Israélite Universelle, and a distinguished Jewish architect who sat on the Vienna city council. Although Herzl hoped that the Rothschilds and other Jewish magnates would fund the mass transfer of Jews from sites of antisemitism and persecution, Herzl's interlocutors threw cold water on the idea. Similarly, Herzl's father, Jakob, thought that supplicating the Rothschilds was undignified and impracticable.

Herzl accordingly decided to bring his ideas "straight to the people, and in the form of a novel."[2] Herzl had in mind a version of the melodramatic work, featuring characters based on his deceased friend Kana and sister Pauline, that he had considered writing in April. But by the fall Herzl had abandoned the novel and decided to produce a tract instead. In December, Herzl began to search for publishers. His first two choices rejected the work, but Herzl's fortunes improved when, in January, the *Jewish Chronicle*, one of the world's most influential Jewish newspapers at the time, published a summary of Herzl's main arguments under the title "The Solution of the Jewish Question." The day after its appearance, Herzl signed a contract with a small publisher based in Leipzig and Vienna.

The *Jewish Chronicle* piece attracted smatterings of both

support and derision, but the unpublished proofs of the pamphlet turned out to be a far greater cause of concern for Herzl when his editors at the *Neue Freie Presse*, Bacher and Benedikt, got hold of them. They urged Herzl not to publish the work, which would, as Bacher put it, endanger the Jews' positions in their current fatherlands without guaranteeing them a new one. Herzl pointed out that, with the appearance of the pamphlet's summary in the *Jewish Chronicle*, the cat was already out of the bag. Herzl stood his ground, but in the coming days he suffered episodes of heart palpitations and shortness of breath. On 14 February 1896, Herzl received a bundle of five hundred complimentary copies of his pamphlet, titled *Der Judenstaat: Versuch einer modernen Lösung der Judenfrage* (The Jewish State: An Endeavor for a Modern Solution to the Jewish Question).

At just over twenty thousand words, *The Jewish State* is perhaps the shortest example of the waggish definition of a "classic" as something that is often praised but rarely read. For over a century, snippets from the pamphlet have been quoted in the writings and speeches of Zionist activists and Israeli politicians, mainly to demonstrate Herzl's prescient understanding of the dangers of antisemitism and his vision of a Jewish state that would be a model of social justice and technological progress. These qualities are indeed present in the text, but much of the original meaning of Herzl's discussions has gotten lost. What is more, these discussions are highly revealing about Herzl's own intellectual and psychological state—which aspects of his selfhood had changed since his burst of frenzy just a half year previously, and which remained the same.

The pamphlet adopts a taut, muscular, and above all unemotional style. Herzl examines antisemitism "without fear or hatred," seeing it as an inevitable reaction to what he calls "commercial jealousy." These jealousies affect the Jewish upper and middle classes as well as the poor and proletarian Jewish masses. Herzl does not focus on the plight of Russian or Romanian Jews, who at the time were the center of concern for Jewish nationalists in eastern Europe and Jewish philanthropists in the West:

> In Russia, imposts are levied on Jewish villages; in Rumania, a few persons are put to death; in Germany, they get a good beating occasionally; in Austria, antisemites exercise terrorism over all public life; in Algeria, there are traveling agitators; in Paris, the Jews are shut out of the so-called best social circles and excluded from clubs. Shades of anti-Jewish feeling are innumerable. But this is not to be an attempt to make out a doleful category of Jewish hardships.
>
> I do not intend to arouse sympathetic emotions on our behalf. That would be a foolish, futile, and undignified proceeding. I shall content myself with putting the following questions to the Jews: Is it not true that, in countries where we live in perceptible numbers, the position of Jewish lawyers, doctors, technicians, teachers, and employees of all descriptions becomes daily more intolerable? Is it not true that the Jewish middle classes are seriously threatened? Is it not true that the passions of the mob are incited against our wealthy people? Is it not true that our poor endure greater sufferings than any other proletariat? I think that this external pressure makes itself felt everywhere. In our economically upper classes it causes discomfort, in our middle classes continual and grave anxieties, in our lower classes absolute despair.[3]

Although Herzl worries about the harm that antisemitism can do to middle-class Jews, that harm has limits. Jewish emancipation, Herzl asserts, cannot be undone because the modern world is wedded to the concept of the *Rechtsstaat*—the state regulated and legitimized by law. Besides, any attempts to rescind Jewish emancipation would send Jews into the arms of revolutionary movements. Therefore, "no weapons can be effectively used against us, because these injure the hands that wield them." With the hindsight of history, we know that Herzl was wrong about the invulnerability of Jewish emancipation, which was in fact rescinded in much of Europe during the 1930s and 1940s and preceded the Nazi genocide.

Another surprising aspect of Herzl's pamphlet is its positive attitudes toward Jewish assimilation and to Jews who did not wish to move to the Jewish state. Herzl expresses no disapproval of assimilation but asserts that it is impossible due to pervasive resentment directed against Jews. This will all change, however, when a critical mass of Europe's Jews, who are seen as economic competitors to Gentiles, have left for their state. Herzl has in mind not only the Jewish poor but also the educated proletariat of Jewish attorneys and journalists who scramble for a living in Europe's major cities. (This critique was self-referential, in that Herzl was trained to be an attorney and worked as a journalist.) Herzl further claims that Jews who leave Europe will transfer their property at a fair price to Gentiles, who will thereby be enriched. Last but not least, a Jewish state will be a social and technological wonder, attracting Gentile admiration and respect for Jews. All these factors will cause antisemitism to disappear. By no means will all Jews leave for the Jewish state, but once that state exists, Jews who choose to remain in diaspora will lead comfortable and prosperous lives, leading to their complete—and this time successful—assimilation.

Herzl's justifications for the founding of a Jewish state occupy only a small portion of the pamphlet. Most of it is about how the massive transfer of bodies and property across thousands of miles will be accomplished. Herzl calls for the establishment of two bodies: the Society of Jews and the Jewish Company. The Society of Jews will be a "state-making power," that is, a proto-government: "Those Jews who agree with our idea of a State will attach themselves to the Society, which will thereby be authorized to confer and treat with Governments in the name of our people." Although any supporter of Herzl's plan could join the Society, Herzl quickly dismisses the prospect of a democratic organization where issues would be subject to debate and vote. "Such a result," writes Herzl, "would ruin the cause from the outset, and dissidents must remember that allegiance or opposition is entirely voluntary. He who will not come with us should remain behind." Thinking along these lines, Herzl proposed that the Jewish state would be an aristocratic republic. From his experiences in Paris and Vienna, Herzl had come to fear the excesses of mob democracy when exercised by Christians, and he apparently did not hold much more trust in Jews.

The Society of Jews would also carry out statistical studies and environmental research to determine the most appropriate site for mass Jewish settlement. This task provides the context in which Herzl raises the possibility of Argentina as well as Palestine as the site of the Jewish state. On this issue, Herzl tips his hand, for although he briefly acknowledges Argentina's excellent land and climate, his language about Palestine is considerably more passionate. Palestine, he writes,

> is our ever-memorable historic home. The very name of Palestine would attract our people with a force of marvellous potency. If His Majesty the Sultan were to give us Palestine, we could in return undertake to regulate the whole finances of Turkey. We should there form a portion of a rampart of Europe against Asia, an outpost of civilization as opposed to barbarism. We should as a neutral State remain in contact with all Europe, which would have to guarantee our existence. The sanctuaries of Christendom would be safeguarded by assigning to them an extra-territorial status such as is well-known to the law of nations. We should form a guard of honor about these sanctuaries, answering for the fulfilment of this duty with our existence. This guard of honor would

be the great symbol of the solution of the Jewish Question after eighteen centuries of Jewish suffering.[4]

Herzl's association of Asia with "barbarism" is disturbing, and I will address it, along with Herzl's colonialist sensibilities, in the next chapter. Here I want to focus on the difference between Herzl's conception of territory in the pamphlet and in his June diary entries, where he favored a Jewish state in Latin America. What had happened? Herzl was experiencing a gradual but steady process of intensified Judaic identity, and along with it came a greater awareness of, and attraction to, Palestine. No less important, Herzl's conversations with Zionist activists while he was writing the pamphlet indicated, time and time again, that Palestine was the only destination that would mobilize a popular movement.

Herzl deals with the Society of Jews fairly briefly and devotes the bulk of the pamphlet's prescriptive sections to the operations of the Jewish Company, a public utility that would undertake the construction of the new Jewish state. As in the June diary entries, but now in a more subdued and coherent fashion, Herzl lays out every jot and tittle of the company's operations. It will oversee the formation of immigrant groups by place of origin, regulating the pace of migration to the new land. Poor immigrants will precede bourgeois ones, with the wealthy coming last of all. The company will take charge of the liquidation of the emigrants' property in their old homes and purchase real estate for them in their new land. It will employ poor immigrants in building the country's infrastructure and accommodate them in clean and healthful homes, unlike "the melancholy workmen's barracks of European towns." All who are capable of work will be employed via a tutelary administration, "military in character: there will be commands, promotions, and pensions." Men and women will marry young, producing sturdy offspring. Prizes will be given for outstanding economic performance. The company will not enforce religious observance, which will be a matter of individual choice, yet each immigrant group will have its own rabbi, "for we feel our historic affinity only through the faith of our fathers as we have long ago absorbed the languages of different nations to an incredible degree." Similarly, inhabitants of the new state will be free to speak whichever language they wish, but Yiddish will disappear—not because of a dictate from the company, but rather because the Jews' "miserable stunted . . . Ghetto languages" were the "tongues of prisoners," which Jews, once free, will abandon of their own accord.

Undergirding the Jewish Company's paternalism is an imperative for benevolence. Pregnant women will not labor. Work will be carried out in a seven-hour workday consisting of two three-and-a-half-hour shifts, separated by leisure and rest: "We will seek to bestow the moral salvation of work on men of every age and of every class and thus our people will find their strength again in the land of the seven-hour day." In addition to striving for social justice in the new Jewish state, the Jewish Company will adhere to the most stringent ethical standards in its financial activities in the Jews' former homelands. The company will give "every assistance to Governments and Parliaments in their efforts to direct the inner migration of Christian citizens" to formerly Jewish properties. "Every obligation in the old country must be scrupulously fulfilled before leaving. . . . Every just private claim originating in the abandoned countries will be heard more readily in the Jewish State than anywhere else. We shall not wait for reciprocity; we shall act purely for the sake of our own honor." As a sign of their acknowledgment of Jewish honor, writes Herzl, even "honest antisemites" will buy shares in the Jewish Company and take part in the orderly transfer of Jewish property to its new owners.

Herzl's passion—one might say obsession—with planning and central direction of the settlement enterprise helps account for one of the most curious lacunae in Herzl's writing. In the diary entries for 1895 and early 1896, Herzl uses the word "Zionist" to describe others, not himself. Similarly, the word "Zionist" appears only three times in *The Jewish State*, and each time it is used in a critical way. When Herzl first experienced a Jewish awakening, he had never heard of "Zionism," a word coined around 1890 by Nathan Birnbaum, a Viennese Jew of Galician (Austrian-Polish) origin. Birnbaum had been a student activist in Vienna and in 1882 had founded the Jewish nationalist society Kadimah (Forward) at the city's university. By Zionism, Birnbaum meant a Jewish nationalism with an attachment to Palestine. This was an intensification and clarification of the sentimental attachment to the land of Israel espoused by the first generation of primarily eastern European Jewish nationalists, organized in 1884 into a federation known as the Lovers of Zion (*Chovevei Tsion*). When Herzl experienced his frenzy in June 1895, he did not have a word or phrase to describe his newfound cause. And when he did learn of the word Zionism, he associated it with the practices of the Lovers of Zion, who sponsored small-scale, piecemeal Jewish settlement in Palestine. Thus, in his diaries, Herzl described as "Zionists" people who, like himself, had a Jewish national program, but who lacked a grand plan for implementing it. And in *The Jewish State*, the same differentiation applied. Herzl adopted the Zionist label for himself and his enterprise only in the months following the publication of the pamphlet. Herzl appreciated the strength and simplicity of the word, and he applied it to the Zionist Organization and the Zionist Congress, both of which he founded.

The Jewish State did not take the world by storm. It received attention in the Jewish press, but otherwise it was mostly ignored. Only half-jokingly, Herzl described his "warmest adherent" as Ivan von Simonyi, an antisemite in Bratislava who bombarded Herzl with his journalistic writings. In the Jewish world, reactions were definitely mixed. The *Jewish Chronicle* gave the pamphlet an arch review, but the chief rabbi of Sofia, Bulgaria, proclaimed Herzl to be the Messiah. Eastern European Zionists found the pamphlet both familiar and alarmingly audacious. Veteran activists in the Lovers of Zion looked askance upon Herzl's assimilated background and disregard for their own settlement activity in Palestine for the previous fifteen years. They feared that his scheme might infuriate both Palestine's suzerain, the Ottoman Empire, and the reactionary Russian Empire, which outlawed nationalist activity by any of its minorities. Most importantly, many of Herzl's ideas, both diagnostic and prescriptive, had appeared almost fifteen years before the appearance of *The Jewish State*. In 1882, Lev Pinsker, a founder and leader of the Lovers of Zion, published a pamphlet in German called *Auto-Emancipation*. Like Herzl, Pinsker considered the only remedy for antisemitism to be a Jewish national home, and like Herzl he called for the mobilization of international Jewry into a state-building organization. In his diary, Herzl contends that he had never heard of Pinsker before September of 1895 and that he read Pinsker's pamphlet only five months later, when *The Jewish State* was already in press. Herzl acknowledged "an astounding correspondence in the critical part, a great similarity in the constructive one" and confessed he was glad not to have seen it previously, for had he done so, he would not have written his own pamphlet.[5] Since Pinsker died in 1891, Herzl could not communicate his admiration directly to the pioneer activist.

On this issue, as on many others, we may bring to Herzl's diary a quantum of suspicion, as from the start he intended it for publication after his death as a chronicle of his achievements and vicissitudes. There is no evidence, however, of Herzl lying outright regarding events, his personal experience, or his state of mind. *The Jewish State* emerged from the June 1895 diary entries, which, like molten lava, hardened into a solid, coherent form, yet still bore the signs of a volcanic origin. Herzl perceived himself as having few forerunners and no peers, a singular creature possessed of a unique vision and ability to realize it. "I shall be the Parnell of the Jews," he noted in October 1895, likening himself to the Irish nationalist leader Charles Stewart Parnell, who had died just four years previously.[6] (The two men, in fact, had much in common—Parnell came from a wealthy, Anglo-Irish family that was in many ways similar to Herzl's assimilated Austro-Hungarian one. Both men died young—Herzl at forty-four, and Parnell at forty-five.)

Herzl's friend Nordau certainly shared the view of Herzl as a uniquely gifted leader. His response to *The Jewish State* was immediate and profound:

> I have read your *Jewish State* twice. I don't have time today to discuss it. But here is my impression in brief: objectively the work may be judged in certain ways; subjectively it is simply a great deed. If you had never written another line, if you never wrote one again, this brochure assures you a lasting place among heroes. Heroically, for a writer passionate about style—renouncing any showy language, the modest, austere terseness of the presentation; unspeakably heroic is the burning of all bridges behind you. You have given up being a "German writer" or [Austrian] patriot. Henceforth you can only continue to act as you have—calling forth the deepest humanity from the reader. For you, the more common emotions that are evoked by playing the strings of patriotism, of territorial associations, etc., must from now on remain mute; and highly heroic is this more than brave, indeed, fearless unto death, recognition of the ultimate feeling, which all Jews until now have borne in the deepest recesses of their soul. Uriel Da Costa did less; Luther at Worms did no more. It was not your intentional effect that I would think primarily about the subjective, about you, and not on the

work. But you must be able to empathize with me that I do this. For I do not know what will become of this work, but I do know that you have revealed yourself in this brochure.[7]

Like Nordau, eastern European Zionists admired Herzl's passion, but they were concerned where it might lead. In March of 1896, the Hebrew newspaper *Ha-Melitz* noted approvingly that although Herzl had been raised "without Torah," "with scarcely a sign of Jewish spirit, like a dry bone," he fulfilled the prophet Ezekiel's vision of dry bones coming back to life. Herzl has "returned with complete penitence; his soul shall kindle hot coals and his heart burns with the heat of the love of his people . . . 'in the place where penitents stand even the completely righteous do not stand.'"[8] The article even contends that Herzl is more focused, talented, and renowned than the beloved and departed Pinsker. Yet at the same time, it cautions, Herzl's dreams are too grandiose. If there is to be a Jewish state, it will arise gradually, and it will take in only a modest number of Jews. Nahum Sokolow, editor of another major Hebrew newspaper, *Ha-Tzefirah*, was more blunt, dismissing Herzl as a "Viennese feuilletonist who is playing at diplomacy," and likened him to a child playing with matches near a grain silo. The silo here was the Ottoman Empire, which, Sokolow correctly acknowledged, tolerated Palestine's small Jewish community but periodically acted against Jewish migration, and would not stand for a mass influx of Jews.

In 1896, Sokolow was a middle-aged man. (He was thirty-seven, a year older than Herzl.) Other leaders of Russian Zionism were approximately the same age. Asher Ginsberg, a major figure in Hebrew letters who wrote under the pen name Ahad Ha-Am (One of the people), was four years older than Herzl. Menachem Ussishkin, one of the Lovers of Zion's most influential leaders, was three years younger. Tensions between Herzl and Russian Zionists stemmed from many sources. Differences in approach—quiet versus public, gradual versus orchestrated—blended with cultural differences between the highly assimilated Herzl and Russian Jews who were intimately familiar with the Jewish tradition, were often native speakers of Yiddish, and had learned Hebrew at an early age. Russian Zionists, for the most part, were not Orthodox, and most had had a formal secular education, but one cannot compare even the most secularized among them with Herzl, who was so non-observant that he did not have his son Hans circumcised. When the chief rabbi of Vienna came to visit Herzl at his home in December of 1895, Herzl was decorating the children's Christmas tree.

Herzl's Judaic ignorance did not, however, put off David Wolffsohn, a genial Lithuanian Jew with a thorough yeshiva education and a successful career as a timber merchant. As a youth, Wolffsohn studied under Rabbi Isaac Rülf, a leader of the Lovers of Zion in the city of Memel in East Prussia. Wolffsohn was fluent in German and spent most of his life in Cologne. Wolffsohn admired Herzl with a deep and unshakable, yet not naïve, loyalty, and he became Herzl's most effective and long-serving lieutenant. Wolffsohn was blessedly free of the competitive drive that takes hold of so many men in the prime of their lives. In this sense, he was light-years apart from Nathan Birnbaum, who both emulated Herzl and resented his spectacular entry into the Viennese Zionist community. That community congregated in the Zion Union of Austrian Societies for the Colonization of Palestine and Syria, also known as the Zion Society. Here, Herzl gave lectures in which he met Zionists from all walks of life; many of them were medical students who viewed him with wide-eyed veneration.

Adulation from the young was satisfying, but it would not get Herzl the access he wanted to world leaders and major financiers. He also needed experienced leaders for his Jewish Company. Herzl believed he had found such a man in Colonel

Albert Goldsmid, who was the highest-ranking Jew in the British armed forces and a zealous supporter of the Lovers of Zion. In November of 1895, Herzl met Goldsmid and his family at their home in Cardiff. After dinner, when the men withdrew to the smoking room, the colonel dramatically told Herzl that he was akin to Daniel Deronda, the hero of George Eliot's 1876 novel about an Englishman raised as a Christian gentleman but who discovers that he is, in fact, a Jew. Similarly, said Goldsmid, he was raised as a Christian, learned in early adulthood of his Jewish origins, and subsequently converted. He married a woman like himself—that is, a Christian of Jewish descent—and they both became Orthodox. Goldsmid insisted to Herzl that the Jewish state could be founded only in the ancient Jewish Holy Land and not in Latin America, as Herzl was considering. Goldsmid further expressed his aspiration to dismantle the Church of the Holy Sepulchre "stone by stone" and divide it between Moscow and Rome. Despite this fantasy of assault against one of Christendom's most holy sites, Goldsmid believed that "the pious Christians of England would help us if we went to Palestine. For they expect the coming of the Messiah after the Jews have returned home."[9]

About three months after the dinner in Cardiff, one such pious Christian came to call on Herzl. William Hechler, chaplain of the British embassy in Vienna, had learned of Herzl through the Polish journalist and Zionist activist Saul Landau. Hechler dwelled on the fringes of a movement within Protestantism, primarily in Britain and America, that had, since the 1830s, advocated the restoration of the Jews to Palestine as a precondition for the second coming of Christ. A graybeard with the look of a prophet, Hechler had calculated that the Jews would return to Palestine en masse within the coming two years. Hechler expanded upon his messianic vision when Herzl visited him in his office at the embassy. Herzl recounted:

Even while I was going up the stairs I heard the sound of an organ. The room which I entered was lined with books on every side, floor to ceiling.

Nothing but Bibles.

A window of the very bright room was open, letting in the cool spring air, and Mr. Hechler showed me his Biblical treasures. Then he spread before me his chart of comparative history, and finally a map of Palestine. It is a large military staff map which, when laid out, covered the entire floor.

"We have prepared the ground for you!" Hechler said triumphantly.

He showed me where, according to his calculation, our new Temple must be located: in Bethel! Because this is the center of the country. He also showed me models of the ancient Temple. "We have prepared the ground for you."[10]

Herzl considered Hechler to be a "naïve visionary," but this visionary had worldly political connections. Hechler had been a tutor to the son of the Grand Duke of Baden, Friedrich I, who was the uncle of the German emperor, Wilhelm II. Hechler secured an invitation for Herzl from the Grand Duke, and they first met in the Badenese capital, Karlsruhe, on 21 April 1896. That date marked the onset of Herzl's diplomatic Zionism, an enterprise that took off with dizzying alacrity.

After pressing the elderly, affable duke for an introduction to Wilhelm, Herzl wangled his way into a meeting with the Papal Nuncio in Austria. The meeting did not go well. Roman Catholicism was cold to Protestant biblical philo-semitism, and the return of Jews to Palestine did not figure prominently in Catholic doctrine. Not surprisingly, the representative of the Bishop of Rome did not see any reason to support Herzl's proposal. Landau then directed Herzl to a shady Polish aristocrat, Baron Philip de Nevlinsky, who served as a diplomatic agent for hire on behalf of several European states as well as the Ottoman Empire. In exchange for a considerable amount of cash, Nevlinsky promised to open doors for Herzl in Constantinople. By mid-June, the two men were on the Orient Express, which, just seven years earlier, had established a direct rail link between Vienna and Constantinople. It was a journey that Herzl would make four more times in his life.

Once in the Ottoman capital, Herzl met with imperial underlings, but the sultan, Abdul Hamid II, would not grant him an audience. Communicating with Herzl through Nevlinsky (who may well have been on the sultan's payroll), the sultan made it crystal clear that he would under no circumstances hand Palestine to the Jews. Herzl and Nevlinsky hashed out different stratagems to win over the sultan. The first was to offer to raise from Jewish bankers a sum sufficient to retire the empire's massive sovereign debt. For decades, the empire had borrowed heavily from the West, and in 1875, it defaulted on its loans, amounting to a quarter billion pounds. Six years later a Public Debt Administration, subject to international supervision, was founded, and the debt was trimmed to just over one hundred million pounds. Still, debt service was consuming about one-third of the empire's total revenues. Herzl claimed that he could raise twenty million pounds—only a fraction of the actual debt, but still an eye-popping amount, equivalent to the United States' annual federal budget at the time. Herzl further asserted that once the syndicate of Jewish bankers had restructured the debt and dismantled the Public Debt Administration, current bondholders would receive even higher interest rates than they did at present. That would have been hard to do, given that the Ottoman bonds were already paying an average of 5 percent, a return with a considerable built-in risk premium, and twice as high as rock-solid British government bonds.

Nevlinsky had a more realistic, or more opportunistic, approach. He suggested that Herzl, as an eminent journalist connected with one of Europe's most influential newspapers, could be of great service to the Ottoman Empire's public relations regarding its persecuted Armenian minority. Accordingly, Herzl provided his newspaper a flattering interview with the Grand Vizier, Halil Rifat Pasha, and a pro-Turkish account of recent mass killings in Armenia as well as the empire's conflict with Greece over Crete. Herzl was not unsympathetic to the Armenian cause, but he believed that Armenian "revolution-aries" were bringing misfortune upon themselves and, in a meeting in London with the Armenian nationalist leader Avetis Nazarbekian, urged him to order his followers to lay down their arms. Herzl may well have viewed the Armenians with compassion, but he also knew that so long as the "Armenian Question" exercised the sultan, he would not brook any consideration of concessions to another non-Muslim minority.

Herzl's goal, he confessed to his diary, was to convert money and bodies into political power. Once the loan was fully subscribed and immigration had reached a critical point, there would be "so many Jews in Palestine, accompanied by Jewish military power, that one need no longer fear that the Turks will attempt to get a stranglehold on them."[11] He wanted Goldsmid to join the ranks of the Ottoman military's foreign officers and to secure the command of Palestine. "Upon the breakup of Turkey," Herzl wrote to Goldsmid, "Palestine would then fall to us or to our sons as an independent country."[12]

Herzl saw no contradiction between this aggressive stance and a willingness to consider something short of sovereignty, such as an autonomous, tributary state like Egypt or Bulgaria: nominally part of the empire yet possessed of its own laws and army. In the short run at least, Herzl believed, it was in the Zionists' best interests for the empire to remain stable and intact. If Abdul Hamid were deposed, Herzl feared, a more effective ruler could come to power, and such a man would be able to raise capital on his own without needing Herzl's promised (but nonexistent) Jewish bankers. During the Greco-Turkish War of 1897, Herzl supported raising funds for wounded Turkish soldiers and wrote approvingly of young Turkish Jews volunteering to fight on behalf of the empire. He assured the sultan that the Zionists had no intention of dispossessing anyone in Palestine: "Ownership is a private right and cannot be violated." Moreover, the Jews would strengthen, not weaken, the empire: "The energy and importance of the Jews in commerce and finance are well known. It is a river of gold, of progress, a vitality which the sultan will admit into his empire with the Jews, who since the Middle Ages have always been the grateful friends of the Turks."[13]

While he was flattering the Ottoman sultan, Herzl also attempted to convince the British foreign minister, Lord Salisbury, that an intact Ottoman Empire with an autonomous Jewish vassal state would be in Britain's best interest. Such a state would support the building of a British railroad linking the Mediterranean with the Persian Gulf and connecting with rail links through Central Asia to India. "England," Herzl wrote, "would have these benefits without expense and without the world's learning of her participation."[14] If the British were to lose Egypt, they would be dependent upon a Jewish Palestine to secure the Suez Canal, Britain's lifeline to India.

For Herzl, diplomacy meant pursuing multiple interlocutors, sending contradictory messages, and exploiting every opportunity, no matter how improbable or remote, that came his way. Fortunately, his work for the *Neue Freie Presse* required frequent travel. Herzl was dependent on Europe's intricate and integrated rail network, which by the end of the nineteenth century reduced the journey from Vienna to Paris to just over a day. (Within five days, one could get from London to places as far flung as northern Scandinavia, North Africa, Asia Minor, and the Urals.)

Herzl cannily piggy-backed Zionist activity onto journalistic assignments. In September Herzl covered the German emperor's visits to Breslau and the Saxon city of Görlitz. Over his days at Görlitz, Herzl did not receive an audience with Wilhelm, but Herzl observed him closely:

> This Supreme Warlord would be rejected by the medical board if he were an ordinary man called up for military service. His pathological predilection for all things military may stem from this. Nor can he adopt any natural pose, because he must always think of how to conceal his defect [his withered left arm]. He loves dazzling, shiny uniforms and gleaming helmets which attract, distract, the eye.
>
> However, he is, it seems to me, a likable man; to put it even better and more briefly, a man!
>
> He wants to make a big impression on the crowd, to be sure, and he plays the emperor with might and main. But he wishes to charm those who meet him by amiability. He has an engaging way of shaking hands, like a party leader. He looks everyone with whom he speaks full in the eye by stepping up close to him. . . .
>
> There is no doubt that he is a man of great and varied talents who, however, wants to tackle too many things with his one arm and always has his hands full because he wishes to hide the fact that he has only one hand.
>
> If I understand him aright, I am going to win him for our cause, provided I manage to get close enough to him.[15]

These lines evince a paradoxical blend of insight, wit, and obtuseness—obtuseness about the emperor's weakness of character as well as Herzl's projection onto the sovereign of his own masculine insecurities caused by rejection from military service.

Herzl was the one who was tackling many things and "always" had "his hands full." While Herzl was playing the role of statesman and constantly traveling, he continued to work as a journalist, not only because he needed a livelihood, but because he saw a direct link between journalism and statecraft. One means by which Herzl hoped to win the support of the great and mighty was through the establishment of a newspaper, based in Vienna, that would support the Dual Monarchy's government and commercial elite while vigorously endorsing Zionism. "With such a great paper," Herzl wrote, "governments negotiate as one Power to another."[16] The Austrian prime minister, Casimir Badeni, had first suggested to Herzl that he found such a newspaper, and Herzl immediately warmed to the idea. Not only did he want a vehicle for publicizing Zionism, away from the disapproving eyes of his editors at the *Neue Freie Presse*, but also he yearned to be his own boss. Herzl loved being taken seriously by Badeni, who was a master of the warm handshake and knowing glance, and Herzl had no qualms about supporting the moderately liberal Austrian regime. The establishment of the newspaper, however, required raising a million guilders, more than twice the total of Herzl's considerable family fortune. So the scheme went into abeyance, although it would crop up again down the road.

Herzl longed to be a maker, not an observer, of history. Upon his return from Constantinople, his editor Bacher asked if he was going to write a piece about the city for the newspaper. Herzl retorted, "at Constantinople I had only historical experiences, not feuilletonistic ones."[17] The trip, however, had brought him only to the antechambers of state power. He had nothing tangible to show for his time and expense except a meaningless decoration from the sultan. The European Rothschild dynasty had thus far rebuffed him, and members of the Anglo-Jewish aristocracy treated him with the coldest of courtesy. In Vienna, Herzl's editors were dead set against his Zionist activity. In the journalistic world at large, he had only one helpmate: Sidney Whitman, a roving correspondent for the *New York Herald* who spoke excellent German and spent considerable amounts of time in Turkey. He was also, like Nevlinsky, on Herzl's payroll. For selfless, authentic support Herzl had to look beyond the elites and to the Jewish public. In July of 1896

Herzl found himself simultaneously pursuing diplomatic castles in the air and seriously considering a change in audience and strategy.

Since his days in Paris, Herzl had both pitied and feared the working classes. On the journey to Constantinople, Herzl encountered a different form of mass power when he stopped in the Bulgarian capital, Sofia, and was greeted by an enthusiastic crowd of well-wishers. Reflecting on the masses' political energy, Herzl wrote in his diary a Latin quotation from Virgil's *Aeneid:* "If I cannot bend the powers above, I will move the lower world." Herzl remained ambivalent, however, as to whether and how to exploit that potential. On 12 July, Yiddish-speaking immigrants at London's Jewish Workingmen's Club compared Herzl to Moses and Columbus. The day after the meeting, Herzl wavered between whether to lead a mass movement or to "buy the Rothschilds at the price of my resignation from the movement." Herzl was about to have the opportunity to make that pitch to a Rothschild in person: he and Baron Edmond de Rothschild agreed to meet in Paris on the 18th.

In the early 1880s, the baron had bailed out struggling Jewish agricultural colonies in Palestine, home to about five thousand of Palestine's thirty thousand Jews, and by 1890 he had poured somewhere between six and ten million francs into the settlements (in contrast to the Lovers of Zion, who had contributed less than a quarter million francs). The baron rejected Jewish nationalism, was categorically opposed to a public, international effort to obtain a Jewish state, and insisted on maintaining his enterprise at its current level. He did not want any interference, and certainly not from a wild-eyed journalist without a shred of political backing. The meeting went as badly as one might imagine, and it left Herzl determined to renounce the Jewish financial elite and instead to "move the lower world." Already at the meeting in London, Herzl perceived himself taking on the mantle of a hero: "I saw and heard my legend being born. The people are sentimental; the masses do not see clearly. I believe that even now they no longer have a clear image of me. A light fog is beginning to rise around me, and it may perhaps become the cloud in which I shall walk. But even if they no longer see my features distinctly, still they divined that I mean very well by them, and that I am the man of the little people. Of course they would probably show the same affection to some clever deceiver and imposter as they do to me, in whom they are not deceived."[18]

The summer of 1896 represented a second rebirth for Herzl. A year earlier he had committed himself to the rescue of the Jewish people. Now he was to become not only their rescuer, but also their leader. Making this decision, however, did not immediately grant Herzl a mass following. His fame spread gradually. Most Jews were indifferent or hostile to Zionism. Orthodox Jews usually rejected it as a blasphemous act of supererogation, taking into human hands the act of restoration of the Jews to the Holy Land that should only occur in the days of the Messiah. Jewish socialists—and there were a great many of them in eastern Europe and North America in the late nineteenth century—rejected Zionism as a utopian attempt to solve the problem of antisemitism, whose roots, they believed, lay in the capitalist system of production. They were confident that once capitalism was overthrown, antisemitism would disappear. In contrast, prosperous Jews in the Western world saw Zionism as a threat to their own claim to be fully a part of their homelands' societies. Even if they had compassion for poor and oppressed Jews elsewhere, they were still discomfited by Herzl's strident proclamation in *The Jewish State:* "We are a people. *One People.*" And even those Jews who identified with Zionism, as we have seen, often found Herzl preposterous, if not dangerous.

Facing these formidable obstacles, Herzl devoted himself to the building of a Zionist organization and the convening of a Zionist Congress. Entering into a flurry of correspondence with Zionist activists throughout Europe, Herzl attracted much interest, if not always allegiance. Herzl and the veteran Lovers of Zion remained poles apart on the issue of fostering small-scale Jewish immigration to Palestine, which Herzl dismissed as "infiltration." He wanted to hold off on any immigration until the international community had recognized the Jewish claim on Palestine and a charter or protectorate had been granted for the territory. Herzl did, however, gain enough traction to move toward the goal of a Zionist Congress. In Vienna, he mobilized a somnolent group of sympathizers into what he called an "Actions Committee." The committee was composed of amiable loyalists, including Johann Kremenezky, an electrical engineer and lightbulb magnate who enchanted Herzl with the possibility of extracting chemicals from the Dead Sea.

In Cologne, Herzl had the support of Wolffsohn and the attorney Max Bodenheimer. There were several bands of Zionists in Berlin, with considerably differing orientations—Orthodox, nationalist, and purely philanthropic. It required all of Herzl's persuasive powers to align these groups behind the convening of a Congress that would be more than just a meeting of charitable organizations. Herzl stuck to the idea of a Congress as a national parliament that would meet regularly and would authorize the creation of a council to manage the diplomatic enterprise as Herzl conceived of it. In other words, Herzl wanted a Congress that would create his envisioned Society of Jews.

Throughout the first seven months of 1897, Herzl encountered one challenge after another to his plans. Hermann Adler, the chief Ashkenazic rabbi of the United Kingdom, had been cold to Zionism from the start. In his view it violated the principles of the Jewish faith, which placed Torah and the Ten Commandments, not nationhood, at the center of Jewishness. The chief rabbi of Vienna, Moritz Güdemann, may have privately expressed sympathy for Herzl—Herzl's diaries assert that he did, but Güdemann's own memoir denies it—but whether out of conviction or fear of taking an unpopular stand, he publicly condemned Zionism. The Congress was to be held in Munich, as it was easily reached via rail from eastern Europe and offered decent kosher dining facilities. But the city's organized Jewish community refused to host it. In July, five prominent German rabbis—two Orthodox and three Liberal—issued a joint denunciation of Zionism as a violation of both Jewish religious obligation and the Jews' duties to honor their fatherlands.

These assaults physically wore Herzl down. Since the fall of 1895, he had suffered from heart palpitations and fatigue, and in March of the following year, Herzl's family physician diagnosed him with heart disease and warned him of potentially dire consequences. At the end of 1896, Herzl was sunk in depression, convinced that his mission had failed. He drew up his last will and testament. He wrote with bitterness, self-pity, and a touch of paranoia about the obstreperous lot whom it was his fate to lead. "Even the demonstrations of support," he added, "don't give me any pleasure, because behind the masses who are applauding me I already see the ingratitude, the future envy, the possible vacillation of the next day."[19] Herzl maintained this dour view even after his movement was well launched. In late 1898, Herzl bemoaned that "what obscure, indescribable battles I have had to fight over every little step I took will never be suspected or appreciated by the ungrateful Jews, who will show enmity toward me soon after success has come."[20]

Herzl was an exquisitely anxious person. He frequently worked himself into a panic about his relationship with Bacher and Benedikt, who, he feared, were about to sack him because of his commitment to Zionism. Yet he would rather lose his plum job than give up on Zionism, which had become the source of his identity, creative drive, and will to live. Herzl took upon himself the role of martyr to a great cause, a Moses who would lead his people yet not see the Promised Land.

In March of 1898, Herzl explicitly compared himself with Moses as he considered writing a novel about the biblical hero that was clearly self-referential: "I imagine him as a tall, vital, superior man with a sense of humor. The drama: how he is shaken inwardly and yet holds himself upright by his will. He is the leader, because he does not want to be. Everything gives way before him, because he has no personal desire. He does not care about the goal, but about the migration. Education through migration. . . . The aging Moses keeps recognizing Korah, the Calf, always the same procession of slaves. He is exhausted by all this, and yet he has to lure them onward with ever renewed vigor. It is the tragedy of any leader of man who is not a misleader."[21] Herzl claimed that as a child he dreamed that the Messiah presented him to Moses. Whether or not he had that dream, until Herzl was in his mid-thirties Jewishness affected only his personal identity, not his public one, and it was more a source of shame or anxiety than pride and compassion. But from late 1895 on, Herzl wrote and spoke with increasing frequency on what Jewishness meant to him and what it should mean to others.

In November 1896 Herzl delivered an address, which was later published in an Austrian-Jewish weekly, entitled "Judentum." *Judentum* is an ambiguous word that can refer to both Judaism as a religion and Jews as a collective. It is clear from the article's content that Herzl meant the latter, just as his pamphlet *Der Judenstaat* did not mean "Jewish state" in a religious sense. Herzl spoke of the power of *Judentum* to sustain the Jews throughout centuries of persecution, and he proclaimed "that we shall once more retreat into *Judentum* and never again permit ourselves to be thrown out of this fortress."

Yet what did it mean to be Jewish? Herzl's definition was

entirely functional: "We are noticed, we are a group, a historical group of people who clearly belong together and have a
common enemy; this seems to me an adequate definition of a
nation. I do not think the nation must speak only one language
or show uniform racial characteristics. This quite moderate
definition of nationhood is sufficient. We are a historical group
of people who clearly belong together and are held together by
a common foe. That is what we are, whether we deny it or not,
whether we know it or not, and whether we desire it or not."[22]
Even in an essay titled "Judentum," Herzl had little concrete to
say about Jewishness as a state of mind or a system of belief and
instead focused on the external factors that defined Jews as a
people. He also devoted a good deal of attention to his beloved
themes of technology and geopolitics. The printing press, telegraph, and railroad, European colonial conquests in Africa, and
the Sino-Japanese War were all jumbled together as evidence
that the restoration of Jews to Palestine was as feasible as it was
necessary.

Herzl's early Zionist writings did not ignore religion, but
for him it had little to do with transcendence, providence, or
obligation. It was, instead, a framework in which collective identity takes form. Herzl's appreciation of this aspect of Judaism
emerges in his revealing short story "The Menorah," published
in December of 1897. By this time, Herzl had given up celebrating Christmas, and Hanukkah gained a newfound attention in his eyes. "The Menorah" is a painfully autobiographical
tale about an artist in a state of psychological crisis: "Once
there was a man who deep in his soul felt the need to be a Jew."
The man is a successful artist, but he is bedeviled by antisemitism and is searching for his own identity. He finds that identity
by sharing in the suffering of his fellow Jews, by being, as the
narrator puts it, "one bleeding wound." Only by joining the
Jewish people's long history of suffering can he rid himself of
his personal anguish. Given that Herzl himself was a deeply

unhappy man, afflicted by depression and a horrendous marriage, throwing himself into a national cause was not only heroic but also therapeutic.

From the summer of 1896 on, Herzl's relationship with Julie improved, partly because he felt more personally fulfilled, and partly because he was rarely at home. Tensions between the two of them still remained, however. Julie never approved of Herzl's Zionism, which gave her husband a reputation as a crackpot and brought him into close contact with men below his and Julie's social station. Worse still, he supported the nascent movement through not only his own resources but also Julie's dowry. If Herzl were to lose his job at the *Neue Freie Presse*, they would be ruined. Erwin Rosenberger, a medical student and one of the editors of the Zionist newspaper *Die Welt* (The World), recalled a day when the two men were working on the newspaper at the family's elegant home in the Berggasse. Julie approached Herzl from behind, kissed him gently on the neck, and asked, "why does everyone like you so much?"[23] Rosenberger, who was young and venerated Herzl, mistook Julie's comment for a sign of affection, when it was far more likely to have been an expression of incomprehension if not outright hostility.

Herzl was not fazed by Julie's disapproval, but he frequently complained to her of overwork and fatigue, and he told her he planned to retire from Zionist activity and spend more time with her and the children as soon as he could be assured that his project would succeed. Since Herzl wrote similar things in his diary, it is likely that he thought he meant it. Herzl also considered himself a loving father, yet he spent little time with the children. In June of 1897, he noted that his son Hans was turning seven when in fact the boy was celebrating his sixth birthday. Nonetheless, in feuilletons written for the *Neue Freie Presse*, Herzl described his children with insight and sentimentality. He marveled at their linguistic and artistic development, and he expressed concern for their well-being. (In one particularly macabre feuilleton of 1896, Herzl wrote of a waking nightmare in which he imagined his daughter Trude's death.) One might dismiss these public displays of fatherly love as a journalistic convention, but in fact, Herzl was beside himself when his daughter Pauline fell seriously ill in June of 1898. For over a month, Herzl stayed home and did not write in his diary, leaving Zionist affairs in the hands of Wolffsohn, to whom Herzl sent updates regarding his daughter's health. By mid-August she had recovered, and Herzl was soon back on the road and back to absent parenthood, writing to Pauline that he was too busy to respond at length to her letters.

As Herzl's Zionist activity intensified, the lines between his Zionist writings and his feuilletons for the *Neue Freie Presse* began to blur. Some of the feuilletons harped on Herzl's pre-Zionist experiences and obsessions. For example, in the story "Sarah Holtzman" (1896), the irretrievable girl-woman from Herzl's past takes the form of a beautiful but sad-faced lass whose brassy, bejeweled mother is having an affair. The story is told by a friend of the family, a tortured and struggling artist—a stand-in for Herzl himself—whose love for the girl is both avuncular and romantic. But two other feuilletons from 1896 made obvious references to the recent change in the course of his own life. The first is about an unhappily married man on the verge of drowning himself, but who is rescued and learns that "despair is a precious substance, from which the most wonderful things may be generated: courage, self-denial, resolution, sacrifice. . . . To the stubbornest I recommend self-realization in a great task, and they have achieved the most. . . . As I look back in the past, it seems to me that all of the great men of history were once at the river's edge and turned back so that their despair bore fruit."[24]

In the second story, "The Steerable Airship," the hero is a man of thirty-five who discovers how to build a flying machine and is so emotionally overwhelmed by his invention that he bursts into tears. The inventor attempts to raise millions of guilders for its construction, but is ridiculed by friends, colleagues, and even the girl he loves. The inventor is put in an insane asylum, but he puts on an air of calm serenity to get himself released. The man makes a fortune on various inventions, and the girl who jilted him begs him to take her back, but the inventor sends her packing. He sails off to an undiscovered island and releases the ship into the ether. "The Steerable Airship" hews closely to Herzl's own life story and self-perception, and the end, in which the inventor and his invention disappear, illustrates Herzl's fears that his Zionist project was unattainable.

A further melding of Herzl's Zionist and journalistic work came in the form of the newspaper *Die Welt*, which first appeared on 4 June 1897. Herzl oversaw its editing and production, although he had helpmates, including Landau and Rosenberger. As its first issue declared, the newspaper was intended to promote the Zionist goal of creating a homeland "for those Jews who cannot and do not want to assimilate in their present lands of residence." It proudly proclaimed itself to be a *Judenblatt*— a "Jew rag"—and to claim this antisemitic term as a badge of honor. It was to be "the paper of the poor, the weak, the young, and also of those who, if not themselves oppressed, have nonetheless found their way back to their tribe." Herzl drove the point home by printing the first page in yellow, the color of the medieval Jewish badge. Despite its specifically Jewish message and content, the paper insisted that Zionism was a universal cause "capable of inspiring nobler human beings, whether they be Christians, Mohammedans, or Israelites."[25] In this spirit, an early issue featured an article by Father Ignatius, a Welsh Christian Zionist. "The Jews," he wrote, "have already made divine truth known to all the peoples of the earth. The name Zion has become a blessing and an inspiration for untold myriads. . . . The Jews are God's chosen instrument; they have, as their prophets foretold, performed many wonders among the peoples of the earth, and in the future they shall also carry out the other prophecies."²⁶

Herzl did not appear on the masthead out of deference to his anti-Zionist employers at the *Neue Freie Presse*, but in the first issue he contributed the lead article under his own name. Thereafter he wrote at times anonymously or under the letter "H," but some of his most strident pieces were written under his Hebrew name, Benjamin Zev. Herzl no longer sought to hide his Jewish identity, as he had when he asked his friend Schnitzler to submit *The New Ghetto* to the Burgtheater in 1894. Herzl savagely attacked assimilationist anti-Zionists in the pages of *Die Welt*. One such screed, "Mauschel," from September of 1897, refers to a German pejorative for Judeo-Germans, inextricably linked with connotations of sharp dealing, cheating, and insincerity. The infinitive *mauscheln* connotes engaging in duplicitous speech and dishonorable behavior. Employing the proper noun *Mauschel* (akin to "kike"), Herzl declaims: "In poverty Mauschel is a despicable schnorrer; in wealth he is an even more despicable show-off." The distinction between the good Jew and the wicked Mauschel is that the latter has no honor: "What is honor? Who needs honor? If business is all right and one's health is good one can live with the rest." Herzl concludes that "no true *Jew* can be an anti-Zionist; only Mauschel is one."²⁷

Herzl was willing, even eager, to expose himself as a Jew on the world stage at the forthcoming international Zionist Congress. He found a soulmate in the extroverted Nordau, who had eagerly agreed with Herzl's assessment in *The Jewish State* that for almost two millennia Jews had lived like "prisoners of war," but who added that "only through another act of war can we become free men."²⁸ Nordau saw the Congress as an opportunity to educate the Jewish masses about the necessity for a bold Zionist geopolitics that would engage the Ottoman Empire, the United Kingdom, and Russia. While Nordau and Herzl eagerly exchanged views about the Congress, Russian Zionists saw a potential for disaster. Ussishkin feared it would provoke the wrath of the Russian and Ottoman regimes. In the words of Joshua Buchmil, a Russian delegate to the Congress who himself supported Herzl, Russian Zionists considered Herzl to be a "weird and peculiar dreamer, a furious madman whose bellowing can only tear down everything that Baron Rothschild has built with his money."[29]

Many Russian Zionists did, nonetheless, agree to attend, although until late July Herzl did not know where the Congress would take place, given the refusal of the Jewish community of Munich to allow the event to take place in their city. Herzl had originally considered holding the event in Zurich but decided against it because of the city's substantial community of émigré Russian revolutionaries, and Herzl, taking his Russian colleagues' concerns seriously, did not wish to kindle the suspicions of the tsarist government. With Munich no longer an option, Herzl chose Basel, a sleepy city with a small Jewish community and a pliable chief rabbi. Kosher slaughtering was illegal in Switzerland, but meat could be brought in from Germany. The venue that Herzl's man in Basel had arranged to rent for the gathering turned out to be a rather seedy music hall, but the City Casino, a public building with a large concert hall, was an attractive and available alternative.

Some two hundred and fifty attendees came to the Congress. There were no elections beforehand, and so the attendees could not be considered delegates in any formal sense of the word. About seventy represented Jewish communities or organizations, and the rest, including ten non-Jewish sympathizers, were invited by Herzl himself. About one-third of the attendees were from eastern Europe. In terms of the overall strength of the Zionist movement, Germany, with forty-two attendees; Switzerland, with twenty-three; and France and Britain, with eleven each, were strongly overrepresented. Twenty-two attendees were women.

Julie Herzl was not one of them. She refused to take part in what she thought was a ludicrous spectacle that was consuming her family fortune. Herzl stayed alone at the Three Kings Hotel, overlooking the Rhine and a ten-minute stroll from the casino. The weather was pleasant, in the high sixties Fahrenheit. The cool temperatures made it easier for the assembled participants to obey Herzl's decree that, as a sign of the gravity of the occasion, they wear formal dress (white tie and tails) for the opening session on the morning of Sunday, 29 August. In every respect, Herzl engineered the aesthetics and structure of the three-day meeting. On the day before, Herzl attended synagogue and recited the Hebrew blessings for the Torah reading. He did so partly out of deference to the religious sensibilities of many of the attendees, and partly out of a genuine sense of return to *Judentum*. At the opening session, Herzl allowed a Hasidic Jew, Aron Marcus, to wear a caftan rather than formal garb. To appease the Lovers of Zion, the opening address was given by an elderly activist in the organization, Karpel Lippe from Jassy, Romania.

Herzl arranged for the Congress's speakers to be a mix of trustworthy allies and rivals who had to be given a hearing. The agenda was to be strictly followed, with time limits for speeches and debate. In his opening remarks, Herzl coolly noted that whereas Jews' first responses to modern antisemitism were astonishment, pain, and anger, now it was possible to view the situation with utter calm and to devote the Congress's energies entirely to developing the most effective means to enabling mass Jewish settlement in Palestine. Herzl's attempt to set a pragmatic, unemotional tone, however, was belied by the outburst of emotion that accompanied his first approach to the dais. There was a storm of applause, waving of handkerchiefs, and stomping of feet. Many men grasped, and some kissed, his hands. Amidst the commotion, which lasted for a full quarter of an hour, the Russian Zionist journalist Mordechai Ben-Ami wrote, "That is no longer the elegant Dr. Herzl of Vienna, it is a royal descendant of David risen from the grave who appears before us in the grandeur and beauty with which legend surrounded him. Everyone is gripped as if a historical miracle had occurred . . . it was as if the Messiah, the son of David, stood before us." Ben-Ami could not prevent himself from shouting *"yehi hamelekh* [long live the king]!"; others soon joined in.[30]

Nordau, whose speech followed Herzl's, had a charisma of his own. His peroration about the grave peril facing Jews the world over, and in particular about Russian depredations toward the Jews, flew in the face of Herzl's own attempts to avoid even mentioning Russia so as not to upset the Russian Zionists or their government. But there was an undeniable appeal about Nordau, described by the Anglo-American Zionist Jacob de Haas as "a radical Parisian writer, debonair, square shouldered, with an imperial beard, one of the most modern of the intellectuals, who a year before was not even known to be a Jew." In "throbbing accents, [he] intone[d] Jeremiah, 'A voice is heard in Ramah, lamentation and bitter weeping, Rachel weeping for her children,'" and the rabbinic interpretation of that verse, promising the Jews' return to Eretz Israel.[31]

Some of the eastern European attendees were unimpressed. Ahad Ha-Am sniffed that the Congress could have had value had it met for just one day and been purely symbolic, but it erred in moving into organizational work designed to foster the creation of a Jewish state. A Jewish state is an impossibility, Ahad Ha-Am wrote, and even if there were one, it would be a weak, minuscule country that was threatened by its neighbors and forced into "groveling" diplomacy to keep afloat. Herzl, Ahad Ha-Am maintained, was akin to the notorious seventeenth-century false messiah Shabbetai Zvi. Reuben Asher Braudes, who covered the Congress for the Hebrew newspaper *Ha-*

Maggid, tepidly described Herzl's opening speech as "fine" and Nordau's as "straight as an arrow." His overall assessment, however, was positive: "The Congress was like a wonderful dream, a fabulous, divine spectacle. . . . It was an extraordinary event, not because it arrived at any great decisions, witnessed any great debates, or produced any great insights, but in and of itself. . . . It is enough for our people to know that it now has something to hope for, that it still has the will to live, that it has taken its future into its hands."[32]

Herzl's charisma, however, cast a spell on many others. Reuven Brainin, writing in *Ha-Melitz*, described Herzl as "the Hebrew type at its purest, with a rare charm, an Oriental grace, and two dark eyes, burning like coals."[33] Nahum Sokolow, who had been skeptical about Herzl, was transformed by their encounter at the Congress: "And I saw before me a man tall in stature . . . the first impression he made upon me was that of a man of a handsome, serious, and thoughtful visage. . . . It was his way to stare directly into the face of his conversation partner, in his piercing, hawk-like gaze, in his most beautiful eyes and in the strength of their authority. . . . From the first moment there was the impression of an extraordinary personality, there was an element of suffering in his exterior form. His head was large and somewhat oval, wonderfully symmetrical, a blend of strength and grace."[34]

Herzl was, perhaps predictably, elected president of the Congress and presided over a series of earnest, and at times raucous, discussions about the consolidation of the world's diffuse Zionist groups into a united Zionist Organization. In addition to creating the structure of the new organization, the Congress debated its political program. There was a stark division between those attendees who wanted to pursue statehood, and to declare that goal explicitly, and those who preferred, for either substantive or tactical reasons, to speak only of a homeland. Herzl, who wanted to maximize his freedom of negotiation with the Great Powers, tended toward declaratory mini-malism. The program committee, whose members included Nordau, Bodenheimer, Birnbaum, and the mathematician Her-mann Schapira, hammered out a compromise statement that, with further tweaking by the plenum, became the official pro-gram of the Zionist Organization for almost half a century: "Zionism aims at establishing for the Jewish people a publicly and legally assured home in Palestine. For the attainment of this purpose, the Congress considers the following means service-able: (1) the promotion of the settlement of Jewish agricultur-ists, artisans, and tradesmen in Palestine; (2) the federation of all Jews into local or general groups, according to the laws of the various countries; (3) the strengthening of Jewish feeling and consciousness; (4) preparatory steps for the attainment of those governmental grants which are necessary to the achieve-ment of the Zionist purpose."[35]

Every word of this program represented a compromise between differing factions—between proponents and opponents of immediate settlement activity in Palestine; between aspira-tions for a centralized Zionist organization and for the auton-omy of each national federation; and between those for whom Zionism was inseparable from the promotion of Hebrew and Yiddish culture and those like Herzl for whom Jewish culture had far less significance. To assuage the fears of assimilated Jews, the Congress repeated the words in the first issue of *Die Welt* that Zionism was directed only at Jews who could not or would not assimilate in their respective dwelling-places.

Herzl understood that east European Jewry would pro-vide the bulk of his support at future Congresses and in the work of the new Zionist Organization (ZO) in general. But he also wanted the freedom to operate unhampered, and he was well aware that the eastern European Zionists viewed his dip-lomatic ventures with suspicion, if not disdain—feelings with which he regarded the eastern Europeans' devotion to ongoing settlement activity in Palestine. Accordingly, he created two executive committees: a small, five-man "Inner Actions Committee" that sat in Vienna and would essentially serve as a rubber stamp for his initiatives, and a "Greater Actions Committee," consisting of the smaller committee plus eighteen elected representatives, fully half of whom would come from Russia, Galicia, and Romania. (In contrast, Palestine received only one seat, with one more for the entirety of Middle Eastern and North African Jewry.)

Herzl faced a thornier problem with the Orthodox. He enjoyed the support of some prominent Orthodox rabbis, such as the French chief rabbi Zadoc Kahn, Shmuel Mohilewer in Bialystock, and Isaac Rülf in Memel. But in *The Jewish State*, Herzl had written that the state would keep its rabbis in their synagogues just as it would keep its soldiers in their barracks. Herzl was determined to keep control over the nascent movement away from the rabbis. He ensured that none would sit on the ZO's five-man inner executive committee and placed only two on the twenty-three-member external committee. Aware that most Orthodox Jews opposed Zionism, Herzl appreciated the importance of the Congress's declaration that "Zionism did not intend to take any steps that would offend the religious sentiment of any Jew, whatever his opinions."[36]

There was one group whose sentiments were not taken into consideration at the Congress—women. At the outset of the Congress, Herzl said patronizingly that women were welcome as guests but would not have voting rights. According to Brainin, "the women, some of them writers and intellectuals, accepted quietly, but with broken hearts. Then one of the men participants remarked, 'If the women have no rights, we have not gained anything!'"[37] One female attendee, Marie Reinus, insisted on speaking and voting. (In the preparations for the Second Congress a year later, women were accorded the right to vote for congressional delegates, and women delegates were allowed to vote and address the floor.)

This act of rebellion by Zionist activists against Herzl was but the first of many.

Moreover, when things did go Herzl's way—and more often than not, they did—neither the decisions made by the Congress nor those made by its new institutions were his alone. Much of the ZO's administrative structure was created by committees, such as the one that created the ZO's primary revenue stream, an annual membership fee called the shekel, equivalent to forty Russian kopeks or one British shilling, German mark, or French franc. Herzl came to a meeting of minds with other Zionists about initiatives such as a national bank, or a fund for land purchase and reforestation. But Herzl alone had imagined, convened, and publicized the event, and immediately after its conclusion, he threw himself into preparing *Die Welt*'s special "Congress Issue," which would chronicle the historic gathering for Jews throughout the world.

As many as a dozen journalists at the Congress represented the Jewish press, which covered its deliberations extensively, if not always positively. The Yiddish author Sholem Aleichem wrote a pamphlet on the Congress that quickly sold thirty thousand copies. News coverage translated into action; in eastern Europe, the number of branches of the Lovers of Zion, which were mostly incorporated into the ZO, leaped by a factor of five between 1896 and 1898. Herzl was less successful, however, in using the press to gain approval of his movement in the non-Jewish world. Virtually all of the journalists for the world press were freelancers who submitted terse, purely descriptive reports for multiple newspapers or wire services. In the British and French press, the Congress left few positive impressions. The liberal and Dreyfusard paper *Le Matin* expressed respect for Herzl but considered the entire scheme outlandish.

In the United States, the *New York Times'* first descriptions of Herzl were rather puckish: "Whatever the merits of this undertaking, the doctor brings to its execution the vigor of maturity and a large amount of varied experience. . . . Dr. Herzl's scheme is entirely practical—whatever may be the case as to its practicability."[38] The placement of this story is telling; it was put in the "Topics of the Times" column, which was filled with droll tidbits about subjects such as tax dodging by the assessors of Lewiston, Maine, efforts by Prince Ferdinand of Bulgaria and the Ottoman sultan to recruit competent assassins, and an unusual friendship in a local menagerie between a rhinoceros and a cat.

The Congress did win Herzl some Gentile friends. The prominent German Orientalist Johannes Lepsius attended, and his impressions, published a few months after the Congress's conclusion, indicated how deeply he shared the Zionists' ardor: "Whoever experienced the fanatical, enthusiastic applause with which Dr. Herzl was greeted at the Basel Congress must have the impression that here was not only a party leader in the midst of his supporters, but rather a great lord in the midst of his retinue. A tall, manly appearance, of a classical, semitic type, he would have done no dishonor to his forefathers had he sat on the 'throne of the governor of the province beyond the River' [Nehemiah 3:7] in Ephraim's Gate in Jerusalem, which was once held by Zerubavel. But also, the tranquil harmony of a commanding spirit and the moral solemnity, which saturates the greatness of the project, appear to be rooted within him."[39] Herzl's effects on people reflected both his own charisma and his interlocutors' deepest desires. To Lepsius, Herzl was a biblical king. To eastern European Jews, he was a latter-day Moses, raised in the Pharaoh's court but now restored to his people. To young Zionists, Herzl was a father figure who inspired adoration and awe. Women flirted with him and sent him love letters.

Remembrances of Herzl routinely described him as majestically tall, yet his actual height was 5'8". That was about three inches taller than the average central European male of the time. Given that the average North American male today is about 5'9", if a similarly proportioned Herzl lived among us today, he would be just over six feet tall—a pleasing but by no means unusual or imposing height. A father or king, however, is always tall in the eyes of those who revere him.

Herzl had certainly become taller in his own eyes. On 3 September, he wrote in his diary:

> Were I to sum up the Basel Congress in a word—which I shall guard against proclaiming publicly—it would be this: at Basel I founded the Jewish State. If I said this out loud today, I would be answered by universal laughter. Perhaps in five years and certainly in fifty, everyone will know it. The foundation of a State lies in the will of the people for a State, yes, even in the will of one sufficiently powerful individual (*L'état c'est moi*—Louis XIV). Territory is only the material basis; the State, even when it possesses territory, is always something abstract. . . . At Basel, then, I created this abstraction which, as such, is invisible to the vast majority of people. And with infinitesimal means, I gradually worked the people into the mood for a State and made them feel that they were its National Assembly.[40]

It was Nordau, however, who grasped the consequences of the Congress for Herzl as an individual. Admitting that he was unwilling to make Herzl's own commitment to the Zionist cause, Nordau warned:

> Each man is free not to initiate a movement such as Zionism. But no one is free to lightheartedly (or even heavy-heartedly, in my view) detach from such a movement once he has brought it into being. Only death can liberate one from self-imposed duties. Any other form of self-liberation is rubbish. . . . I don't know if you have kept the letter that I wrote to you when I read *The Jewish State*. There I predicted what

would in future become of your life. I saw the tragedy of your decisions. That is why I greeted a hero, almost a *moritorus* [a warrior about to die]. Jason cannot abandon the Argos at the halfway point of the journey. He must be victorious or die. Therein lies the definition of the word "hero." Always take that into account.[41]

Herzl indeed took the gravity of his decisions into account. By 1898, he had become, in his own eyes and in the eyes of his followers, what the philosopher Hegel called a world-historical figure, a shaper of human affairs. There was no turning back.

4

Reaching for the Stars

Between 1898 and 1901, Herzl's Zionist career was at its zenith. The Zionist Congresses, which continued to meet regularly, were only the tip of the iceberg. The Zionist Organization's central office in Vienna, and the main offices of the Zionist federations of Germany and the United Kingdom, were beehives of activity. Herzl oversaw the foundation of a Zionist bank, a fund for the purchase of land in Palestine, and a flurry of initiatives to win support for Zionism in Europe and North America. Most importantly, these were the years when Herzl finally gained access to the German and Ottoman emperors. In scenes more colorful and dramatic than any of his plays or stories, Herzl met Kaiser Wilhelm II in Palestine at an encampment just beyond Jerusalem's city walls and Sultan Abdul Hamid II in the splendor of Constantinople's Yildiz Palace. Herzl was convinced that victory was within reach, and that

Palestine would become a German protectorate or an Ottoman vassal state.

Herzl's social circle was now entirely circumscribed by the Zionist movement. He and Nordau continued to be intellectual soulmates. There remained nonetheless a certain formality in their relationship, as evinced by the fact that despite the close bonds between them, in their correspondence they always used the *Sie* form to address one another, rather than the more casual *Du*. Herzl did, however, develop a more intimate rapport with two other men. In 1903, after years of acquaintance, Herzl began to use *Du* when writing to Alexander Marmorek, a physician and bacteriologist whom Herzl had met in Vienna through the student group Kadimah, and who served on the ZO's Greater Actions Committee. Herzl admired Marmorek deeply for his commitment to finding a cure for tuberculosis and wrote that he "loved him very much."[1] Herzl's closest colleague, however, or at least the man upon whom he relied most heavily, was David Wolffsohn. In 1898 Herzl began to call him by the nickname "Daade," and two years later the two men adopted the *Du* in their voluminous correspondence. Wolffsohn was an easygoing, affable man, and he and his wife, Fanny, got along well enough with Julie that the Herzls and Wolffsohns dined out together on occasion.

Whereas Herzl treated Nordau with deep respect, his tone with Wolffsohn veered between condescending familiarity and anger born of frustration and disappointment. He praised Wolffsohn for his devotion, but Herzl could quickly become peremptory, accusing Wolffsohn of incompetence, faint-heartedness, and disloyalty. Herzl frequently wrote that Wolffsohn should never forget that he was the deputy and Herzl was the leader, as only he possessed the courage and stamina to handle the extraordinary pressures placed upon him. Herzl testily wrote to

Wolffsohn that unlike so many of his indecisive, risk-averse Zionist colleagues, "I don't shit in my trousers!"[2]

Herzl's sense that he was duty-bound to fulfill extraordinary obligations extended to his family. Herzl frequently wrote to friends, and in his diary, that he would quit the *Neue Freie Presse* were it not for his duty to support his wife and children. In January of 1900, when one of his children had pneumonia, and two years later when Julie was ill, he stayed at home until they were well enough for him to go back on the road. He constantly fretted about the children's financial future after his death. Despite these displays of parental tenderness and authority, Herzl continued to misremember Hans's birthday, and he failed to display an interest in his children's upbringing or education. However, during a brief visit home in early 1901, Herzl asked his children to add a Hebrew prayer to the German one that they customarily recited at bedtime. Most of the time, when Herzl thought of his children, he saw them as a reflection of himself; in May of 1901, as he was about to leave Vienna for Constantinople, he wrote that the children were unaware of the great fate that awaited their father.

Herzl's work at the *Neue Freie Presse* was also a ceaseless source of stress. In addition to churning out feuilletons on a regular basis, Herzl was responsible for all of the material that was submitted to, and published in, the newspaper's literary section, which included essays and reviews in the social and natural sciences as well as belles lettres and the fine arts. Herzl supervised the work of contributors from all over the continent. (One of them was Nordau, who, from his perch in Paris, constantly carped to Herzl about insufficient payment and too much editorial control.) Job fatigue did nothing, however, to quench Herzl's ambition. In late 1899 he surmised that Bacher was about to retire and threatened to leave the paper if he was not given Bacher's position. Bacher was not going anywhere, so he and Benedikt tried to appease Herzl by awarding him "the highest salary of any staff member of the *Neue Freie Presse*—3000 guilders more than [Hugo] Wittmann gets."[3]

The job also had nonmaterial benefits. For one, it gave Herzl access to the Austrian governing elite. Shortly after assuming office in early 1900, the head of Austria's government, Ernest von Koerber, solicited Herzl's advice about a proposal for Viennese electoral reform. A few weeks later, Herzl wrote a long speech for Koerber to deliver in parliament regarding the empire's most sensitive issue: the official status of the welter of languages spoken in the Austrian half of the monarchy. (Czech nationalists were particularly adamant in their demands that schooling and government services be provided in their language.) Koerber actually used very little of Herzl's text except for a flourish stating that the new language legislation was "the purest expression of the collective will." Herzl was piqued by the slight, and he wrote in his diary that he was ingratiating himself to the prime minister solely so that Koerber would put in a good word for him with the Austrian foreign minister, who Herzl hoped would then intervene with the Ottoman sultan on Herzl's behalf.

Herzl still dreamed of being his own boss and having access to a major newspaper that could promote the Zionist cause. He did not want to escape from journalism so much as to transcend the constraints of his job by either acquiring an interest in his employers' newspaper or starting his own. Not mollified by his raise, Herzl made another effort to become the publisher of his own newspaper, which would be nominally independent yet sympathetic to the government. This time around he had a would-be patron in Count Leopold Auersperg, a prominent industrialist who owned an insurance company and a munitions factory. Auersperg gathered a consortium of investors, and negotiations went on for about three months, between October of 1900 and January of 1901. Over this time, Herzl and

Koerber stayed in close contact, so much so that one evening Herzl dropped by the private residence of the prime minister, who greeted him in an undershirt and slippers.

The newspaper negotiations were so time-consuming that Herzl neglected Zionist diplomatic work, but he expected a great victory that would place him in an immeasurably more influential position. Sadly for Herzl, the venture failed. At first, Herzl blamed himself for demanding too high a salary; then he mused that his Zionist activity had made the investors skittish. Herzl realized dejectedly that he was attractive to the Austrian magnates solely for his attachment to the *Neue Freie Presse*, which the investors were angling to buy, and for which purpose they wanted to use Herzl as their agent.

Herzl's failure left him feeling trapped. He longed to leave Vienna, and London was a tempting alternative. By the end of the century, Herzl had begun to feel that the fortunes of the Zionist movement would depend upon its relationship with the United Kingdom. He demanded that Bacher and Benedikt transfer him from Vienna to London, where he would leave behind the dreary work of a literary editor and return to being a foreign correspondent, as he had been in Paris. The editors were inclined to agree, but Herzl's parents refused to move yet again to a foreign country, so he had no choice but to stay in Vienna.

Adding to these professional frustrations, Herzl's attempts to return to the theater were disappointing, if not disastrous. His comedy *Our Cathy* (1899) got mired in controversy as its theme—the hypocrisy of a bourgeois marriage versus the honesty of a common-law union between two proletarians—opened Herzl up to accusations of radicalism and indecency. In the following year, the premiere of his comedy *I Love You* was met by hissing from the audience and hostile reviews.

Not only was *I Love You* flat and unfunny, Herzl had become a common object of satire, derision, and even hatred. In the increasingly toxic atmosphere of Karl Lueger's Vienna, Herzl was a visible target for antisemites, while bien-pensant Viennese Jews considered him an embarrassment. Occasionally, Herzl found an unexpected sympathizer, such as the writer Hermann Bahr, who had been in Herzl's student fraternity, Albia, and at the time had been a vicious antisemite. Years later he repented and became a Zionist sympathizer. More common, however, were those who sniped at Herzl, or who hounded him—if not because they hated Jews or opposed Zionism, then because they embraced Zionism rather too fervently. Herzl called such people "Messiahs of every stripe." One of these fanatics was Joseph Marcou-Baruch, a Turkish Jew who packed into his short life stints as a soldier in the wars for Italian unification, an anarchist (who may have been involved in the assassination of the French president Sadi Carnot), and an itinerant Zionist activist in Egypt and the Balkans. Marcou-Baruch pestered Herzl so frequently and so passionately that Herzl feared for his personal safety, even feeling relieved when Marcou-Baruch committed suicide in 1899, at the age of twenty-seven.

The slings and arrows of fortune took their toll on Herzl. Zionist work continued to consume Herzl's income and eat away at his and his wife's savings. In the second half of 1899 and August of 1901, he was stricken by a painful writer's cramp, an understandable condition given the several hours every day he spent at his desk composing letters and articles. More ominous, from 1899 on, Herzl complained increasingly of palpitations, shortness of breath, an irregular pulse, and what he called "brain anemia," a faint-headedness caused by reduced blood flow to the brain. All of these symptoms could have been psychogenic, but they also could have been, and most likely were, indicative of heart disease. In early 1901, although Herzl was only forty, he already felt that he was entering the autumn of his life.

As overwork took its steady toll on Herzl's health, his journalistic writing changed—and for the better. From the start of his career, Herzl had in his feuilletons affected an ironic and somewhat melancholy tone that was typical of bourgeois Viennese literary culture. But from 1898 until his death, his feuilletons assumed a softer, more introspective tone, with a mood of detachment, even resignation. As in the past, Herzl continued to write in a self-referential mode, noting the fine line between artistic genius and madness. Quoting Gustave Flaubert, Herzl observed in 1900 that "the pearl is the illness of the oyster"[4]— that is, there can be no pearl without the grit against which the oyster produces layers of nacre. But the kinetic, even chaotic energy that had characterized "The Steerable Airship" and other stories from 1896 began to abate. Herzl's writings now exuded a sense of impending mortality: "Whoever has already lived and suffered much—both are the same—for him a farewell doesn't necessarily seem the bitterest thing of all."[5]

In essays from 1900 and 1901, Herzl obliquely referenced his own struggles to balance his sense of mission with the contingency of events that rocketed him to fame. On the one hand, "In the light of history unique persons were presumably not as rare as one might think. . . . Only rarely would time, place, circumstances bring about the meeting of the right conditions that are no less important for the appearance of the great person than is their character." Yet whatever the circumstances are that bring the leader onto the historical stage, he is an indispensable figure: "the masses never think in terms of ideas but always in terms of persons."[6]

Herzl clearly saw himself as the one who would personify the masses' yearnings. He continued to apply to himself a Roman legal concept mentioned briefly in *The Jewish State*, that of the *negotiorum gestio*, or self-appointed actor, who, in an emergency, volunteers to assist his fellow even without express consent. But Herzl's later feuilletons have few saviors or leaders who accomplish, or who inspire the people to accomplish, great things.

They reflect Herzl's anxieties about his shortcomings as a leader and the possibility that everything he was striving for might come to nothing. In 1900 he published "Solon in Lydia," a tale set in ancient Greece, about a young man named Eukosmos ("beautiful world" in Greek) who invents a machine that manufactures wheat out of air and promises to end all hunger. The sage Aesop advises the king of Lydia to put the machine into action—and once he does, the populace grows lazy, greedy, and violent. Solon the lawmaker then orders that Eukosmos be killed.

Whereas Eukosmos unintentionally leads the people astray, the central figure of another story from 1900, "The Beloved of Venus," is a powerful man who wants to return to a simpler life.[7] The story is based on Plutarch's narrative of the life of the ancient Roman dictator Lucius Cornelius Sulla. In Herzl's version, Sulla relishes the newfound freedom of walking unarmed in the public square. A centurion upbraids him for what he sees as a sign of weakness, yet for Sulla, in Herzl's rendering, walking in public, unarmed or, as he puts it, "exposed," is a sign of masculine strength. This may be a reference to Herzl's own self-exposure as a Jew, and clearly, Herzl finds this behavior to be honorable, but in the story Sulla does not come to a happy end. He sleeps with, and in flagrante delicto is murdered by, his enemy's mistress. As in Herzl's earliest feuilletons, Venus symbolizes the corrupting force of erotic love, which, Herzl feared, can destroy even the greatest of men.

There were few Venuses in Herzl's world. He flirted with young women at the Zionist Congresses or in the streets of Vienna, but his heart belonged to the movement. The only woman who came close to his inner circle was the Austrian peace activist Bertha von Suttner. Suttner belonged to Herzl's small coterie of Gentile supporters, but unlike the likes of Hechler, her sympathy for Zionism had little to do with Christian messianism. She was drawn to Herzl's charismatic personality and saw in

Zionism a vehicle of liberation for an oppressed people. Suttner was seventeen years Herzl's senior, possessed of a charisma of her own, and happily married, although she balanced that marriage with a long-lasting romantic relationship with Alfred Nobel, the munitions inventor turned antiwar activist. Suttner may have been something of a mother figure to Herzl, who in April of 1898 confessed to her that he was experiencing depression: "I don't want to hide from you that I am once again experiencing a crisis, in which I don't believe that one can improve humankind with magnanimity and noble thoughts. *J'ai le printemps triste.* The whole city of Vienna weighs upon my breast; under such circumstances it is rather hard to breathe."[8] Herzl also saw in Suttner a valuable asset, as she was a celebrated author, whose novel *Lay Down Your Arms!* (1889) was a best seller, and who would win the first Nobel Peace Prize in 1905. The relationship between Herzl and Suttner was symbiotic, as each needed the other. For all her fame, Suttner was hard up for money, and Herzl paid her to accompany him to the 1899 international peace conference at The Hague. Two years later, Herzl and Suttner were in Paris together to attend a gathering in honor of Paul-Henri d'Estournelles de Constant, a French politician and visionary who predicted a United States of Europe.

Herzl hoped that attending meetings celebrating international cooperation would improve Zionism's visibility and luster. But Herzl continued to believe that the shortest path to a Zionist diplomatic victory would be through direct negotiations between himself and the Great Powers' rulers and highest officials. At the same time, he strove to build up the movement from the inside, by increasing membership in the ZO and its constituent national federations and shoring up its financial resources. There was an obvious contradiction between Herzl's two selves: on the one hand, a man alone, deciding the fate of the Jewish people through secret diplomacy, and on the other, an elected leader of a democratic movement, who was obliged to delegate as well as arrogate authority. Nordau urged Herzl to set diplomatic activity aside and focus on winning over Jewish communities to Zionism. Only once Herzl led a truly mass movement, Nordau claimed, could he legitimately claim to represent world Jewry before world leaders.

Herzl rejected Nordau's critique, but the two men agreed upon the necessity of establishing a Zionist bank. Herzl saw Jews as having two possible sources of power—words and money—and it is not surprising that he invested most of his organizational work into a Zionist newspaper and bank. Herzl had always both admired and envied the wealthy, and he felt personally betrayed by magnates such as Baron Maurice de Hirsch and Baron Edmond de Rothschild. In the June 1895 diary entries, Herzl vowed to "smash" and "demolish" Hirsch. At the end of 1897, Herzl wrote of the Zionist bank as a "national financial instrument," serving the interests of the Jewish people, and if the Rothschilds tried to stand against it, he would launch a "barbaric attack" against them: "If they force us to march off without boots, like the soldiers of the First Republic [during the French Revolution], we shall take revenge for our distress."[9] Four months later, Herzl told France's chief rabbi, Zadoc Kahn, that it would behoove Rothschild to support the bank as an act of self-preservation. Herzl warned that antisemitism in France was on the rise, French Jews might find their freedoms limited by special legislation, and the Rothschild bank might be forced to liquidate. If Rothschild could overcome what Herzl called his "money-lender's mentality," there could be a mutually beneficial alliance between "financial aristocracy" and "financial democracy." (This idea followed from Herzl's notion that a successful Zionist movement would reduce antisemitism by restoring Jewish honor.)

Intriguingly, although the Jewish bank was to be a national endeavor, Herzl insisted that the word "national" not appear in its name, lest it put off the Ottomans. Therefore Herzl preferred to call it the "Jewish Colonial Trust," even though the word "colonial" was only "window-dressing, hokum, a firm-name"—not only less frightening to the Ottomans, but also more impressive to the Europeans.[10]

The establishment of the bank was decided at the Second Zionist Congress, held, like the first, at the Basel Casino at the end of August. Unlike the first, this one had elected delegates from Zionist federations all over the world. During the preparations for the Congress, Herzl was keen to attract delegates from Asia and Africa as well as Europe and North America. Jacques Bahar, a French Zionist activist with connections to the Maghreb, promised to deliver "an Algerian in native dress" and "as many Tunisians and Moroccans as we want" so long as the ZO paid their way. Bahar related that the editor of an Algerian newspaper, whom Bahar called "fully assimilated, more Arab than Jew," wanted to come to the Congress and would mobilize not only North African Jews but "even a black Jew" from the Algerian Sahara. Herzl was excited by the prospect of securing the attendance of what he called "authentic" North African Jews: "We absolutely must have [them] at the Congress because of the color they would convey." Herzl also thought it essential to draw attention to the baleful growth of antisemitism in Algeria with the intensification of the Dreyfus affair. Nordau demurred, grumbling, "I do not believe in the Zionism of the Algerians. . . . I have not been able to detect the slightest trace of a Jewish national soul among them."[11]

Herzl very much wanted Nordau to play a starring role at the Congress, but Nordau had been attacked in the European Jewish press for having recently married a young Danish Protestant, Anna Dons-Kaufmann, and Nordau felt that he should lay low. Herzl reassured him, "If our work had already been accomplished, so, most certainly, it would not be forbidden for a citizen of the Jewish state to marry a foreigner."[12] Nordau did attend the Congress, delivering another passionate, and ecstatically received, address about the abundant threats facing world Jewry. In many ways, however, the Second Congress was different from the first. It had nearly twice as many attendees and received considerably more press coverage. Women were welcomed as delegates, and at an evening gathering, Bahar recited a poem in praise of the heroism of Jewish women, from biblical times to the present. ("O Jewess, my goddess!" he intoned.)

There was a festive feeling in the air. A group of Swiss soldiers passing by the Casino shouted, "Hurrah for the Jews!" At the opening ceremony, a local orchestra played music from Wagner's *Tannhäuser*—the opera that in June of 1895 had soothed Herzl's overstrained mind, like the music from David's harp in the presence of mad King Saul.[13]

The Congress approved as its official flag a design similar to one that had been used in Palestine since 1891—blue stripes, reminiscent of a prayer shawl, and a blue star of David at the center, against a white background. On a more practical note, not only did the Congress authorize the establishment of the Zionist bank, it also passed a proposal that Zionists engage in national politics throughout the diaspora—in particular in the Russian, Austro-Hungarian, and Ottoman empires—for the improvement of Jewish civil rights.

Despite Herzl's grand statements, the bank could not simply be willed into existence. No major investor would touch it, so the bank issued one-pound shares, which could be bought on installments, and pledged to begin operating once it had holdings of 250,000 pounds sterling. It took three years for the bank to reach this modest goal. Ever the technological enthusiast, Herzl wanted the bank to invest in experiments by Marmorek to find a cure for tuberculosis. (The experiments failed, and Marmorek had a breakdown, which worried Herzl greatly.) Nor was it an easy thing to balance the demands of Zionist activists for political and cultural work in the diaspora with the mounting fears of even those few Orthodox rabbis who were sympathetic to Zionism. Behind what the Zionist movement later called *Gegenwartsarbeit* (work in the present) was a direct promotion, or implicit validation, of a Jewish secular nationalism that would undermine Jewish observance and the authority of the Jewish textual canon as well as the rabbis who interpreted it.

Despite his autocratic leanings, in internal ZO affairs Herzl had no choice but to work within groups—permanent and ad hoc committees, the boards of institutions like the Jewish Colonial Trust, and the Congress itself. In his diplomatic work, Herzl made a show of working alone, yet to make inroads with foreign powers, and especially with the Ottoman Empire, he employed a crew of raffish adventurers of dubious character. One of these men, Philip de Nevlinsky, died in April 1899, having accomplished nothing and having cost a great deal. Within a couple of months he was replaced by Arminius Vambery, an elderly Hungarian Jew who held a professorship in Oriental languages at the University of Budapest. As Herzl described him, he "doesn't know whether he is more Turk than Englishman, writes books in German, speaks twelve languages with equal mastery and has professed five religions, in two of which he has served as a priest. . . . He told me 1001 tales of the Orient, of his intimacy with the sultan, etc. He immediately trusted me completely and told me, under oath of secrecy, that he was a secret agent of Turkey and of England."[14] Yet another of Herzl's agents, the journalist Sidney Whitman, jaunted across Europe on Herzl's behalf, meeting with luminaries ranging from the Roman Catholic bishop of Westminster to the king of Romania. The meetings came to naught. Romania's King Carol was particularly cold, remarking that he found Zionism "interesting," but that Dreyfus deserved to be on Devil's Island, and that Jewish publicans must not be allowed to get the peasants drunk.[15]

At Herzl's behest, these men worked behind closed doors,

far from the public eye. Herzl wanted to avoid entanglements such as one that at the end of 1897 enmeshed him with an Austrian archaeologist named Eduard Glaser. Some years earlier, Glaser had proposed establishing a Jewish state in Arabia. Perhaps out of pique that the Zionists did not run with his idea, Glaser published a newspaper article accusing Herzl of conspiring with Britain to establish a Jewish state in Palestine and dissolve the Ottoman Empire, thereby working against the interests of Germany, France, and Russia. Nordau and Herzl, along with a staff journalist at the *Neue Freie Presse*, issued a volley of articles attacking Glaser, and Herzl even considered challenging him to a duel, but the matter blew over.

Was Glaser right? Was Herzl scheming to partition the Ottoman Empire? On the one hand, Herzl enthusiastically supported European colonialism. In 1898, during a public debate about Zionism in Berlin, Herzl said: "Don't you know what a colonial age we are living in? As a consequence of overpopulation, and of the resultant ever more acute Social Question, many nations are endeavoring to found overseas colonies in order to channel the flow of immigration back. This is the policy which England has been pursuing for decades, and which has been regarded as exemplary by many nations. I believe that Germany, too, has taken steps to become a Greater Germany, since it has looked across the seas and has striven to found colonies everywhere."[16] On the other hand, like most European statesmen of the time, Herzl's designs on the Ottoman Empire were more about influence than conquest. Herzl told the Second Congress that "the partition of Turkey is still a long way off" and "no serious politician now thinks of partitioning Turkey." He did not hide his aspirations for a European protectorate over Palestine, which would represent a significant limitation of Ottoman sovereignty—as was the case in Egypt, which at the time was an autonomous province of the Ottoman Empire but effectively controlled by Britain. But Herzl remained open to a direct relationship between the Jewish state and the Ottomans, as he laid out in a detailed proposal of 1901, in which he proposed that citizens of the Jewish state would be loyal Ottoman subjects and perform military service for the empire.

Glossing over the considerable differences between these two scenarios, Herzl proclaimed in public that the Zionists presented no threat to the Turks or to anyone else: "If there is such a thing as a legitimate claim to any piece of the Earth's surface then all the peoples who believe in the Bible must recognize the right of the Jews. And they can do so without envy or concern, for the Jews are not a political power and will never be one again." Or as Herzl said at the Berlin debate, "Well what is a state? A big colony. What is a colony? A small state." Even under a protectorate, Herzl insisted that the Holy Places in Jerusalem would remain internationalized—or, as he put it given his penchant for Roman legal terms, *extra commercium:* "This land presumably cannot, and never will, become the property of any single great power, for it is the best-guarded land of all. It is carefully guarded not only by its present proprietor but by everyone else as well."[17]

Herzl's writings about Constantinople were filled with Orientalist stereotypes, but he respected the empire as the seat of (as he would put it) a once-great civilization that would be revived by Western guidance and technology. Herzl had more negative views of, and drastic plans for, sub-Saharan Africa, which he wrote about in feuilletons for the *Neue Freie Presse* when exhibits of exotic peoples were staged at Vienna's Prater park. (There were hundreds of such exhibitions in Europe and North America in the late nineteenth and early twentieth centuries.)

Touring a display of Ashanti villagers in the Prater in 1897, Herzl described them as "primal men . . . authentic primal men, notable for their simplicity and cruelty, their savagery, which is only [an expression of] fear, for their tools, their childlike art and their faith."[18] Two years later, Herzl was back at the Prater to view an exhibition of Bisharin, members of a Beja tribe concentrated in Sudan and southern Egypt. Herzl described them as "a people of the ambush, of spoil, and whoever conquers them can only improve them, for they stand on one of the lowest levels of human consciousness, and bear barely a trace of concepts of bodily and moral purity." He wrote that they were "doomed to extinction," and "their annihilation as barbarians will take place with increasing speed in our time and in the near future." Herzl averred that their "annihilation" would be peaceful, and that it had already begun in Vienna and everywhere else the Bisharin performed. They were developing self-awareness and resourcefulness by negotiating contracts, learning the value of money, and, when necessary, going on strike. Their performance for the paying customers was just that, a performance: they "must not behave tamely, like government officials, but must balefully roll their eyes, threateningly brandish their crude weapons, and fill the petty bourgeois with fear."[19] By learning how to act, they were learning how to be proper specimens of Western humanity.

Karl Kraus, an acerbic Viennese-Jewish journalist and foe of bourgeois conventions, was not mollified by Herzl's paternalistic gestures toward the Bisharin. Kraus carried a double burden of resentment against Herzl, both for being the staid *Neue Freie Presse*'s literary editor and for his Zionism, which Kraus, who renounced his own Jewishness and called for complete assimilation, found abominable. Kraus was also anticolonialist. He condemned the display of humans under any circumstance but was particularly irked by Herzl's attempts to base serious ethnographic observations on a vulgar and degrading spectacle. Kraus linked Herzl's enthusiasm for the exhibit to his Zionism: "His interest in the Prater colony is easily explained: he is determined in the near future to place Europeans at the foot of Mount Lebanon."[20]

Whether Herzl perceived a connection between his writings on Africa and his long-term plans "to place Europeans at the foot of Mount Lebanon," and whether his mollifying statements about the Ottoman Empire were sincere or calculating, we can be certain of one thing—the Ottoman sultan did not want the Jews in Palestine. As Abdul Hamid put it, "Why should we accept Jews whom the civilized European nations do not want in their countries and whom they have expelled?" Imperial authorities strove to keep Jews out of Palestine altogether or, failing that, to grant them visas valid for only three months. The only thing the Zionists might have to recommend them was money, but Ottoman officials were well aware that Herzl was bluffing. As the Ottoman ambassador to London wrote in June of 1898, wealthy Jews "have not the slightest inclination to exchange their comfort, their habits, their contact with all that is brilliant and elevated in the great capitals of Europe for a restricted and modest existence in Palestine."[21] According to Abdul Hamid's daughter, the sultan said that he would never give Palestine to the Jews while he still breathed: "Only our corpse can be divided. I will never consent to vivisection."[22]

In mid-1898, Herzl's diplomatic initiatives appeared to have reached a dead end. Herzl began to consider a radical solution— a temporary Jewish homeland outside of Palestine. "The poor masses need immediate help, and Turkey is not yet so desperate as to accede to our wishes. . . . Thus we must organize ourselves for a goal attainable soon, under the Zionist flag and maintaining all of our historic claims." Cyprus, or a territory within South Africa or North America, might suffice "until Turkey is dissolved."[23] Herzl had planted the seeds of an idea that in 1903 would almost tear the Zionist Organization apart, and that would in time mature into what became known as the Territorialist movement.

At the moment when Herzl's view began to shift away from

Palestine, the German connection that Herzl had striven to forge through Hechler and Grand Duke Friedrich suddenly came alive. They obtained for Herzl a meeting on 16 September 1898 with Philipp zu Eulenburg, the German ambassador to Vienna. Eulenburg was a tall and courtly Prussian aristocrat whose cold exterior concealed passions for the arts and the occult. He was an avowed racialist and antisemite. He was also discreetly bisexual, and his affairs with equally aristocratic men eventually became public and led to his ruin. Eulenburg also happened to be Wilhelm II's closest friend. Eulenburg was quite taken by Herzl, whom he later described as "undeniably one of the most interesting personalities I have ever met . . . the prototype of a militant Jewish leader from the age of the Jewish kings, without a particle of the type we call 'trading Jew.'"[24] Eulenburg may have found Herzl appealing on many levels: politically, as the author of a plan to get the Jews out of Europe; professionally, as a celebrated journalist who might be useful at some point for public relations (or cover-ups); aesthetically, as a wordsmith and fantasist possessed of charismatic charm; and even physically, as a man of great beauty.

As luck would have it, two days after this meeting, the kaiser and his foreign minister, Bernhard von Bülow, were to be in Vienna for the day. After a meeting with von Bülow, who was warm and affable, Herzl waited nervously at the offices of *Die Welt*, hoping for a call to see the kaiser before his evening train. Herzl had a pair of black gloves at the ready and a band of black crepe around his hat ("so as to appear in proper court attire"). Alas, when the call came, it was Hechler saying that Wilhelm and Eulenburg had departed for the rail station. Undeterred, within a few days Herzl was pressing his case with Eulenburg, pleading not for the imposition of a German protectorate over Palestine by brute force, but rather for Kaiser Wilhelm's intervention with Abdul Hamid to allow for mass migration of Jews into Palestine. They would bring to Turkey an "intelligent, economically energetic national element" that would mean "unmistakable strengthening." "The return of even the semi-Asiatic Jews under the leadership of thoroughly modern persons," Herzl wrote, "must undoubtedly mean the restoration to health of this neglected corner of the Orient. Civilization and order would be brought there. Thus the migration of the Jews would eventually be an effective protection of the Christians of the Orient."[25]

Unbeknownst to Herzl, the kaiser was kept in the loop about Herzl by Eulenburg and by his uncle Friedrich, the Grand Duke of Baden. Wilhelm's reaction, as he wrote to his uncle, was that "we are dealing here with a question of the most far-reaching importance. . . . I am convinced that the settlement of the holy land by the wealthy and industrious people of Israel will soon confer on the former unexpected prosperity and blessing." Not only would Jewish money restore the Ottoman Empire to financial health, "the energy, creativity, and practical ability of the tribe of Shem would be diverted into more honorable channels than battening on the Christians" and fomenting socialist revolution. Wilhelm acknowledged that most Germans would, on religious grounds, oppose his generous and sympathetic support for a Jewish cause, but although "the Jews have killed the Savior; this God knows even better than we do, and He has punished them accordingly." Besides, Germany must acknowledge the "immense power that international Jewish capital . . . represents in all its dangerous implications. It would be an enormous gain for Germany if the world of the Hebrews looked up to it with gratitude!"[26] That is to say, Germany needed to support Zionism as a means of self-defense.

Two days after the kaiser wrote this letter, Herzl heard from Eulenburg that the kaiser would receive him and a Zionist delegation in Jerusalem during Wilhelm's upcoming pilgrimage to the Holy Land. Herzl was stunned. Shortly after that, he was called to Berlin for a whirl of meetings with Eulenburg,

Friedrich, von Bülow, and, for the first time, the German chancellor, Prince von Hohenlohe. Herzl was giddy to be among the elite of the Prussian aristocracy that he had venerated since his youth: "This is the forthright grand old style!" he enthused, "open and above-board!" Von Bülow, however, was cooler than in their previous meeting, and Hohenlohe was downright nasty, asking Herzl if Jews would truly abandon their beloved stock exchange. Herzl's optimism did not dim, rooted as it was in the belief that ultimate power lay in the hands of the kaiser. The Zionists would now surely have their protectorate, or Ottoman suzerainty, or both. In his diary, Herzl gushed, "To live under the protection of this strong, great, moral, splendidly governed, rightly organized Germany can only have the most salutary effect on the Jewish national character."[27]

Herzl badly misread the long-term effects of German political power on the Jews. He also seems not to have understood that the kaiser, although far more powerful than a constitutional monarch, did not rule Germany single-handedly, or that Wilhelm was mercurial and that his whims of the moment could quickly shift. It was inevitable that as soon as Wilhelm raised the issue of Zionism with Turkey's ambassador in Berlin, Ahmet Tevfik Pasha, the initiative would be dead in the water. But the kaiser himself had issued the invitation to meet Herzl, first in Constantinople, and then in Palestine. Herzl hurriedly assembled a delegation consisting of himself, Wolffsohn, Bodenheimer, the physician Moritz Schnirer, and the engineer Joseph Seidener. On 14 October, Herzl was on his way to Constantinople, where he waited nervously for the kaiser at a palace that had been purpose-built for Wilhelm's use. When the two men met, Herzl was captivated: "He has truly Imperial eyes. I have never seen such eyes. A remarkable, bold, inquisitive soul shows in them. . . . He is exactly as tall as I am." The kaiser was also impressed; in his memoirs, he described Herzl as "an enthusiastic idealist with an aristocratic mentality." The two men chatted amiably about global politics and the Dreyfus affair (Wilhelm thought Dreyfus was innocent) before Herzl unfurled his Zionist program, which he summed up as a "Chartered Company under German protection." Wilhelm said he would take that request to Abdul Hamid, after which the kaiser and Herzl's delegation would meet in the Holy Land.[28]

On the ship en route to Jaffa, Herzl wrote a lyrical feuilleton for the *Neue Freie Presse* about the eastern Mediterranean, but he did not even mention his destination. Herzl had forewarned his editors about the journey, and they were anything but pleased to see their star staff member bring Zionism, which they continued to find outlandish and embarrassing, to the world's most powerful leaders. Herzl was both excited and apprehensive about the upcoming audience with the kaiser, and he became increasingly fearful that Turkish officials opposed to Zionism might do him physical harm. These emotions overpowered whatever anticipation he may have felt about the prospect of being physically present, for the first time in his life, in the land of Israel. It is not at all clear that Herzl had any particular desire to visit Palestine. He only went because of the kaiser's invitation, and he stayed for barely ten days. He spent the entire time in Jaffa, Jerusalem, and their environs. He never went back. Before the visit, Palestine was an abstraction to him; during it, it was a considerable disappointment.

Herzl knew next to nothing about Palestine—its geography, demography, climate, flora, and fauna—until long after he published *The Jewish State*. In early 1897, the director of Jerusalem's Rothschild Hospital told an astounded Herzl that Palestine's soil was not barren, that orange trees grew there, that there were Jewish laborers (who had been coming since the early 1880s), and that the majority of Jerusalem's inhabitants were Jewish (as had been the case since the middle of the century). In January of 1898, Herzl met the botanist Otto Warburg, an expert in colonial agriculture and a recent convert to Zionism. Although Warburg worked mainly on Africa and the South Pacific—the regions in which the German empire was establishing colonies—he had a keen interest in the Middle East, and he was involved in German initiatives to grow cotton in Anatolia. Herzl obtained from Warburg detailed information about Palestine's flora and climate. This rather clinical education does not appear to have been matched by reading on Palestine's history or its numerous and highly diverse Jewish communities, the Muslim and Christian Arabs who constituted more than nine-tenths of the land's population, and the significance of Jerusalem in Islam.

While in Palestine, Herzl made only two references to Arabs in his diaries. One was to the countryside south of Jaffa as "neglected in Arab fashion." The other was that the work of draining malarial swamps might best be done by local Arabs who were, he believed, immune to malarial fever. A few months after the journey, Herzl had a brief correspondence with Youssuf Zia al-Khalidi, a former mayor of Jerusalem, in which al-Khalidi expressed sympathy for Jewish suffering and the Jews' ancient connections with the land of Israel, but observed that the land was populated and that neither the Palestinians nor the world's three hundred million Muslims would tolerate Jewish domination in the land. Herzl's response was that the local Arabs had nothing to fear from the Jews, who would neither displace nor enslave them but would improve and enrich their lives through Western technology. Herzl had a capacity for duplicity as well as fantasy, but there is no reason to believe that Herzl's assertions to al-Khalidi were insincere.

It is somewhat more difficult to reconcile disparities between the myth and the reality of Herzl's visit to Palestine. For example, in 1929 a Russian Zionist activist, Z. H. Masliansky, wrote that in 1908 Wolffsohn told him of the night before the Zionist delegation's arrival in Jaffa. According to the story, all the men went down to their cabins for the night except Herzl, who remained on deck. In the middle of the night, Herzl woke Wolffsohn up, saying that they must both go up to the deck to see the approach to their beloved motherland. Herzl was "attired as for an audience with an emperor." As they spied the minarets of Jaffa, Wolffsohn and Herzl fell "into each other's arms, and tears rose to our eyes as we whispered softly: 'our country! Our mother Zion!'"[29] Herzl's own diary entry about that same night is rather anticlimactic in comparison: The whole group slept on the deck, as it was hot underneath. When they spied the "Jewish coast," Herzl writes, "we approached the land of our fathers with mixed feelings."[30]

Another legend is based on the true story that on the Friday afternoon when Herzl and his retinue traveled by train from Jaffa to Jerusalem, Herzl was ill with fever, and due to delays the train arrived after the onset of the sabbath. From here, however, the story departs from reality, narrating that Herzl insisted, despite his illness, upon walking to his hotel, a journey of over half an hour, rather than desecrate the sabbath by riding in a carriage. Herzl's diary makes clear, however, that he very much wanted to take a carriage, but that his traveling companions "made long faces," "so I had to resign myself to walking in the city, weak with fever though I was."[31]

Herzl indeed experienced mixed feelings over the course of his brief stay in Palestine. He summarized Jaffa, Palestine's commercial hub, as "poverty and misery and heat in gay colors." But Herzl perked up at the agricultural settlement of Rehovot, where a group of young Jews on horseback thrilled Herzl and his colleagues by performing equestrian stunts while singing Hebrew songs. The delegation teared up at the sight of the horsemen, "into whom our young trouser salesmen can be transformed." Herzl also had a memorable experience at Mikveh Israel, a Jewish agricultural school near Jaffa. Knowing that the kaiser and his retinue were scheduled to pass by, Herzl had prepared the school choir to sing Prussia's royal anthem as

the kaiser approached. He and Herzl exchanged a few words—
the kaiser mounted on his steed, Herzl below:

> "And how has the journey agreed with your Majesty, so far?"
> He blinked grandly with his eyes.
> "Very hot! But the country has a future!"
> "At the moment it is still sick," I said.
> "Water is what it needs, a lot of water!" he said from
> above me.
> "Yes, your Majesty! Irrigation on a large scale!"
> He repeated, "It is a land of the future!"[32]

Shortly after that, the kaiser and his retinue trotted off, while
the choir reprised the royal anthem.

Jerusalem, however, was not quite so uplifting, for reasons
that went beyond Herzl's mercifully brief illness. Although on
the Friday night of his arrival the silhouettes of the Old City
were beautiful, in the heat of the day Herzl saw only filth and
squalor. He hoped to "clear out everything that is not something sacred, set up workers' homes outside the city, empty the
nests of filth and tear them down. . . . I would build around the
Holy Places a comfortable, airy new city with proper sanita-
tion." The Wailing Wall was "pervaded by a hideous, wretched,
speculative beggary."[33] Herzl was confronted by not only the
city's decay but also the "superstition and fanaticism" of its
Jews and even of his traveling party, which refused to enter the
Via Dolorosa and would not allow Herzl to set foot inside the
Church of the Holy Sepulchre or onto the Temple Mount.

Herzl had come to Palestine not as a pilgrim or a tourist,
but as a statesman on a mission. His thoughts were entirely focused on the audience with the kaiser. Its date and time had not
been fixed, so Herzl and his colleagues whiled away their days
in sightseeing and fretted about whether they would miss their
ship home. Shortly after arriving in Palestine, Herzl had submitted to Eulenburg a lengthy draft of a speech he wished to

declaim to the kaiser. On 1 November, the draft was returned to Herzl, with all specific reference to Zionist political goals deleted. If Herzl was aware of this walk-back from support for Zionism, he did not admit it even to his diary. What mattered at that moment was that the audience was set for noon the following day.

The next morning, the exquisitely anxious group donned formal attire and proceeded in blazing heat to the German imperial retinue's compound of tents, just north of the Old City. Once in the presence of the kaiser and von Bülow, Herzl read his speech, after which Wilhelm spoke for a few minutes, making banal references to the land's need for water and Western influence for the benefit of its local inhabitants. There was time enough for Wilhelm and von Bülow to make an antisemitic crack that "the money which is such a problem for us you have in abundance."[34] Shortly after that, the audience was over. Three days later, Herzl and his crew were on an orange freighter sailing from Jaffa to Alexandria, and thence to Naples.

Thus ended Wilhelm and Herzl's short-lived relationship. Herzl and Grand Duke Friedrich continued to correspond, and Herzl and Eulenburg continued to see each other, but the kaiser never reentered Herzl's life. Yet Herzl could not let go. Nine months after the fiasco in Jerusalem, Herzl fell into a panic when he feared he had lost a letter from Eulenburg avowing the kaiser's sincere interest in the Zionist cause. A year after that, Herzl was still blaming himself for the failure of his encounter with the kaiser in Jerusalem. Had he only met Wilhelm at the Old City's Dung Gate, the entry to the ancient Jewish Quarter, Herzl fantasized, the kaiser would have seen that Herzl was, indeed, the king of the Jews. In 1901, Herzl wrote to the journalist Maximilian Harden that he still had a soft spot for the kaiser, "although perhaps he sometimes makes mistakes. He is a man, and a king, through and through."[35] A few months before his death, Herzl dreamed of Wilhelm: "He and I were alone on a barque at sea."[36]

With his hopes for German sponsorship dashed, Herzl returned to wheedling with the Ottoman regime, although so far that strategy had led nowhere. In 1899, he twice turned to the Ottoman deputy foreign minister, Artin Dadyan Pasha, painting a rosy scenario of an Ottoman Empire made independent thanks to Jewish financial assistance. Desperate for an audience with the sultan, Herzl offered a bribe to Mehmet Nuri Bey, chief secretary of the Ottoman foreign ministry, but that gambit failed. The situation remained stagnant until late 1900, when Herzl's intermediaries in Constantinople informed him that the government was in the market for a 700,000-pound loan, and that the Zionists should be the ones to arrange it. Herzl, who had for years been selling a fantasy about Jewish bankers conjuring millions of pounds, suddenly had to produce something concrete. Fortunately for Herzl, he had an ally in Jacobus Kann, a Dutch banker who was part of the team setting up the Jewish Colonial Trust. For two months, Herzl worked with Kann to assemble the loan, but the Ottoman government chose another lender.

Cut to the quick, Herzl lashed out in his diary, declaiming that he would prevail upon the great Jewish bankers to cut off all ties with the Turks. Once again, he quoted Virgil: "If I cannot bend the powers above, I will move the lower world." Each time he invoked that phrase, however, it lost some of its power. The first time was before his decision to convene a Zionist Congress, which was a great success. The second time was after the realization that major Jewish bankers would not support his movement and that he would have to base the Zionist bank on small contributions. The bank took years to get off the ground and was badly under-resourced. And now Herzl indulged in a tantrum that was, in fact, a confession of impotence. Herzl attempted to mask his weakness with haughty dignity, as when, in early 1901, he requested an audience with the sultan, noting, "Only that gracious act can atone for the errors committed by your officials. Then I will come and place complete loyalty at the foot of your throne."[37] Herzl's thoughts, however, were never focused solely on the sultan. A week before sending this letter, Herzl returned to his idea from 1898 that Cyprus might be an alternative to Palestine.

It would be too harsh to dismiss Herzl's diplomacy as an outright failure. He never won the coveted German protectorate or charter from the Ottoman sultan, but he made Zionism into a known quantity on the world stage. In the final year of his life, Britain would grant the Zionist movement an unprecedented level of recognition. Until then, however, Herzl's major accomplishments lay in the development of the ZO and the penetration of Zionism into European Jewish communities. By 1900, he had gained enough clout in Vienna to prevail upon Austrian Jewry's most substantial philanthropy, the Israelitische Allianz zu Wien, to have three Zionists appointed to its directorial board. The line between diplomacy and internal Jewish politics could be a blurry one, as was the case with Herzl's attempts to meet the tsar "to make our movement appear as recognized in Russia through the fact of this audience."[38] Herzl explicitly denied that he wanted the tsar to endorse Zionism, which, given the virulence of antisemitism in Russia, could be seen as "a deportation decree."

The Zionist newspaper *Die Welt* had to follow a similar balancing act. From its first issues, it reported on antisemitic incidents throughout Europe, but it had to be cautious in its coverage of anti-Jewish incidents within Austria-Hungary, to whose law the newspaper was subject. In July of 1897, an issue of *Die Welt* was the object of a confiscation decree when it reproduced a Polish newspaper's report about an Austrian army unit that ran amok in Tarnów, Galicia, "beating and stabbing any Jew who crossed their path. The police drove the people off the streets but did not interfere with the soldiers in their 'work.'"[39] Two years later a Jewish man, Leopold Hilsner, from the Bohemian town of Polná, was accused of the ritual murder of two Christian women. When he was convicted and sentenced to death, *Die Welt* had to exercise restraint because journalistic criticism of a court decision was a criminal offense. But Herzl allowed Rosenberger (now the newspaper's executive editor) to be blunt about the poisonous antisemitic rhetoric in the courtroom and the flimsiness of the prosecution's case.

Herzl took justifiable pride in *Die Welt*, which was a newspaper of quality and over which he exercised complete (albeit unofficial) control. His other pet project, the Jewish Colonial Trust, was far more frustrating, as he wanted to control that as well, but given the complexity of the undertaking, he had no choice but to delegate authority to others. Herzl had a low opinion of Kann (despite his being a professional banker) and accused Wolffsohn of knowing nothing about finance, although Wolffsohn was a successful businessman and far more expert in money matters than Herzl. On the bank and many other matters, Herzl and Moses Gaster, the chief rabbi of Britain's Sephardi community, had a particularly intense mutual hostility. In part, the source of these tensions was the fault line between veteran Lovers of Zion activists like Gaster, and Herzl, who was perceived as an interloper and a Judaic ignoramus. Vanity, rigidity, pettiness, and ambition on the part of Herzl's colleagues-*cum*-rivals certainly played a role as well, as did Herzl's inability to heed criticism and his profound distaste for compromise. As Herzl vented to Ussishkin, "It simply suffices for me to speak out on a matter, which then awakens the spirit of independence of one faction or another, and then, in order not to follow the will of the 'tyrant,' any number of reasons to speak against it."[40]

There was also a cultural clash between eastern European Zionists and Herzl, but this should not be exaggerated. Herzl could be derisive of his Yiddish- and Russian-speaking colleagues, yet he also saw eastern European Jews as repositories of nobility and authenticity, qualities that he prized above all others. Thus Herzl wrote of eastern European Jews as "not Caliban, but Prospero!"[41] Herzl's haughtiness toward Wolffsohn should not be seen as merely a display of arrogance by a "Western" Jew over an "Eastern" one. Herzl demanded unquestioning loyalty from everyone, including British and American Zionists.

The structures that Herzl had established were strong enough to withstand the squabbles that fill up so much of Herzl's diary and correspondence. The real question was whether Herzl himself would be strong enough to continue. The Fourth Zionist Congress took place in London in mid-August of 1900. Shortly after his arrival in London, Herzl fell ill with a 104-degree fever and suffered bouts of angina. For three days he was unable to get out of bed. Among the delegates, rumors spread that he would not attend. But then, according to the Hungarian Zionist Samuel Bettelheim: "Suddenly there resounded the cry of a thousand voices! Everyone turned towards the entrance at the lowermost part of the hall, whence the noise came. Herzl is coming! His glorious head towers over the throng, like Saul, with his head and shoulders above the rest. Reality exceeds all images of him from portraits. So majestic and at the same time so primal-Jewish, no one had anticipated."[42] Herzl's presence at the Congress was essential for reasons that went beyond managing the ZO's affairs. He had deliberately moved the Congress venue from Basel to London in order to attract the attention of the British government and public. His opening address was a calculated exercise in flattery, praising Britain as the last place on earth where "God's people were not persecuted" and where they enjoyed "absolute freedom."[43]

The press took the bait. The *Glasgow Herald* remarked that "the compliment paid by the president of the Zionist Congress to this country is all the more welcome for being not only sincere, but also well deserved." The *Birmingham Post* also appreciated Herzl's "gratitude" to Britain for its toleration of the Jews. The *Leeds Mercury* described Herzl as "somebody to say something for us" at a time when Britain was being "bullied" by the Continent. The press also appreciated Herzl's warnings that Jewish immigration from Russia to Britain would be "disastrous" for both Britain and the Jews, and that a mass migration of Jews from eastern Europe to Palestine would be in everyone's best interests. Although the press uniformly praised Herzl's opening address and identified him squarely as the "originator" or "leader" of the Zionist movement, feelings about its feasibility were mixed. As the *Glasgow Herald* archly put it, "A garret in a Whitechapel slum may not be a very desirable inheritance, but at least it is more substantial than visionary acres on the barren hills of Galilee or Judea." A Welsh newspaper noted the gap between "the pious idea which is at the root of Zionism" and the skepticism of wealthy Anglo-Jews who "stand aloof from the movement."[44]

Herzl could not bridge that gap. The eminent bankers Nathaniel Mayer Rothschild and Samuel Montagu opposed Herzlian Zionism, as did the communal activist Claude Montefiore. Herzl repeatedly attempted to win over the Anglo-German banker Isaac Seligman, without success. King Edward VII and Lord Salisbury, the British foreign minister, remained unreachable, although Herzl "talked a blue streak" at Salisbury's private secretary.

Herzl continued to plug away on all three fronts—trying to kindle a flame with Britain, blow life into the cooling embers with Germany, and transform random sparks into fire with the Ottoman Empire. For months after the Congress, nothing happened, and then Vambery's interventions paid off. On 8 May 1901, Vambery informed Herzl that the sultan would meet with him, "not as a Zionist but as chief of the Jews and an influential journalist." Vambery cautioned Herzl not to mention Zionism, and he also threw out a deflating comment that the sultan did not recognize Herzl's name. But Herzl was happy, figuring that all he needed was an hour of the sultan's time in which to make a brilliant speech to establish his case. Herzl's family was in the midst of moving to a different apartment, but he hurriedly packed his bags and set off for Constantinople, accompanied by Wolffsohn and a member of the ZO's Vienna executive, the architect Oskar Marmorek (Alexander's brother). Fearful that the volume of the diary he was currently writing might be stolen, Herzl began a new one.

The timing was auspicious, not only because of the upcoming journey to Constantinople, but also, as Herzl noted, because the holiday of Pentecost was approaching—the sixth anniversary of Herzl's psychic whirlwind that sent him into, and landed him atop, the Zionist movement. The first issue of *Die Welt* had come out at the same time of year, and upon its publication Herzl had written, "I am going to remember this Pentecost week."[45] The fact that Pentecost is a Christian holiday, celebrating the descent of the Holy Spirit to Jesus's apostles, did not stop Herzl from marking key events in his life according to it.

By 13 May he was in Constantinople, staying in the same suite at the Hotel Royale where he had been five years before, with the same stunning view of the Golden Horn, the waterway separating Byzantine Constantinople from newer parts of the city. Yet Herzl felt "like a changed man. . . . Beauty no longer moves me." Herzl endured days of grilling by haughty functionaries and perfunctory sightseeing, his mood decidedly darker than it had been in anticipation of his meeting with the kaiser in Jerusalem. Yet his mind raced with plans as to how to make the best possible use of what he called "the fairy-tale moment of attaining my wish." Sitting in his bath on the morning of the 17th, Herzl practiced aloud what he would say (in French) to the sultan, and wondered, "How much of this will I be able to get in?" Later that morning, he received word that the sultan would see him. Two days later, he wrote jubilantly in his diary, "I got everything in."⁴⁶ The long-awaited audience had taken place.

Herzl wore an overcoat he had had custom-made two years earlier, for just this event. As in 1896, he was taken to the Yildiz Palace, and once again he viewed the weekly demonstration of imperial power known as the *selamlik:* "Every Friday the same thing. Troops start marching and form walls more impenetrable than stone. The court, eunuchs, princesses in closed landaus, pashas, dignitaries, flunkeys and lackeys *de toutes les couleurs.* All move past to the accompaniment of music. Over yonder, the Bosphorus gleams wondrously blue. The muezzin calls from the minaret, and the Padishah [sultan] drives in his partly closed carriage to the mosque."⁴⁷ Herzl described Abdul Hamid briefly as "short, skinny, with a large hooked nose, a full dyed beard, a small tremulous voice." By his own account, Herzl did most of the talking, spinning tales of technological wonders that the Jews could bring to the empire, the wealth they could generate through electricity and railroad monopolies, and the willingness of Jewish financiers to restructure the Ottoman debt. Herzl did not so much as mention Zionism, although at the end of the audience he asked vaguely for what he called a "pro-Jewish proclamation."

Herzl had a visceral distaste for the Ottoman court, and his flattery of the emperor was heartily insincere: "I pretended to be delighted at the prospect of coming under the old reliable and glorious scepter of Abdul Hamid," he wrote. Although Herzl had been shabbily treated by Kaiser Wilhelm, he continued to venerate him and to believe in the high-mindedness of German policy-making. Not so with the sultan or his court:

> I got into the power of a despot whom I had every reason to regard as half-demented. . . . My impression of the Sultan was that he is a weak, cowardly, but thoroughly good-natured man. I regard him as neither crafty nor cruel, but as a pro-

foundly unhappy prisoner in whose name a rapacious, infamous, seedy camarilla perpetrates the vilest abominations. . . . Abdul Hamid Khan II is a collective name for the most depraved pack of rogues that have ever made a country unsafe and unhappy. I never even suspected that such a gang of crooks was possible. The shamelessness of this business of tip-taking, which begins at the palace gate and ends only at the foot of the throne, is probably not even the worst of it. Everything is a business, and every official or functionary is a crook.[48]

Despite these profound negative feelings, in his communications with Ottoman officials after returning to Vienna, Herzl promised that Jews in an autonomous Palestine would be loyal defenders of the empire and would carry out military service on its behalf. Piling one fantasy upon another, in June Herzl proposed to the sultan a Jewish-initiated joint-stock company with capital of five million pounds that would flow into the empire. In his meeting with the sultan, and again in this proposal, Herzl invoked the story of Androcles and the lion, casting himself as Androcles, removing the thorn from the sultan's paw and earning his gratitude as a result.

Two months after his return from Constantinople, Herzl and his family spent their summer holiday, as was their custom, at Altaussee, a spa town about two hundred miles from Vienna. They were still there on Yom Kippur, and, despite Julie's unceasing arguments with Herzl and her mother-in-law Jeanette, Herzl was in good spirits: "Today I sat by the lake, which was beautiful. I thought how it would be if next Spring I can sit by the Lake of Gennesaret [the Sea of Galilee] like this." He jotted down the next set of world leaders whom he would find a way to meet—the South African magnate Cecil Rhodes, Tsar Nicholas II, King Edward VII, and the American president, Theodore Roosevelt, who had just assumed office following the assassination of William McKinley.[49]

Advances on the diplomatic front came as a fillip to Herzl. They were a pleasant distraction from his relationship with the ZO, which was becoming increasingly tense and had begun to resemble that of a parent and a rebellious adolescent. The Zionist Congress evolved from a meeting of individuals within the framework of national delegations to a parliament composed of political parties. The first such parties were a product of the movement's critical mass in eastern Europe. From the ZO's first days, eastern European Zionists from the Lovers of Zion favored immediate settlement activity, which Herzl thought to be a waste of money and an irritant to the Ottoman government. Herzl did, however, agree with the eastern Europeans on the need to establish an agency for land purchase in Palestine. Herzl himself had raised the idea in 1896, and at the First Zionist Congress the following year, the Russian-Jewish mathematician Hermann Schapira proposed a fund whose land purchases would never be resold, but would remain the eternal possession of the Jewish people. Schapira died in 1898, but at the Fifth Zionist Congress in 1901, Herzl oversaw the establishment of the Jewish National Fund (JNF). This gesture encouraged settlement-oriented Zionists, but Herzl had no intention for the JNF to buy land until Palestine was securely in Jewish hands.

An overlapping yet distinct group of Zionists was less interested in settling Jews in Palestine than in fostering a national Jewish culture. The group was inspired by the veteran Zionist Ahad Ha-Am. Ahad Ha-Am dismissed Herzlian dreams of a Jewish state and believed that what the Jewish people needed most was a cultural renewal, based in the Hebrew language and a modestly sized, yet vibrant, Jewish community in Eretz Israel. Ahad Ha-Am distanced himself from the ZO, preferring to lob criticisms from the safety of his newspaper, *Ha-Shiloah*. Opposition to Herzl from within the ZO came from a former ally, Leo Motzkin, one of the few Russian Zionists who had endorsed Herzl's political program. Motzkin was joined by a knot of young men that included Chaim Weizmann, who at that time had just completed his doctorate in chemistry, and the scholar Martin Buber. In 1901, these men and some thirty others organized themselves into a body called the Democratic Faction, which comprised about 10 percent of the Fifth Congress's delegates. In part, the name reflected its members' pique at Herzl's autocratic rule of the movement. But in a broader sense, for these men, Jewish culture and democracy were inseparable, as the former was an emanation of the people's will, and the latter was the exercise of that will.

Herzl was not indifferent to Jewish culture. Like the *Neue Freie Presse*, the Zionist newspaper *Die Welt* contained historical and literary essays as well as news. Herzl had only a minimal knowledge of Hebrew, but he appreciated its importance among the eastern European Zionist elite. He had *The Jewish State* translated into Hebrew immediately upon its publication, and he ensured that the ZO newspaper would have a Hebrew as well as German edition (*Ha-Olam*, which like *Die Welt* means "the world"). Herzl worried, though, that the Zionists most committed to developing new forms of Jewish culture were, in one way or another, advocates of the secularization of Jewish life. This entailed the subordination of the traditional textual canon to modern concepts of historical development and of natural science, and a selective approach to the observance of ritual commandments.

Herzl himself was non-observant, and he did not care how his colleagues lived their lives, but the cultural Zionists infuriated the Orthodox Zionists whose support Herzl badly needed to make inroads into the eastern European masses. Those Orthodox Jews who did warm to Zionism saw it as a purely humanitarian movement to rescue Jews from poverty and oppression. On that, they and Herzl could agree. Thus an odd alliance developed between the arch-secular Herzl and the Orthodox

Zionists, who in 1902 organized their own faction, known as Mizrahi, an acronym for *Merkaz Ruhani* (spiritual center). Herzl provided the fledgling faction with financial assistance to get it off the ground and form a counter to the cultural Zionists.

In addition to swirling factionalism within the ZO, Herzl confronted an indifferent, even hostile, reaction by the eastern European Zionists to his diplomatic maneuvers. They were upset that he had drawn on the bank's reserves for the trip to Constantinople (though Herzl insisted it was only a short-term loan) and considered the whole business a waste of money. An embittered Herzl wrote in his diary:

> Once the Jewish state is in existence, everything will appear small and obvious. Perhaps a fair-minded historian will find that it was something after all if an impecunious Jewish journalist in the midst of the deepest degradation of the Jewish people and at a time of the most disgusting antisemitism made a flag out of a rag and a people out of a decadent rabble, a people that rallies erect around that flag.
>
> But all this and my skill with negotiating with Powers and princes are nothing.
>
> No one can appreciate what I have done and what I have suffered.[50]

Four days after writing these lines, Herzl fainted while riding in a carriage in Paris's Bois de Boulogne. He lay down across two chairs in the woods and then drove home "with greatly diminished consciousness."[51] A few months later, he wrote to Wolffsohn that he had overstrained his nerves and had premonitions of a sudden death. He entrusted Wolffsohn "as a sacred testament" to set up, immediately after his death, a fund for the support of his children. His wife's family was not to get a cent.[52]

Herzl was down, but he was not out. As difficulties piled up around him, writing fiction provided a balm. He was determined to produce a novel that would express his deepest feelings and desires about Zionism. It was not to be an extended feuilleton, not an escape from Zionism but, rather, an alternative means to its realization. This idea had been on his mind, in one form or another, ever since those febrile weeks in the summer of 1895. His ideas for the plot kept changing, but Herzl was always the hero. In early 1898 he considered writing the story of an upstanding Jewish journalist who becomes a Zionist and sails off to the Promised Land with a lovely woman at his side. A year later, he started down a very different path. At the Third Congress, Herzl announced that he had started work on a novel, which he directed *Die Welt* to describe as "depicting conditions in the projected new Commonwealth twenty years after its creation."[53] The day after Herzl sent in that directive, the title of the novel popped into Herzl's head while he was on a bumpy bus ride in the outskirts of Vienna. The book would be called *Altneuland* (Old-Newland), after the medieval Altneu synagogue in Prague. *Die Welt* dutifully announced this news as well.

In the years that followed, Herzl did his utmost to steal time away from his myriad responsibilities to write the novel, and he berated himself when he had to step away from it, lest it "grow worse and worse and more and more insipid." But he felt compelled to complete the work: "My hopes for practical success have now disintegrated," he confided to his diary in 1901. "My life is no novel now. So the novel is my life."[54] Herzl was referring here to his entire life, not just the years since his turn to Zionism, and to his drive to be recognized as not only a leader but also a serious author. "I am in a field," he wrote, "where I have accomplished next to nothing intellectually . . . in the Jewish Question I have become world famous as a propagandist. As a writer, particularly as a playwright, I am held to be nothing, less than nothing. People call me only a good journalist. Yet I feel, I know, that I am or was a writer of great ability, one who simply didn't give his full measure because he became disgusted and discouraged."[55] In fact, the final act of his life would involve more than a novel. There would be a true diplomatic breakthrough, which would lead to an offer by a Great Power of a territory for the benefit of the Jewish people. There was, however, a catch: it was not Palestine.

5

If You Will It, It Is Still a Dream

ON FRIDAY, 24 January 1902, Herzl awoke in the early hours of the morning in a reflective mood. "Zionism was the sabbath of my life," he wrote. Without elaborating, he then moved on to a moment of candid self-assessment: "I believe my effectiveness as a leader may be attributed to the fact that I, who as a man and a writer have had so many faults, made so many mistakes, and done so many foolish things, have been pure of heart and utterly selfless to the Zionist cause."[1] These statements reflected a state of emotional intensity, but not the melodrama that often featured in the pages of his diary. Instead of blaming others and indulging in self-pity, as he was wont to do, Herzl acknowledged his own failings as well as his strengths.

The analogy Herzl drew between his relationship with Zionism and that of the Jewish people with the sabbath was an admission of the need of even this most secular of men for the sacred. It was also a poignant statement about Herzl's stance toward *Judentum*—that ambiguous German word that can mean both "Judaism" and "Jewry." Herzl's "sabbath" was not a sacred time, separated from the profane work week, just as the Holy Land, in his eyes, was not particularly holy. Zionism was, instead, a project, a framework that gave Herzl's life structure and meaning. For all the stress Zionism caused him, it was actually the eye of his psychic storm, and a source of inner calm.

That calm was induced by action, not sabbath rest. Action would make dreams into reality—dreams of alleviating Jewish distress and putting an end to the industrial unrest and economic inequity that racked the European continent. In Herzl's finest play, *The New Ghetto*, the "Jewish Problem" and "Social Problem" were intertwined. The same was the case in Herzl's novel *Altneuland*. The key difference between the two was that in the novel both problems are solved. The novel's epigraph, *wenn ihr wollt, ist es kein Märchen* (if you will it, it is no fairy tale), became a watchword of the Zionist movement and the state of Israel. For Herzl, the novel became a repository of dreams that bore little resemblance to the desperate, fourth-quarter diplomatic plays that preceded his death.

Herzl was a social reformer but hardly a radical. In 1898, he assured the German foreign minister von Bülow, who suspected Jews of orchestrating international Marxism, that Moses had invented individualism as a rejection of pharaonic socialism. The message of his feuilleton "Solon in Lydia," that inequity and the struggle to survive are necessary evils, continued in one of Herzl's last feuilletons, written in 1903, about a march of unemployed men in London. Observing the mass of impoverished humanity, Herzl felt great pity for them yet wrote that the fear of falling into poverty and the attempt to avoid it are key to all social success. Herzl remained enchanted by capitalism so long as it was not corrupted by avarice or fraud. In 1901, Herzl wrote in praise of an essay titled "The Psychology of Business," by the powerful German-Jewish industrialist Walther Rathenau. The essay was a piece of fiction, claiming to be the memoir of the nephew of a recently deceased ethnic German Russian state counselor. The fictional uncle was presented as a Prussian nobleman who combined aristocratic honor with heroic financial risk-taking. Herzl was thrilled by the essay's depiction of a businessman who is a natural ruler: strong, robust, and honest. In his review of the article, Herzl praised the entrepreneur's gift to "recognize and create need"—to function as a dramaturge, creating desire, yet doing so without manipulation or dishonesty.

When Rathenau revealed to Herzl that he had in fact made the story up, Herzl did not bat an eye, but saw it as an entrée into conversation with a man whom he yearned to win over for Zionism. The two men had crossed paths before. In 1897 Rathenau wrote a scathing essay, titled "Hear O Israel," attributing antisemitism to what he called the Jews' own boorish and unethical behavior. At that time, Herzl wrote to the editor of the periodical that published the piece, saying that Rathenau was not entirely wrong—that Jews did, in fact, need to transform themselves from the inside out—and he held himself up as an example: "You do not know me, but if you had known me previously, you would not recognize me now. One such idea works upon men as a magic well, from which new forms go forth when they are immersed. The Jews must delve into that well." Four years later, Herzl and Rathenau corresponded directly. This time around, Herzl did not speak of the Jews' need to transform themselves but rather of the "many wonderous possibilities [that] lie in the resurrection of the Jewish people." Once restored to its homeland, it would carry out "land reform, social reform, and reform of the Orient."[2]

Herzl had been using this kind of language since completing *The Jewish State*. In 1896, he remarked that agriculture in the Jewish state would be carried out by cooperative societies with credit from the Jewish Company. In Paris in June of 1899, Herzl gave sustained thought to the social foundations of the Jewish state. His imagination was stimulated by an automobile exhibition, to which he responded by envisioning fleets of electric cars and a network of "cement roads" and charging stations throughout Europe. This fantasy network of cement and electricity led him to think about the dependence of human beings upon each other. Strolling along the rue Cambon and through the Tuileries as he had done precisely four years earlier, once again he had a burst of inspiration, albeit more controlled than his first one. Herzl hit upon the word "mutualism" to describe the social philosophy he was striving for: "the middle ground between capitalism and collectivism." It would be characterized by producers' and consumers' cooperatives, along the lines of existing cooperative enterprises in Europe and America.[3]

At the Fifth Zionist Congress in 1901, Herzl proclaimed that "each settlement should administer its own affairs as an agricultural productive association in accordance with the principles which experience and science suggest to us even now."[4] Later that year, Herzl met the German economist Franz Oppenheimer, a tireless supporter of agricultural cooperatives as a means to give the poor access to land and credit. Oppenheimer was himself Jewish and attracted to Zionism out of philanthropic concern for eastern European Jews as well as a desire to demonstrate to antisemites that Jews were indeed capable of working the land. Herzl and Oppenheimer corresponded while he was writing *Altneuland*, and Herzl commissioned Oppenheimer to write a series of articles for *Die Welt*.

These articles exerted a deep effect on Herzl. After reading the last of them in January of 1902, he wrote in his diary: "The final appeal, the comparison of the experiment of Rahaline [a cooperative settlement in Ireland in the 1840s] with the Berlin-Zossen experimental railroad struck me, and I immediately decided to carry out Oppenheimer's experiment."[5] Herzl refused, however, to set up a cooperative farm in Palestine prior to the receipt of an Ottoman charter or the establishment of a European protectorate. Instead, he resolved to place the farm in what he called "Egyptian Palestine," that is, El-Arish in the northern Sinai Peninsula, which was under British administration. Herzl was not sure if this would be a "national affair," "for Zionist propaganda purposes," or whether it should be "started in all secrecy." Either way, the end goal of the experiment was to enable efficient and effective agricultural settlement of Jews in Palestine.

Three months after this diary entry, Herzl finished his novel, and he eagerly anticipated its publication. Herzl's joy, however, was soon overwhelmed by sorrow when his father Jakob died in June. While in London, Herzl received a telegram from his wife that his father was seriously ill, but although he hurriedly arranged for his departure for Vienna, he was still in London when news arrived that Jakob had died. Herzl was devastated: "What a support he was to me all the time! What a counsellor! He stood by my side like a tree. Now the tree is gone." Jakob had apparently read the entire draft of Herzl's novel save for its conclusion, which, Herzl lamented, he would never see. Nor would his father know that Herzl had been scheduled to meet the next day with Nathaniel Mayer Rothschild, a meeting "that might have been decisive for Zionism."[6]

Herzl sent a telegram to his colleague Kremenezky in Vienna ordering that there should be no speeches and only Hebrew prayers at Jakob's funeral. After he returned home, Herzl arranged for his father to be placed in a temporary grave, not a mausoleum, as the day would soon come, Herzl thought, when Jakob would be disinterred and then reinterred in Palestine. While harboring these hazy dreams, Herzl was also faced with the more immediate question of care for his widowed and aging mother, Jeanette. After the funeral, Herzl took her and the rest of his family to Altaussee for the summer. Herzl was away from them from early July to mid-August, when he shuttled between Paris and London before undertaking a three-week journey to Constantinople. When he was not traveling, Herzl insisted on receiving Zionist luminaries in Altaussee so that he would not have to leave his mother. He wanted David and Fanny Wolff-sohn to get to know Jeanette so that she would feel comfortable with them should the two families ever live in the same place. Herzl's thoughts were entirely with Jeanette, not Julie, with whom he was still sharply at odds. He complained to her cousin Moriz Reichenfeld that Julie was a shrew and a liar, and that he had stayed with her only because "I cannot leave my poor unfortunate mother alone; I also want to preserve a paternal household for my children."[7]

Carrying out Zionist business from his summertime "paternal household," Herzl corresponded with Rothschild, with whom he had held a rescheduled meeting in London in July. Rothschild was unyielding in his opposition to a Jewish state: "I tell you very frankly that I should view with horror the establishment of a Jewish Colony pure and simple; such a Colony would be an *imperium [in] imperio*; it would be a Ghetto with the prejudices of the Ghetto; it would be a small, petty Jewish State, orthodox and illiberal, excluding the Gentile and the Christian." Referring to his novel, Herzl retorted that "I worked for three years on a coherent reply to this and similar misgivings."[8]

Altneuland, then, functioned on multiple levels: it served to convince skeptics of Zionism's feasibility and to convince Herzl of his own literary talent. It also represented an opportunity for Herzl to exorcize psychological demons that had haunted him throughout his life and that repeatedly figured in his writings. "Somewhere in the depths of depression," the novel begins, "Dr. Friedrich Lowenberg sat around a marble-topped table of his coffeehouse."[9] It invokes Herzl's dead friends from youth, Heinrich Kana and Oswald Boxer, as Friedrich has lost his two closest friends: one to suicide and one to tropical illness while establishing Jewish settlements in Brazil. As the story moves forward, details from Herzl's own life blend with his long-standing self-perceptions, beliefs, prejudices, and longings.

Friedrich is a poor man, a barrister's assistant, in love with a wealthy and spoiled Jewish woman who breaks his heart by getting engaged to the son of a wealthy banker. Escaping a gathering of rich and vulgar Jews, Friedrich flees to his café, where he is approached by an east European Jewish beggar and his son. Friedrich accompanies them to their hovel, gives them some money, and is surprised when he says to them, "May God be with you." "Since the days of his boyhood," Friedrich thinks, "when he used to go to synagogue with his father, he had never thought of the 'God of his fathers.'" He is unwittingly under-going the beginning of a process of rebirth and return.

On the verge of suicide, Friedrich responds to a mysterious newspaper advertisement seeking a "cultured and despairing young man willing to try a last experiment with his life." The man who placed the advertisement, Kingscourt, is a middle-aged German aristocrat who has also been unlucky in love. Kingscourt has been living on a desert island with his mute Tahitian servant, who is yet another lonely, brokenhearted man. Plainspoken yet good-natured, Kingscourt is searching for a traveling companion and finds one in Friedrich, who sees the journey as "taking leave of life." He has only one request of Kingscourt—a substantial gift of money for the poor family that Friedrich had encountered a few nights before.

En route to their desert island, the two men stop in Pales-tine, where they encounter "poor Turks, dirty Arabs, shy Jews . . . blackened Arab villages whose inhabitants looked like brig-ands. The children played in the dust, naked." The hills are also naked, for they have been "denuded of soil." There is a bright moment at the Jewish colony of Rehovot, where the colonists' youths perform an equestrian fantasia, much to Kingscourt's delight. Yet this display does not prevent Friedrich from sinking into depression, and the two men sail off to their desert hideaway.

Twenty years later, in 1922, the men return to Palestine. Over the years, Friedrich has grown muscular and tanned, and Kingscourt derives considerable pride and pleasure from this transformation. Just as Friedrich has regenerated himself, so has Palestine. The men disembark at Haifa, which now resembles "an Italian port." Its All Nations Square is home to sundry European trading and banking houses, and the presence of churches, mosques, and Buddhist and Hindu temples as well as synagogues testifies to its cosmopolitan population. Friedrich and Kingscourt are greeted by David Litwak, a handsome young man who turns out to be that same boy whom Friedrich had encountered at the café, and whose family members are now healthy and prosperous thanks to Kingscourt's generous gift, which allowed them to start new lives in Palestine. Litwak is a leader of Palestine's New Society, the name given to Palestine's government because it is not a sovereign state. David's sister, Miriam, is virtuous and demure, "of singular beauty." Another major character, Reshid Bey, is an Arab with fluent German who has studied at the University of Berlin.

Once the characters have been introduced, the rest of the book is fairly static, consisting of depictions and demonstrations of the technological paradise that Jews have created in Palestine. The only real tension is between Litwak and Rabbi Geyer, a xenophobic nationalist who caters to the mob and who is running against Litwak for the presidency of the New Society under the slogan "against the stranger in our midst." There is a melodramatic flourish at the end, when Litwak's little boy falls gravely ill, and the gruff Kingscourt, who has become attached to the lad, is distraught. But the boy pulls through, though David and Miriam's mother dies, leaving Friedrich free to marry Miriam without having a domineering mother-in-law to darken his life.

Litwak is modeled after Wolffsohn; not only do they share the same first name, they are both traditional eastern European Jews of an extraordinarily even disposition. Litwak wins the election for the presidency of the New Society, foreshadowing Herzl's anointing of Wolffsohn to be his successor as head of the ZO. The bacteriologist Steineck, who is searching for a cure for malaria, is an avatar of the Zionist activist Alexander Marmorek, who Herzl had hoped would find a cure for tuberculosis. The beauteous Miriam bears a striking resemblance to Herzl's deceased sister, Pauline. And Friedrich is, of course, Herzl's alter ego.

A depressed, lost young man finds love and purpose in the old-new Jewish homeland. What impresses Friedrich most about the Jews of Palestine is that they have reclaimed the honor that they lost due to shameful assimilation. They have become, as Herzl longed to be, "proud and free." It is no coincidence that one of the novel's final scenes, and arguably its most powerful, is Friedrich's lengthy internal monologue in Jerusalem on the sabbath eve, sitting in the rebuilt Temple. The Temple has not restored animal sacrifice, but it is filled with biblical motifs connoting continuity, strength, and dignity—limestone walls, a bronze altar and basin, and the twin pillars that, in the Second Temple, were called Boaz and Jachin ("in His strength" and "He will establish"). In this setting, Friedrich reflects that "Jewry has a look so different now because it was no longer ashamed of itself. . . . The strong, the free, the successful had also returned home—and they received more than they gave. . . . Only here had the Jews again developed a free commonwealth in which they could work for the good of mankind. . . . In the ghetto they were without honor, without rights, without justice, without defense—when they left the ghetto, they ceased to be Jews. Yet a man, to be a man, must have both freedom and the feeling of community. Only when the Jews had both could they rebuild the house of the Invisible and Almighty God." The

Temple epitomizes Jewish particularism, but for Friedrich, as for Herzl, the purpose of Zionism is the integration of Jews into the community of independent nations. The Temple square also houses a vast Peace Palace—a site for international congresses, a residence for scholars and artists, and a source of charitable assistance for victims of catastrophes throughout the world.

Not everyone in the old-new land is possessed of honor. Those who do not make an honest living from the production of goods, the provision of an essential service, or science and the arts may not be part of the New Society. The snobbish and bejeweled women who cropped up in so many of Herzl's plays and stories show up here as well. The woman whom Friedrich loved in his youth is now elderly and faded, overdressed, and displaying a fallen décolletage. The New Society has a Legion of Honor, membership in which is determined entirely by achievement, not by wealth. The sign of membership in the Legion is a small yellow ribbon; it is the same color as the patch imposed upon European Jews in the Middle Ages. "This sign of ignominy has become an emblem of honor!"

The counterpart to internally generated honor is respect from others. Having received a charter from the Ottoman Empire, the New Society lives at peace with its neighbors, and rail lines link it with Damascus and Baghdad. It has no army. In Europe, the reduction of the Jewish population has caused antisemitism to disappear, and in some countries Gentiles so value Jews that they entreat them not to leave. Thanks to the new Jewish homeland, Jews are fully emancipated in the diaspora. Reshid Bey ventriloquizes the Palestinian Arab population with expressions of gratitude to the Jews for bringing Western technology to a benighted land. Reshid takes part in an ecumenical Passover seder along with the novel's protagonists and Christian clergy from various denominations, but no imam or rabbi is present.

The purpose of the seder is not to celebrate the Jews' miraculous exodus from Egypt but the technical miracles wrought by the old-new Jewish homeland. The focal point of the evening is the playing of a phonographic recording by Joe Levy, director of the Department of Industry. Levy's recital of technical and administrative processes goes into exhaustive detail and takes up several pages. What is this monologue doing at a Passover seder? The traditional Passover liturgy, the Haggadah, is read aloud, just as Herzl was wont to read *The Jewish State* aloud, and just as the main character in Herzl's play *The Glossary* saves his marriage by reciting an abstruse Roman legal code to his straying wife. Here, as throughout Herzl's life, the spoken word has a transformative quality.

We learn from Levy, as we learn throughout the book, that Zionism has solved the Jewish Problem not only by bringing poor and persecuted Jews to Palestine but also by turning peddlers and merchants into farmers, manufacturers, and scientists. To prevent the formation of a landless proletariat, all land is publicly owned, leased from the New Society but subject to redistribution every fifty years, following the biblical Jubilee. (Few land reformers of Herzl's generation held such extreme views; most favored heavy land taxes and cheap credit to farmers but wanted to retain private property.) In *Altneuland*, disparities of wealth are further impeded by the maximization of cooperation in the production and purchase of goods as well as the supply of services.

In the novel, Herzl puts aside the pessimistic social sensibilities of his journalistic writings. And unlike his correspondence with Rathenau, in the novel it is rational bureaucratic policy, not heroic capitalist enterprise, that satisfies human needs. In *The Jewish State*, the problems of the Jews were essentially political and legal, and they were to be solved by the international community, on the one hand, and a Jewish aristocratic republic defended by a professional army, on the other.

But *Altneuland* is a democratic cooperative commonwealth, without an army or even an armed police force, which is held together by economic and cultural institutions. Herzl's imagination deconstructs the state that it had constructed in 1896.

This about-face is puzzling, given how enmeshed Herzl was in geopolitics and the thought he had given earlier in his Zionist career to the military means by which a Jewish state might be acquired. One might dismiss the novel's pacific mood as a propaganda ploy to endear Herzl to the Ottoman government, or as daydreaming about an unachievable, utopian future. It is unlikely, however, that Herzl would have devoted three years of his life to the production of a lie, or that he would have considered such a work to be his greatest literary achievement. He also angrily dismissed the applicability of the word "utopian" to his novel, saying that everything in it was all fully realizable within a short period of time—the twenty years from the time of its publication to the characters' visit to Palestine in 1922.

Despite its wild leaps of imagination, the novel is about stasis as much as change, and it reflects many of Herzl's long-held sensibilities. In the New Society women have equal rights, but nubile women give up public life to care for their husbands and children. Only "spinsters and lonely women" work, and their purview is limited to the caring professions such as nursing and teaching. The New Society bristles with technological innovation, but for the most part it has further developed existing technologies rather than prefigured entirely new ones. (The "telephone newspaper," an ancestor of the radio or internet, is an exception.) Friedrich describes the New Society as a testament to peaceful social evolution: "The old state need not be superseded; it can coexist with this economy, can protect it and help it to develop—and the New Society can, in its turn, strengthen and protect the old order." Agricultural cooperatives that root people in the land prevent them from crowding in the cities and becoming a dangerous, rebellious mob. Medical research by the New Society's scientists makes possible the mass migration of Europe's "proletarian masses" to the colonized world, especially Africa. These same medical breakthroughs will enable enslaved or oppressed black people throughout the Western world to return to Africa. Thanks to this little model society in the eastern Mediterranean, the entire Western world will be stabilized.

Few readers today would find literary value in the novel, which has a contrived plot, flat characters, and wooden dialogue. Since Israel's establishment, however, the novel has been a source of pride for Zionists, who see Israel as a fulfillment of Herzl's vision of a tolerant and progressive society. They hail the novel's many accurate predictions, such as the construction of modern Haifa and Jerusalem, and the advanced infrastructure and Western culture that make Israel more closely resemble European states than many of its Middle Eastern neighbors. Its detractors, however, find its Eurocentrism deeply problematic, as the New Society has no cultural connection with the Middle East. Tiberias is a tourist destination for rich Americans and Europeans, who are entertained by musicians from Hungary, Romania, and Italy. When Miriam performs music "of all the nations," those nations are Germany, Italy, France, and Russia. Palestinians are invisible save for Reshid Bey.

Similar criticisms of the novel's Eurocentrism came at the time of publication from within the Zionist movement, although they came not from the perspective of the Arab Middle East but from Jewish eastern Europe. For Ahad Ha-Am, the novel confirmed all of his worst suspicions about Herzl. In a review that was published in Hebrew, Russian, and German, Ahad Ha-Am dismissed *Altneuland* as bereft of Judaic content. The New Society's members speak a pastiche of languages, but there is no identifiable Hebrew culture. Religious symbols such as the Temple or rituals such as the Passover seder are hollow.

(Ahad Ha-Am was neither mollified nor amused by the fact that in the novel the opera house was performing an original work on the life of the false messiah Shabbatai Zvi, to whom Herzl was sometimes compared by his detractors.) Ahad Ha-Am found no value in the novel's ethos of social reform, which was universal, not specific to the Jews' own qualities or needs:

> How would a Negro Altneuland be any different from a Zionist one? I believe it is no exaggeration to say that a few superficial changes would suffice to Africanize [Herzl's] book completely. . . . Imitating others without the slightest originality; going to all lengths to avoid anything smacking of national chauvinism, even if this means obliterating a people's nationality, language, literature, and spiritual propensities; making oneself small to show how great, even revoltingly so, is one's tolerance. . . . All is a monkey-like aping of others with no show of national distinctiveness. The spirit of slavery-within-freedom, the spirit of the Western European Diaspora, is everywhere.[10]

Ahad Ha-Am's attack provoked an even more sulfurous diatribe from Nordau, who accused Ahad Ha-Am of the lowest sort of parochialism and bigotry. ("Ahad Ha-Am does not want tolerance. Aliens should be slaughtered, or at best chased out as they once were in Sodom and Gomorrah. The idea of tolerance disgusts him.") Nordau's polemic provoked a volley of counter-criticisms and defenses. Although criticism of Herzl ran strongest among eastern European Zionists, Herzl and Nordau had defenders from across the Pale of Settlement, including the Russian Zionist Max Mandelstamm, who told Herzl not to mind the "half-Asian yeshiva types. . . . The Russian swamp has come to life and its frogs are croaking." The wittiest defense of Herzl came from the German Zionist Sammy Gronemann, who quipped that if Ahad Ha-Am came "face to face with Achilles, [he] would only see his heel."[11]

Herzl was personally devastated by these attacks. To him,

the New Society's Jewish aspects were substantive, not frivolous. He had revealed his deepest hopes and aspirations, and a book that he thought would unite and inspire the Jewish world turned into a pretext for partisan infighting. The polemics about the novel added to his general feeling of exhaustion and impending death. The spells of "brain anemia" and palpitations became more frequent, and he foresaw that he would soon die. "I am consistently very unwell," he complained to the physician Marmorek. "Heart neurosis! That, and the Jews, will kill me off."[12]

He did not tell his family about his condition. Informing Julie, he noted in his diary, "wouldn't make her any more loving."[13] In March of 1903, Herzl made up a third (and final) will, leaving his children as heirs, but granting his mother a life estate. His son Hans was to be raised in England, the country to which Herzl had developed a profound attachment. Herzl stipulated that he should be buried next to his father until "the Jewish people transfer my remains to Palestine."[14] Any deceased immediate family were to be brought to Palestine as well, except for Julie, unless her own will explicitly requested it. The will singles out Julie for condemnation, accusing her of extravagant spending that consumed her dowry and his parents' fortune.

Herzl spent heavily from those very same sources on the Zionist movement—the newspaper, his travels, and payments to his agents abroad. But despite his escalating worries about money, Herzl consistently refused to take payment for his Zionist activity. Wolffsohn repeatedly urged him to do so, but Herzl angrily retorted, "Don't be mistaken and come back to me with this idiocy, that I should be paid by the movement. That is pure madness and won't happen. Not only because I would despise myself, but also because it would deprive me of all authority."[15] Herzl was, and wanted the world to see him as, incorruptible. As he wrote to Goldsmid, "All my enemies eagerly wait for me to mess up. These people, who are driven by ambition or personal interest, are only dangerous to people like themselves. I possess neither ambition nor personal interests."[16] Financial improprieties on the part of his colleagues infuriated him. When Herzl needed a financial favor from Wolffsohn, he was acutely embarrassed, and swore Wolffsohn to secrecy.

In his final years, Herzl's writing for the *Neue Freie Presse* reflected his self-image as a man above "ambitions and personal interests" as well as concerns with aging and mortality. His 1902 story "The Reading Glasses" is about a middle-aged man who has acquired his first pair of reading glasses and dwells upon their melancholy import: "Reading lenses are the border, the watershed. From here on the water flows to the other side. One must leave this. The glasses are the official beginning of old age."[17] According to the narrator, first we lose our looks, then our passion, and reading is our only remaining pleasure. The narrator is wearing his new lenses while he writes in a hotel salon. He sees—or rather he perceives—a young woman enter the room. Because of the lenses he cannot make her features out clearly, but he catches the scent of her perfume and hears the rustle of her dress. He abandons all ambition to flirt with her or to hide the glasses in her presence so as to conceal his age. The narrator notes that this blurry-faced woman in the salon reminds him of a fourteen-year-old girl whom he had loved as a lad. In this story, Herzl has returned to his own youth, to his love of Madeleine Herz and, eleven years later, Madeleine's niece. But his nostalgia is pallid, and his emotions are subdued. The narrator has achieved the detachment that a younger Herzl, along with his fictional alter egos, had striven for but had been unable to attain.

Despite flagging energy, Herzl mustered enough vitality to push on with his diplomatic efforts. In January of 1902, he prepared a letter to Cecil Rhodes, the governor of the Cape Colony in today's South Africa and one of the most powerful architects of the British Empire. Herzl thought that Rhodes could mobilize investors for a massive loan to the Ottoman Empire, in exchange for which the ZO would receive the long-desired charter for Jewish settlement in Palestine. "You are invited to help make history," Herzl wrote. "That cannot frighten you, nor will you laugh at it." Herzl presented Zionists as constituting a vast and united force: "They obey a command from Manchuria to Argentina, from Canada to the Cape and New Zealand. The greatest concentration of our adherence is in Eastern Europe. . . . Of the five million Jews in Russia, surely four million swear by our program."[18] Herzl never sent the letter, making do instead with attempts through intermediaries to arrange a meeting between the two men. Herzl simultaneously supported efforts by his allies in the United Kingdom to form a consortium of deep-pocketed investors in a Jewish colonization company in Palestine.

Neither scheme worked. Rhodes was cold to Herzl's overtures, and he died in March. Investors kept their distance. Meanwhile, Herzl's negotiations with the Ottoman Empire continued to be fruitless. His journey to Constantinople in July accomplished little and left him even more strongly convinced than before that the emperor's minions were plotting against him. Herzl considered the possibility of acquiring Palestine in bits and pieces, perhaps starting with small concessions in Haifa or Acre. He continued to flatter the sultan with assurances that the Jews would be "sober, industrious, loyal elements, bound to the Moslems by racial kinship and religious affinity."[19] But as his hopes for a positive Ottoman response faded, and as the German front remained dormant, Herzl focused on the United Kingdom. Britain did not control Palestine, but it governed Egypt and Cyprus, either of which might be the site of a temporary Jewish homeland until such a time as Palestine could be secured.

Herzl had been hoping since 1898 to gain entrée with British officialdom, and the Fourth Zionist Congress of 1900 had convened in London for that purpose. But Herzl's great opportunity came only in March of 1902 thanks to the intervention of Leopold Greenberg, a Herzl loyalist as well as a politician and publisher in Birmingham. Greenberg knew Joseph Chamberlain, the colonial secretary, who himself hailed from Birmingham and had begun his political career as the city's mayor. Greenberg secured for Herzl an invitation to testify before the Royal Commission on Alien Immigration, which had been assembled to consider restrictions on the entry of poor and persecuted Jews from eastern Europe into the United Kingdom. Following a one-month delay due to his father's death, Herzl gave his testimony on 7 July 1902.

This was a great opportunity for Herzl, but it presented pitfalls. He did not speak English well, and he could not think on his feet in English as he could in his native German and Hungarian or his near-native French. Herzl had to walk a fine line between arguing against unlimited free immigration to Britain, which would deprive the Jewish state of its potential population, and appearing to endorse antisemitism. In his opening statement, Herzl made clear that eastern European Jewry could not stay in place, and that "if you find they are not wanted here, then some place must be found to which they can migrate, without by [sic] that migration raising the problems that confront them here. Those problems will not arise if a home [will be] found [for them] which will legally be recognized as Jewish."[20]

Herzl considered the Jewish immigrants to Britain to be "industrious, sober, and thrifty," but regardless of their actual qualities, the larger their numbers, the more fear and resentment they would provoke among the local working-class population. England was not an antisemitic country, Herzl assured the commission, "but I'm afraid it could become one someday." Although Herzl presented Zionism as a means of funneling im-

migrants away from Britain, he distanced himself from any notion that British Jews must leave their homes for a new Jewish
homeland. "You must leave that to every man for himself, and
he must decide whether he will assimilate or not, whether he
will go to another nation or belong to his sister nation."

Despite his somewhat awkward English, Herzl's commanding figure and soothing rhetoric impressed his interlocutors.
He also came to a meeting of minds with Lord Rothschild,
whose opposition to Zionism did not dispose him against Jewish settlement in Herzl's new areas of interest—Cyprus and
the Sinai Peninsula, particularly El-Arish, where Herzl had, six
months previously, enthusiastically planned to set up an experimental Jewish cooperative farm. He waxed passionate to Rothschild about how Jewish colonization would strengthen British
interests in the eastern Mediterranean. With Rothschild's and
Greenberg's support, in October Herzl met Chamberlain. Once
again, Herzl was delighted to be in the presence of powerful
men and to feel that he, too, could play a role in global politics.
Chamberlain deftly deferred any discussion of Egyptian territory to Lord Cromer, the British consul-general who was, in
fact if not in name, Egypt's supreme authority. Chamberlain
also pointed out that Cyprus had existing Greek and Muslim
populations that would reject Jewish immigration.

Herzl was nonetheless pleased with the meeting: "The
main result, a tremendous one, which I achieved . . . is that Joe
Chamberlain does not reject outright the idea of founding a
self-governing Jewish colony in the southeastern corner of the
Mediterranean."[21] "Is it possible," he wrote a few days later,
after meeting with the British foreign secretary, Lord Lansdowne, "that we stand on the threshold of obtaining a *British
Charter* and founding the Jewish State?"[22] The foreign secretary's own views were decidedly more jaded. He wrote to
Cromer that El-Arish "may not be exactly the spot upon which
to dump Jews from the East End of London or from Odessa."[23]

The whole scheme, Lansdowne wrote, was "very visionary," a euphemism for utterly unfeasible.

Before tackling any of the vast technical challenges of this "visionary" plan, Herzl had to get approval from his executive committee, which was skeptical if not combative. For several members of the committee, the notion of a Jewish national home other than Palestine ranged from painful to unbearable. Herzl insisted that the needs of eastern European Jewry demanded the immediate creation of a place of shelter. To make the location more palatable, he referred to it as the biblical "land of Goshen" or "Egyptian Palestine." The meeting sent Herzl into a physical breakdown, but in the end he did get the committee's permission to pursue the possibility of settling Jews in Sinai. Two months after this meeting, just before Christmas of 1902, the Foreign Office sent Herzl a telegram saying that "the project for the Sinai Peninsula will be feasible" if an exploratory commission "finds that the actual conditions permit it."[24] Soon thereafter, the commission was assembled. It had a Belgian agricultural expert who had taken part in several expeditions to the Congo and a British civil engineer who was supervising the construction of the Assiut Dam on the Nile in Upper Egypt. The other members were Zionist activists with sundry professions—a mining engineer, a physician, an architect, and a former military commander (Albert Goldsmid, whom Herzl had met at the outset of his Zionist career). They were well equipped with diaries and fountain pens to mail reports to Herzl, and an elaborate system of telegraphic codes that lent a cloak-and-dagger air to the whole affair.

Greenberg now became Herzl's man in Cairo—a choice that Herzl soon came to regret, as he always liked to play the role of chief diplomat. When Greenberg failed to secure a charter from Cromer, Herzl packed his things, and in mid-March of 1903 he headed off to Egypt. After five journeys to Constantinople and the one brief visit to Palestine, this was to be Herzl's last Middle Eastern adventure.

It began, appropriately, with a feuilleton. "A Journey to Egypt" traces Herzl's sea voyage to Alexandria, where he had alighted five years previously en route to Palestine. The essay then depicts the journey to Cairo, with conventional Orientalist observations about the splendor of the Nile, the noise, dirt, and color of Egypt's cities, the fellahin's evocation of the ancient Israelites eating the bread of poverty, and the prevalence of donkeys, camels, and women shrouded in black. The central feature of the feuilleton, however, is not an extended critique of Arab backwardness, but rather a paean to the British colonial presence and its beneficial effects on the country. Observing the tumult of humanity in the square below his hotel room's terrace, Herzl writes:

> In the midst of it all stand a number of guards: severe, with a British air, almost policemen. A company of Highlanders march across: Scottish stockings, dashing young men—the Occupation. Other Englishmen, officers, wear the tarbush, higher on the head than the Turkish fez. And they know how to create order without brutality, without "tropical frenzy" to wonderful effect. Since time immemorial the people of Egypt have been accustomed to being conquered by others. Now a foreigner has come along who certainly appears more wondrous than all conquerors, war lords and despots of past eras—a tyrant who does not bleed the people dry or trample them but instead wishes to elevate and improve them. The puzzling intruder spreads light, creates order, maintains cleanliness, protects public health, brings justice, regulates finances, makes the streets safe, builds dams and husbands the water, the water of the Nile, like no other ruler of Egypt across the millennia. That the tyrant creates all this good for a higher and distinct concept of power is something that the fellah does not know and could not understand even if he did know it.[25]

Herzl rhapsodizes about British irrigation and dam projects in Upper Egypt, projects that have vastly increased the productivity and value of the land, and hence the taxation revenue that derives from it: "This previously bankrupt country now has astonishing surpluses from which public works are financed. . . . It cost a lot of money but now it functions flawlessly. This is the Occupation of Engineers."[26]

Herzl was, no doubt, a colonial enthusiast. Yet he wrote about this "Occupation of Engineers" more candidly, and in a noticeably different register, in his diary on 26 March 1903. Attending a rather boring lecture in Cairo by the British irrigation expert Sir William Willcocks, Herzl found his attention drifting to "the striking number of intelligent-looking young Egyptians who packed the hall. They are the coming masters. It is a wonder that the English don't see this. They think they are going to deal with the fellahin forever. Today there are 18,000 troops that suffice for the big country. How much longer? . . . What the English are doing is splendid. . . . But along with freedom and progress they are teaching the fellahin how to revolt. I believe that the English example in the colonies will either destroy England's colonial empire—or lay the foundation for England's world domination."[27] Three days later, at the pyramids, Herzl wrote in his diary, "The misery of the fellahin by the road is indescribable. I resolve to think of the fellahin too, once I have the power." He later added, "I will have to be patient."[28]

Political circumspection toward both his Viennese employers and his British patrons caused him to exercise self-censorship. He also dared not publicly express his feelings about Lord Cromer, the man responsible for the vast infrastructure projects that Herzl so deeply admired. When the two met, Cromer treated Herzl with thinly veiled contempt, and Herzl found Cromer to be "the most disagreeable Englishman I have ever faced . . . a bit too much arrogance, a touch of tropical madness, and unlimited vice-regalism. I think he didn't like me." In fact, Cromer was not categorically opposed to Jews moving into the Sinai, but he and Herzl disagreed about the length of the lease of territory, the territory's size, and whether it would be contiguous or broken up. Herzl pressed his case, seeking financial support from the late Baron Hirsch's Jewish Colonization Association. He warned Rothschild that without a Jewish enclave to absorb eastern European outmigration, a xenophobic British parliament might prohibit Jewish immigration altogether—which Herzl viewed as "one of the greatest moral losses that we are threatened with."[29]

When Chamberlain and Herzl met in London on 24 April, the colonial secretary tried to wean Herzl off of Sinai and instead suggested what he called "Uganda," territory in British East Africa along the Uganda railway (in today's Kenya). Away from the coast, Chamberlain assured Herzl, the climate was bearable, "even for Europeans," and one could raise sugar and cotton there. Chamberlain had his own reasons for wanting to plant Jews in East Africa. Like recently imported Indians, they could develop the region's agriculture and commerce, and they would not, he felt, be politically troublesome like the South African Boers, with whom the British were at war. Herzl was cold to the idea. He insisted on having a base "in or near Palestine" to give the settlement project what he called a "national foundation." Three weeks after the meeting with Chamberlain, however, British officials formally closed off the Sinai possibility when the undersecretary of state for public works in Egypt determined that settlement there would require five times as much water as the exploratory commission's civil engineer had estimated.

Herzl was crestfallen: "I had thought the Sinai plan was such a sure thing that I no longer wanted to buy a family vault in the Döbling cemetery, where my father is provisionally laid to rest. Now I consider the affair so wrecked that I have already been to the district court and am acquiring Vault No. 28."[30]

As his health deteriorated, Herzl became increasingly volatile, lashing out at colleagues for perceived disloyalty and demanding unquestioning obedience. He also grew increasingly desperate. The situation of eastern European Jewry, which had driven him to push for Jewish settlement in the barren Sinai, became vastly more dire after 19 and 20 April 1903, when a pogrom in the Bessarabian city of Kishinev (today, Chișinău in Moldova) killed forty-nine Jews and attracted global attention. The challenge confronting Herzl was not only the pervasiveness of antisemitism in Russia, the physical danger to Jews who lived there, and the lack of a territory that Jews could call their own and in which they could safely seek shelter. It was also that the Russian government threw up obstacles to block outmigration and considered Zionism to be an illicit form of social radicalism. To solve any one of these problems, he would need to tackle them all.

It took a few weeks for Herzl to pull himself away from the failed Sinai affair, but in mid-May he took the fateful step of writing to the lay leader of the Russian Orthodox Church, Konstantin Pobedonostsev, and the Russian interior minister, Vyacheslav von Plehve. He wrote not to protest the murder of innocent Jews but to humbly beg for an audience with the tsar. Rather than refute accusations that Russian-Jewish youth displayed a proclivity for socialism, Herzl endorsed them, and urged that the Zionist movement be legalized so that it could speed the Jews out of the Romanov Empire, where they were obviously unwelcome, and to Palestine. Bertha von Suttner intervened on Herzl's behalf, as did another influential woman with Zionist sympathies, a Polish noblewoman named Paulina Korvin-Piatrovska, who lived in St. Petersburg and knew Plehve personally. Herzl got permission to travel to Russia for a meeting, and by 7 August he was in St. Petersburg.

Very little about this journey was pleasurable. Herzl did not feel warmth toward, or admiration of, his interlocutors as he did when in Germany or Britain, nor did Russia have the Ottoman Empire's lush Orientalist allure. He and Plehve talked business of the most pragmatic sort. Plehve would support full legalization of a Zionist movement that was devoted solely to outmigration of "several million Jews," particularly those "with weak minds and little property."[31] (Plehve confessed that he would like to keep the wealthiest and cleverest ones.) There would, however, be no tolerance for Zionism if it fostered Jewish political activity within Russia. Yiddish and Hebrew culture were no less suspect. In return, Herzl asked for lifting of the emigration tax and for financial subsidies to pay for Jewish emigration—subsidies that would be financed by taxes paid by Russia's wealthiest Jews. Herzl also asked for Russian intervention with the sultan on behalf of the Jewish claim to Palestine.

Whereas Herzl found Plehve to be cold but receptive, the finance minister, Sergei Witte, was brusque, almost hostile, precisely because he was less dogmatically antisemitic. Witte professed no love for the Jews, saying he would drown them by the millions in the Black Sea if he could, but since that was not feasible, they should stay in Russia and not be further oppressed. Witte expressed his objections to a Jewish state in Palestine in terms of concerns about placing Jews as guards around Jerusalem's Church of the Holy Sepulchre. How could Christendom accept such a thing? Witte asked. Herzl responded indirectly, saying that this was a "familiar objection of Jewish bankers."[32] Herzl's apparent non sequitur reflected his ongoing anger at assimilationist Jewish plutocrats and his belief that they constantly plotted against him. It did nothing, however, to assuage the finance minister.

Herzl did not receive an audience with the tsar but believed that Plehve was an effective intermediary who was acting in good faith. For once, Herzl appeared to be right. He received a letter from Plehve, which was later published in *Die Welt*, supporting a Jewish state in Palestine if it would absorb sizable numbers of Russian Jews. The Russian government would make its support known to the Ottoman government, allow the free operation of Zionist emigration-related activity in Russia, and allow Jewish communities to be assessed a special tax to pay for Jewish migration. The letter acceded to all of Herzl's requests. It even responded to a point he made with Plehve that some concrete measure on behalf of Russian Jews in situ would convince them of the government's good faith. Accordingly, the letter promised to allow more Jews to live outside of the Pale of Settlement, the area of western and southern Russia to which most Jews were legally confined.

It is a great irony that the first endorsement of modern Jewish statehood by a Great Power came from Russia, a historic oppressor of the Jews. It was, to be sure, a carefully circumscribed support, which saw in Zionism a kind of energy source that, if properly harnessed and directed, could be Russia's salvation. Just how dangerous that energy source was thought to be can be seen in Herzl's experience after he left St. Petersburg and stopped off in Vilna for the night en route to Basel to convene the Sixth Zionist Congress. Rumors swirled that the anti-Zionist and socialist Jewish Bund, furious with Herzl for meeting Plehve, might harm Herzl. Local authorities, fearful of disorder, would not allow Herzl to attend the local synagogue or a lunch in town with scores of activists. Visitors and telephone calls to his hotel were carefully monitored. Come evening, Herzl slipped out of town, riding for an hour to a summer house where about fifty guests had gathered for a dinner in Herzl's honor. Throngs of Jewish youth from Vilna walked to the meeting place to meet Herzl, whom one of the guests described as "straight and tall, magnificent to see as he approaches the first line of trees against the background of nature, a picture of glory that lasts for a few instants until his companions emerged from the forests to join him."[33] In Herzl's account, a young man with a blue smock, whom Herzl took to be a revolutionary, announced a toast to *Ha-Melekh Herzl*—Herzl the king. When his carriage returned to Vilna at one in the morning, the streets were packed with well-wishers, who were beaten back by the police.

Less than a week after leaving Vilna, Herzl was in Basel. Herzl went into the Sixth Congress with trepidation about his own health, the perils facing Russian Jewry, and the overwhelming challenge of winning the Congress delegates' support for what he had determined was the only possible diplomatic path forward—Jewish settlement in Africa.

Unbeknownst to all but his closest colleagues, in June Herzl had decided to pursue the East African scheme that Chamberlain had proposed in April. He had also made preliminary inquiries about Portuguese Mozambique, and Jewish settlement in the Belgian Congo flashed through his mind. The linkage of Zionism with Africa did not come easily to Herzl. It was not simply the distance dividing Africa from Palestine. Herzl may have found Constantinople to be decadent and Palestine to be immersed in squalor, but he saw in the Near East the cradle of human civilization, and he respected its ancient glories and future potential for greatness. Herzl did not have such positive feelings about Africa, and when he did write about it, it was often a metaphor for something else.

As early as 1886, Herzl likened himself to the explorer of Africa Henry Morton Stanley, and he did so again at the outset of the Zionist diaries in 1895. In these passages he was indulging in a fantasy, as he did in a late feuilleton in which an unhappily married man (no doubt an avatar for Herzl himself) runs off to Africa to become an explorer. Africa-as-fantasy shows up again in another late story about two childhood friends who dream of running off to Africa to be explorers but whose plans run aground when, shortly after setting off by foot from home, they run out of sausages. When Herzl did write about Africa seriously, as he did in his feuilletons on the human exhibitions of Ashanti and Bisharin in 1897 and 1899, he presented it as on the edge of civilizational abyss.

Until the possibility of settling Jews in British East Africa came along, then, Herzl had not engaged with Africa in a positive way. There was one fascinating exception: a stray line in *Altneuland* about Jewish medical advances curing black Africans of tropical diseases and enabling mass black migration from the Western world to Africa. But this was a future scenario, not an engagement with the present. That engagement took the form of a lengthy memorandum, written by or at least with the approval of Herzl, and submitted by Greenberg to the British Foreign Office in July. The document called for the establishment of a largely autonomous Jewish protectorate in British East Africa.[34] The entity would, as Herzl later announced at the Congress, have a "Jewish administration, a Jewish local government, and a Jewish official at its head." The entity would be called "New Palestine" and feature a distinctive national flag. It would have the right to expand its borders—ostensibly through purchase, not conquest—and although the memorandum makes no mention of an army, the colony would have police powers to "expel from the territory . . . any person," settler or native, who flouted the territory's ordinances.

Was this memorandum a scenario for philanthropic relief for persecuted Jews, or was it a piece of political theater? In Herzl's mind it was difficult to separate the two. Nordau objected strenuously to the scheme, noting that Jewish settlement in East Africa would rely upon black labor, transforming Jews into idle planters. Tropical diseases were rampant, and the "warlike Negro tribes" had resisted pacification by even the European colonizing powers.[35] Tellingly, in his reply Herzl did not refute these claims but took refuge instead in the abstract. The Zionists would obtain what had long been, from the very start, the object of Herzl's desire: a charter, flag, and self-government. Herzl envisioned Jewish chartered companies all over the world as political statements, way stations to the ultimate goal—Eretz Israel. "This British-East African beginning is *politically* a Rishon Le-Zion," Herzl wrote to Nordau, much closer to Zion than anything that Edmond de Rothschild had done.[36] Taken collectively, these temporary points of refuge would alleviate Jewish distress, but more importantly, they would hasten the eventual acquisition of Palestine.

The British Foreign Office responded frostily to the Zionists' demands, noting that the Zionists sought to create a state within a state, with far greater levels of autonomy than the British felt comfortable granting. Undeterred by this admonition, and as yet without a formal offer of African territory, Herzl brought the matter to the Zionist Congress. The recognition of Jewish collective needs by the British government was too great a prize to pass up. Herzl knew he would have his largest audience ever—not just the six hundred delegates in attendance, but also dedicated correspondents from major world newspapers, including the *Times* of London and Italy's *La Stampa*. As usual, he could count on Nordau's powerful oratory. Whatever reservations Nordau had expressed in private, once on stage in Basel, he thundered about the Jews' need for a "night shelter" and the Congress's responsibility to take into account the physical needs of the Jewish people as a whole. Support for the proposal came from unexpected quarters, including some Orthodox Zionists, for whom Zionism was primarily about saving Jewish lives, and if that could be done in East Africa rather than Palestine, which the cultural Zionists wanted to turn into what the Orthodox considered a secular Hebraic travesty, so much the better.

The cultural Zionists were, predictably, aghast. The Russian Zionist caucus held a separate meeting and passed a resolution rejecting any proposal to authorize the executive committee to give the Uganda scheme formal consideration. When the committee's proposal was brought to the plenum, it passed by a margin of 62 to 38 percent, but a quarter of the delegates abstained. After the vote, pandemonium ensued, and the Russian caucus stormed out of the hall. An exhausted Herzl attempted to mollify the enraged dissidents, and the next morning, in his closing address, Herzl raised his right hand and quoted Psalm 137: "If I forget thee, O Jerusalem, let my right hand forget its cunning." He recited these lines in Hebrew—perhaps the only time in his life that he made a Hebrew utterance outside of a synagogue.

The firestorm over Uganda attracted most of the attention at the Congress and most of the headlines thereafter. But Herzl was responsible for something else that happened at the Congress, which drew far less scrutiny. Herzl asked the economist Oppenheimer to address the Congress and to tout the virtues of agricultural cooperatives, administered by professional managers, and employing landless workers. Oppenheimer's speech was politely received, but its real impact became clear when the Congress passed its final resolutions. Oppenheimer was named to a newly created Palestine Commission that would carry out research and exploration in the near future, without waiting for an Ottoman charter, or Great Power guarantee, for Jewish settlement in Palestine. Six months later, Herzl gave up even more ground. He announced that the Jewish National Fund would purchase land for a model cooperative colony to be administered by Oppenheimer's methods. In the final months of his life, Herzl was, at times reluctantly and at times with enthusiasm, transforming the ZO from a purely political organization into a political-economic one, which combined aspects of *The Jewish State*'s Society of Jews and its Jewish Company.

In Palestine and in the ZO, events were outpacing Herzl. A stream of immigration from eastern Europe began in 1903. Most of the newcomers, like Jews who had arrived in the 1880s and 1890s, were not Zionist idealists. They were motivated by a mixture of economic and religious factors and sought livelihoods in commerce, teaching, and crafts in Jaffa and Jerusalem. Some of the new immigrants, however, were young, nationalist enthusiasts determined to work the soil to achieve personal and collective rebirth. The youthful laborers were usually inexperienced and sometimes politically radical, making them less than ideal employees in the veteran Zionist agricultural colonies. They required external assistance, and the ZO would in time become their most important resource for access to land and work.

Meanwhile, in the wake of the Sixth Congress, the ZO was on the verge of a split over the Uganda issue. In November, a Russian Zionist meeting in Kharkov threatened secession if Herzl did not renounce the Uganda scheme and forswear any future colonization gambits other than Palestine. An infuriated Herzl wrote that his Russian colleagues were in "open rebellion." He invoked the now faded specter of the "lower masses" whom he would mobilize against those who opposed him. The passionate energy that Herzl hoped to muster, however, was now deployed against him. In December, at a Hanukkah gathering in Paris, a twenty-seven-year-old student named Chaim Louban shot at Nordau, shouting "Death to Nordau, the East African!" Nordau was not hit, though one person in the hall was grazed by a bullet. On the following day Nordau observed, "Yesterday evening I got an installment on the debt of gratitude which the Jewish people owes me for my selfless labors on its behalf. I say this without bitterness, only in sorrow. How unhappy is our people, to be able to produce such deeds."[37] Herzl feared that "if you are shot, my bullet has already been cast. . . . The connection is hard to establish, but I am convinced that

Louban's revolver was loaded in Russia. In the Kharkovites' ultimatum, I already saw the barrel of the gun."[38]

Herzl had already written a letter to the British Zionist leader Francis Montefiore, confirming that the Jewish Question could only be solved in the land of Israel, but welcoming a British offer of other territories so long as the land was truly habitable and the offer was enthusiastically received by the Jewish people. The letter was published in the *Jewish Chronicle*'s Christmas Day issue. This was a formal, albeit euphemistic, admission of defeat, yet at a Zionist executive committee meeting in January, Herzl refused to endorse the terms of the Kharkov ultimatum. Herzl knew that the Zionist public would never accept Uganda, but he would not let himself be humiliated by his opponents. Ironically, at the end of January the ZO received the formal British offer of five thousand square miles of territory—roughly equal to the size of the state of Israel without the Negev Desert—on the Gwas Ngishu plateau. By then, except for a few Herzl loyalists like Greenberg, the scheme was a lost cause. Besides, British colonists in the area were organizing their own protests against a Jewish presence.

Uganda was Herzl's last battle. It came to a close at the Greater Actions Committee meeting of 11–15 April 1904. Although he was terribly fatigued and short of breath, Herzl fired himself up, upbraiding his Russian colleagues. The issue was, he said, about process, not substance. It was not whether Uganda was a feasible option but the imperative within the ZO to follow the rule of law and obey the will of the Zionist Congress. Without it, Zionism could be nothing more than what it was before Herzl—a cadre of little men who met in little circles and raised little bits of money. Herzl proclaimed that he brought forth "the organizing of the nation, the instrument being the Congress. That is why you must submit to it, even if you are enraged by its decisions." Ultimately, though, the debate about principle devolved into a clash of egos: "I am stronger than you," Herzl declared. "That is why I am conciliatory, because I know that if we fight, I shall win."[39] Herzl did win a token victory in that the executive committee agreed to send an exploratory commission to Africa.

He also won on the quieter front of cooperative settlement that he had raised at the Sixth Congress. The Palestine Commission proposed setting up an experimental station, a training farm, and, at Herzl's insistence, an Oppenheimer cooperative. The Russian Zionists were skeptical of the plan because it called for an expert administrator, something that they found deeply distasteful in the Zionist colonies supported by Baron Edmond de Rothschild, where functionaries slavishly followed the baron's rule and imposed their own on the colonists. They preferred that the ZO pump money into the Jewish Colonial Trust's Jaffa-based subsidiary, the Anglo-Palestine Bank, which had been established two years earlier, and which provided credit for new immigrants. Much as Herzl cherished the bank, he would not waver from his commitment to the cooperative: "There has never been so modern a settlement attempt on these cooperative principles," he said. "For us this is a matter of the utmost importance."[40] This was the voice of the author of *Altneuland*, in which the dream of restoring Jews to their ancestral land was inseparable from the application of managerial expertise and scientific technology. It testifies to the sincerity and urgency that underlay the novel, and how, over the years of his Zionist activity, Herzl's political and social ideas became increasingly intertwined.

In the final months of his life, Herzl found solace in planning for the Zionist future. It is also perhaps not coincidental that his last journey abroad gave him an opportunity to redress a folly of his younger days. In January, Herzl traveled to Italy to meet the recently installed Pope Pius X. Eleven years earlier, when the Jewish Question was beginning to preoccupy him, Herzl had proposed a mass conversion of Jews to Catholicism at a ceremony that would be led by the previous pope, Leo XIII. When Herzl went to Italy in 1904, however, he went with a quite different proposal, although it was no less outlandish— that the pontiff endorse Zionism.

A preliminary meeting with the Vatican secretary of state, Rafael Merry del Val, did not bode well, as the cardinal made clear that the Church could not tolerate Jewish possession of the Holy Land. Herzl offered extra-territorialization of the Holy Places, but Merry del Val would not countenance an enclave similar to the one in which the Vatican, which had lost all its temporal powers with the unification of Italy, was currently ensconced. The day after this meeting, Herzl had an audience with the winner in Italy's struggle between church and state, King Victor Emmanuel III. In contrast to the cardinal, the king was jovial and receptive, and spoke breezily, without a hint of malice, about the prominence of Jews in Italy's parliament, civil service, and officer corps. Of course, there was little Victor Emmanuel could do to convince the pope to support Zionism, but clearly, both men enjoyed the occasion.

There followed the audience with Pius X, "a coarse-grained village priest," as Herzl described him. Herzl declined to kiss the pontiff's hand. The pope opined that it was "not pleasant" that Turks controlled the Holy Land and its sacred Christian sites, but that Jewish rule was out of the question. Pius spoke of a basic decency that unites all of humanity and of his good will toward the Jews. He assured Herzl that if the Jews did come to live in Palestine, the Church would be there, ready to baptize them. With this, the audience was over. Once again, Herzl refused to kiss the pope's hand: "All I did was to give him a warm hand-squeeze and a low bow."[41] His honor and dignity intact, Herzl exited.

After his return to Vienna, Herzl could still display traces of his old energy and majesty, but he was spent. By late April, he was too ill to travel to London. His physician sent him to the

Bohemian spa town of Franzensbad (Františkovy Lázně) for a six-week cure. For years, Herzl had hidden his medical condition from his family and Zionist colleagues, but once in Franzensbad, Herzl admitted to Wolffsohn that he was seriously ill. Only half-jokingly, Herzl admonished his long-suffering lieutenant, "Don't do anything stupid while I'm dead!" Herzl was forbidden by his doctors to do any work, although he cheated and continued to send out a volley of letters, trying to keep his sundry diplomatic initiatives alive. Nonetheless, he was pleasantly bored, with time to read Dickens, listen to music, and write affectionate letters to his family. He and Hans, whom Herzl referred to as "Yankee Doodle," bonded over news reports of the Russo-Japanese War. Exulting over the Japanese defeat of Russia, the Jews' oppressor, Herzl wrote, "What do you say about the Japanese victory? They're the man, no?"[42]

The cure at Franzensbad consisted of daily baths in hot spring water high in carbonic acid. This probably raised Herzl's blood pressure and heart rate, placing a further strain on his weakened constitution. Julie was another source of stress, yet his letters to her were now warm and endearing, addressed to "my beloved, good treasure." Before Julie set out to visit him at Franzensbad, Herzl wrote candidly to her that "the cure is worthless if one gets worked up. Indeed, disquiet is poison for a weakened heart. Both of us need to take note of this for the future, and above all, avoid any unnecessary strife." When Julie returned to Vienna, she and Jeanette fell as usual to fighting, but this time Herzl broke ranks and sided with his wife: "Dear mother, do as you like, but let other adults act freely."[43]

Herzl continued his newfound defense of Julie when he left Franzensbad, less than halfway into the cure, and, after two weeks of resting in Vienna, went to an Alpine spa near Reichenau in eastern Switzerland. With Julie and Pauline at his side, Herzl wrote to his mother, "Her efforts have been beyond all praise, and she has earned your as well as my heartfelt thanks." Over the course of his stay, "she has cared for me constantly and self-lessly, as she has cared for her children, when they were ill."[44] This was the last letter Herzl wrote before his death.

Herzl and Julie's reconciliation did not calm either of their nerves. Although Herzl's condition appeared to improve throughout most of June, Julie was given to fits of hysteria, and Herzl veered between excitability and depression. Nonetheless, a distinguished cardiologist who had been called to Herzl's bedside considered Herzl well enough to travel to his clinic in Hamburg. On 1 July, however, Herzl fell ill with bronchitis, and that night he struggled for breath. The next day, his mother and two younger children were sent for, and on 3 July he developed pneumonia. He hung on long enough, and maintained enough strength, to talk calmly with his mother and children. Then he collapsed and died.

Herzl's body was brought from Switzerland to his home at 29 Haizingergasse. Erwin Rosenberger described the scene: "The coffin lay in Herzl's study, with six unlit candles and tall silver candlesticks on either side. The walls and windows of the room were hung with black drapery; crêpe-covered electric lights and an oil lamp at the head of the coffin provided only feeble illumination. As I stood before the coffin, which was guarded by black-clad members of Vienna's Zionist student societies, I asked myself incredulously: were all the splendid, unique and infinitely varied things that Theodor Herzl had meant to us now confined within this narrow black box?" On 7 July, the day of the funeral, a throng of mourners gathered at the house, filed past the coffin, and gave their condolences to the grief-stricken family. Dr. Alexander Mintz, a former member of the Zionist executive committee and a closed, phlegmatic person, entered the room, stared at the coffin, and then "suddenly, forgetting everyone about him, he clutched at his face and shook with convulsive sobbing."[45]

The funeral at the Döbling cemetery attracted masses of Jews from Austria-Hungary and far beyond. The Austrian writer Stefan Zweig described chaos at the cemetery: "Too many had suddenly stormed his coffin, crying, sobbing, screaming in a wild explosion of despair. It was almost a riot, a fury. All regulation was upset through a sort of elementary and ecstatic mourning such as I had never seen before or since at a funeral."[46]

Reactions in print were more restrained yet no less heartfelt. The poet Naftali Herz Imber, author of the Zionist anthem "Ha-Tikvah," penned a Hebrew acrostic dirge, with the first letter of each line corresponding to the letters of Herzl's name, that began, "Pure of heart, a hero of the people, Herzl was exalted above the rest. . . . O woe! Zion mourns, Rebuild my ruins, Jerusalem entreats."[47] Even Herzl's rivals within the Zionist movement were, for the most part, generous. Ussishkin wrote of Herzl as a "national-political hero," unlike the spiritual, scholarly, and ethical heroes of the Jewish past: "And lo, Herzl's light shone upon us. Since the days of Nehemiah we have not known a hero so great in political deeds as he. . . . He was a revered symbol in the days of our revival; he is the hero without whom no people can create for itself its collective life in a political sense."[48] The anti-Zionist, ultra-Orthodox rabbi Isaac Breuer wrote in praise of Herzl, singling out his dedication, purity of motive and intent, the clarity of his goals, and his spirit of self-sacrifice. Only someone as utterly removed from the Jewish tradition as Herzl, Breuer claimed, could so boldly and baldly demand from the Gentiles that they give the Jews their homeland.

Herzl was no less mourned by a different kind of anti-Zionist: his assimilated editors at the *Neue Freie Presse*. In a front-page obituary, published, appropriately enough, "below the line," that is, on the bottom half of the page where the feuilleton section traditionally began, Bacher and Benedikt praised Herzl's exemplary journalism—his political reportage, cultural critique, and literary writing. The obituary also noted Herzl's "entirely unique" devotion to his parents. In a brief chronicle of Herzl's life later in the issue, the editors acknowledged, for the first time, that Herzl was "the creator of today's Zionist movement, which he brought from small beginnings to wide dissemination. . . . As leader of the Zionists he was received by several European sovereigns, by the emperor of Germany, the Sultan, the current Pope, and the king of Italy."[49]

Martin Buber, who was both an admirer and a critic of Herzl, never quite understood him, and that misunderstanding was shared by a great many of the Zionist faithful in central and eastern Europe. In his obituary of Herzl, Buber wrote that for Herzl, the Jewish Question was a collective and mechanical one, which would be solved through the creation of the Jewish State. Buber accused Herzl of neglecting, or of being too ignorant to ask, the question of *Judentum*, of what it means to be Jewish and how one will choose to live a Jewish life. Herzl, in fact, fashioned himself as a certain kind of Jew—a member of a nation, yet liberal, cosmopolitan, and outward-looking; non-religious but respectful of religion's aesthetic and inspirational qualities; and, above all, proud to identify as a Jew in the face of ridicule and hatred.

More than a decade after Herzl's death, Buber was more generous, at least in terms of comprehending Herzl's effect on others: "There was something captivating about him, which could scarcely be resisted. . . . The people's imagination wove a delicate legend about him, draped his actions in the twilight of mystery, bejeweled his forehead with messianic glory." He projected "the image of a sunny, harmoniously-wrought figure. No one doubted the purity of his being, the constancy of his devotion, the sincerity of his actions." Elsewhere, Buber put it more simply: "And now I feel, as I have never felt before, that we have been orphaned."[50]

EPILOGUE

The View from Mount Herzl

I WROTE THE CHAPTERS of this book in Canada, but I am writing its epilogue in Israel. At the moment I am in Tel Aviv, which more than anywhere else in Israel realizes Theodor Herzl's vision of a Western city in the Middle East: a bustling and cosmopolitan commercial and cultural center, looking outward toward the Mediterranean and the world beyond, and thoroughly secular (although there are synagogues for those who want them). Tel Aviv takes its name from a biblical phrase that means "mound of spring." Connoting both archaeological antiquity and contemporary revival, it was the title of Nahum Sokolow's Hebrew translation of Herzl's novel *Altneuland*. Other, more explicit, references to Herzl abound in Israel. Just north of Tel Aviv is the affluent town of Herzliya. Every Israeli town has a Herzl Street or Boulevard. From 1969 until 1986, Herzl's face adorned the one-hundred-pound (later, ten-shekel) banknote. Most importantly, Israel's national shrine, on a hill in the western outskirts of Jerusalem, is called Mount Herzl. It is home to the Holocaust memorial and museum Yad Vashem, the country's primary military cemetery, and the graves of many Zionist and Israeli leaders. Israel's official independence day celebrations are held here.

By housing both Yad Vashem and symbols of the Israeli state, Mount Herzl represents the Jews' transition from power-lessness to power, and from destruction to rebirth, that has been at Zionism's core since World War II. Mount Herzl is what the French historian Pierre Nora called a *lieu de mémoire*—a place where collective memory is simultaneously constructed, pre-served, and presented. It has a quiet and rather modest beauty. Herzl's tomb is a simple black slab of granite surrounded by a semicircular esplanade. It is unguarded. Many visitors visit the tomb as they would that of a relative or friend, following the Jewish custom of placing a stone on the slab as a sign of respect and remembrance. The tomb of the fiery right-wing Zionist leader Vladimir Jabotinsky, located a short distance away, is similarly understated.

On a recent visit to the mountain, I chatted with a group of Israel Defense Force officers coordinating a ceremony at the esplanade for a couple of hundred soldiers in a special unit for those born abroad. As the soldiers milled about, waiting for things to start, the officers explained to me that normally they would have held the ceremony at the Western Wall, but the lo-gistics hadn't worked out, so they were using Herzl's tomb as an alternate venue.

Herzl would not have liked to be a second choice. But since Israeli forces conquered Jerusalem's Old City in 1967, Mount Herzl, the symbol par excellence of the state of Israel, has been overshadowed by the Western Wall, representing the biblical land of Israel. It was a land that Herzl loved in an abstract rather than concrete way—a land he visited only fleetingly, and parts of which, especially Jerusalem, he regarded with disappointment and distaste.

Even Herzl's resting place on the eponymous mountain might have caused him unease. Herzl never specified in writing where he wanted to be buried, but his colleagues said that he mentioned the Carmel ridge in Haifa, the beautiful city of the future in *Altneuland*. In 1949, however, the Israeli interior minister, Yitzhak Gruenbaum, determined that Herzl needed to be buried in Jerusalem in order to strengthen Israel's claim on the city, which the U.N. Partition Resolution had determined would be an international enclave. And so in August of 1949 Herzl's remains were brought from Vienna to Jerusalem. They were reinterred in an elaborate burial ceremony, dubbed "Operation Herzl," featuring marching soldiers, drums, the blowing of shofars, and forty-four banners, one for each year of Herzl's life. In the previous year, the day of Herzl's death on the Hebrew calendar, 20 Tammuz, had been combined with "Army Day," a celebration of the infant country's armed might. Like his burial in Jerusalem, the close link between the military and Herzl's own vision might have bothered the genteel Viennese journalist. On the other hand, given his yearning to restore Jewish honor and pride, Herzl might well have shared the sentiments of that year's Army Day issue of Israel's *Yediot Aharonot* newspaper that "this army is our savior and defender, for this army accomplished a miracle; it transformed us from sickly pacifists to a normal and healthy people."[1]

In 2004, the Israeli parliament passed a law, commemorating the centennial of Herzl's death, to "bequeath Binyamin Zeev Herzl's vision, heritage, and achievements for generations, to commemorate him, and to bring about the education of future generations, and the structuring of the state of Israel, its institutions, goals and image, in accordance with his Zionist vision." But what was that vision? A sovereign state or an imperial dependency? A land whose native population has been "spirited across the border," as he wrote in his diary in 1895, or one in which, as in *Altneuland*, Arabs and Jews live together as equal and loving brethren? A state with a strong army, as Herzl wrote in his early diary entries, or the peaceful paradise of Herzl's novel?

In this book, I have argued that Herzl experienced a rapid maturation over his brief and meteoric Zionist career. The Herzl of 1902 was a very different man, with very different ideas, from the Herzl of 1895 or 1896. But regardless of the vast changes that Herzl underwent, he consistently fashioned himself as a symbol of Jewish pride, agency, and striving for collective rebirth. That is, if Herzl became a universal symbol of Zionism, no matter how it was defined, it was precisely because he so successfully transformed himself into an icon.

In his own lifetime, Herzl's striking image was made known the world over in paintings and photographs, starting with E. M. Lilien's iconic 1898 photo depicting Herzl on the balcony of his room at the Three Kings Hotel in Basel and overlooking the Rhine. After his death, Herzl became the personification of Zionism. Herzl's face gazed down upon countless classrooms in Jewish schools and offices in Zionist and Israeli government institutions. He was, and still is, widely referred to in Hebrew as *hozeh ha-medinah* (the visionary of the state). In textbooks and children's biographies, Herzl's image is both the George Washington and Abraham Lincoln of his people: a forefather, commander, liberator, unifier—and martyr.

The challenge of representing the life of a man who was larger than life fell upon the Herzl Museum. The museum was opened in 1960, for the centenary of Herzl's birth. It was a modest affair, with a reproduction of Herzl's study in Vienna, photographs and artifacts from his life, and earnest narrative placards. With the passage of time, its approach became increasingly old-fashioned, and attendance languished. The museum closed in the mid-1990s for renovations, and it reopened in 2005. I paid a return visit to the museum when I was last at the mountain.

The new exhibit contains the old artifacts, but its main attractions are videos. The first is set in France in 1894, featuring two military cadets, speaking in French-accented Hebrew, grumbling about a certain Jewish captain who has crossed all bounds and who needs to be put in his place. There follows the story of Dreyfus's trial and degradation, and the onset of Herzl's frenzy of Zionist inspiration. A second video is about an Israeli director (the late Micah Lewensohn, as himself) who has written a play about Herzl and has cast into the title role a nondescript and unmotivated young actor named Lior (played by Zak Berkman). We are told the story of Herzl's life, and as Lior watches, he becomes increasingly absorbed and passionate about his part, until at the end he performs Herzl speaking at the First Zionist Congress. A third video features Lior, in Herzlian evening dress and sporting a beard, observing today's Israel as an inspiring, if still incomplete, fulfillment of his vision.

The museum is a national institution, designed to inculcate not only historical knowledge but also pride and patriotism. It is pedagogic and entertaining. But there is much about Herzl that the museum does not relate. He is a man alone, without the acolytes who anointed him their leader and the rivals who wore him down. We see Herzl striving, but not suffering. We see his vision but not his pain. He is a man without foibles. There is no mention of his miserable marriage or of his family's tragic fate.

Julie, whose children were taken away from her by the terms of Herzl's will, died of ovarian cancer in 1907, at the age of thirty-nine. In violation of Jewish law, her remains were cremated. Pauline suffered from morphine addiction and died in Bordeaux in 1930. Hans was circumcised at the age of fifteen, studied at Cambridge, converted to numerous religions, and was psychoanalyzed by Freud, who determined that he suffered from an Oedipus complex. Hans became a fervent anti-Zionist. "My father was a great man, whom I loved," he wrote, "but I've come to see that he made a great historical error in his attempts to rebuild the Jewish state. . . . My father did not realize the true mission of the Jewish people, which has proven that the living and fertilizing spirit does not need territorial boundaries, and that people can live and exist even when fortifications and borders have disappeared." Hans was shattered by Pauline's death: "I am destitute and sick, unhappy and bitter. I have no home. Nobody pays any attention to the words of a convert. What good is the penance which the church has ordained for my 'spiritual healing'! I torture my body in vain; my conscience is torturing me far worse. My life is ruined. . . . Nobody would regret it if I were to put a bullet through my head."[2] On the day of Pauline's funeral, Hans did just that.

Trude married Richard Neumann, a Jewish industrialist twenty-seven years her senior. Trude had had a nervous breakdown before the marriage, and after giving birth to her son Stephan Theodor, she fell into depression and suffered from delusions of grandeur. Trude spent long periods in psychiatric hospitals. In September of 1942 she was deported to Theresienstadt, where she died six months later. In 1935, Stephan Neumann was sent to England, where he changed his name to Stephen Norman. He attended Cambridge and served in the British army during World War II, rising to the rank of captain. In 1946, he got a British diplomatic position in Washington, D.C., where he received news that his parents had perished during the war. Devastated, he jumped to his death from the Massachusetts Avenue bridge. Only in 2006 and 2007 were the remains of Pauline, Stephen, and Hans—the last two being prohibited from burial in a Jewish cemetery on account of their deaths by suicide—brought to Israel and laid to rest near their grandfather, Jakob.

Until the late twentieth century, in Israel only a handful of writers and dramatists dared reveal the tragic story of Herzl's family and his own troubled soul. In recent decades, the conversation about Herzl has become more open, but it is no less fraught. Herzl has continued to serve as a symbol, but whereas in the past he stood for the state and its mission of *kibbutz galuiyot* (ingathering of exiles), opposing political camps have more recently claimed him for one of their own. The secular and liberal left celebrates Herzl as champion of a humane, tolerant, and peace-loving democracy. Herzl's Zionist vision lies at the core of books like *Herzl Reloaded: Kein Märchen* (2015) by Doron Rabinovici (an Israeli-born Austrian) and Natan Sznaider (a German-born Israeli). In this imagined prolonged email exchange between a resurrected Herzl and the authors, passages from Herzl's writings provide a foil for the authors to wrestle with their own conceptions of Zionism and Israel.

The same premise, but with a sharper political bite, is at work in the 2018 production, by Jaffa's Gesher Theater, of *Herzl Said*, a musical comedy-drama that features Herzl popping out of his coffin just as he is about to be moved from Vienna to the state of Israel in 1949. While a skeptical and increasingly frustrated Orthodox rabbi, IDF officer, and Israeli functionary look on, Herzl reenacts the story from *Altneuland*, whose predictions of a peaceful, tolerant, and equitable society stand in stark contrast to the realities of the new Jewish state. When Prime Minister David Ben-Gurion is alerted to Herzl's startling resurrection, he sends back a message to Vienna that it is Herzl's bones—and by implication, not his living body—that are to be transferred to Jerusalem. Accordingly, the Israeli functionaries scheme at ways to get him back into his coffin, only to fail, until Herzl himself willingly climbs back in once the performance of his novel has finished. Before his voice is stilled for eternity, Herzl reminds his interlocutors that the novel's famous epigraph, "If you will it, it is no fairy tale," is paralleled in the epilogue by the warning "and if you do not will it, it is and will remain a fairy tale." He adds for emphasis, "If you do not wish it, there is nothing! You don't want it? You don't need it! [*Im tirtsu, ein! Lo rotsim, lo tsarich!*]"

These phrases have become ubiquitous in Israeli popular culture. In "Gabby and Debby," a music video from the early 2000s by the Israeli hip-hop band Hadag Nahash, youthful Israeli time travelers from the present journey to Basel in 1897 for the First Zionist Congress. The youngsters come across Herzl and berate him about the desperate straits of today's Israel, only to learn that Herzl's dark, swirling eyes betray the influence of hallucinogenic drugs, which he encourages the youth to ingest, saying, "If you take it, it is no fairy tale [*Im tikehu, ayn zo aggadah*]."[3] Several years ago I found in Jerusalem a T-shirt with Herzl's face and the slogan *Im tirtsu, ein*. Graffiti featuring a stencil of Herzl's face and the words *Lo rotsim, lo tsarich* are scattered throughout Tel Aviv. "*Lo rotsim, lo tsarich*" was the title of a 2009 mixtape produced by an ensemble of Israeli recording artists celebrating Israel's sixty-first birthday. The phrase is ambiguous, as it might connote a rejection of Zionism (we neither want nor need a state), but in colloquial Hebrew its meaning is more admonitory: if you act as if you don't want something, then it will be taken away—but you will regret your decision.

These texts and images are steeped in irony, a literary technique of which Herzl was a master. Herzl appreciated the strength of irony as a means of confronting, managing, and overcoming adversity. It was the opposite of cynicism, which he saw as an admission of defeat. It is irony, not cynicism, that dominates representations of Herzl in today's Israeli popular culture, be they images of Herzl riding a donkey—a reference to the biblical prophecy that the Messiah shall enter Jerusalem upon an ass—or of Herzl's face marred by a birthmark (or perhaps a dueling scar) that is a map of the West Bank, or of Herzl as a consummate hipster, complete with an impeccably groomed beard and an earring.

Herzl remains, to be sure, open to other interpretations. There have been attempts by the Israeli right to present Herzl as a fervent nationalist whose ideas centered around the uniqueness of the Jewish people, its right to the land, and the necessity of a Jewish state. Since 2006, the Israeli NGO *Im Tirtsu* has used the famous phrase from *Altneuland* to express the power of the will to overcome what they see as threats from within Israeli society, most particularly from universities and NGOs that seek Israeli-Palestinian reconciliation. Some adherents of Israeli national-religious Zionism juxtapose against the liberals' Herzl—cosmopolitan, socially progressive, and determined to let people decide their approach to religion—a fiercely religious man who underwent a spiritual reawakening in 1895, trembled with reverence at synagogue prior to the First Zionist Congress, foresaw the rebuilding of the Temple, and, at the height of the Uganda controversy, passionately defended his love of Zion.

In Israel, every political camp, and each generation, has invented its own Herzl. Herzl cast himself in his own legend as a second Moses: raised in the court of Pharaoh, a stranger to his people, who returned to them, led them out of bondage, but had to die before they could enter the Promised Land. After Herzl's death, his followers embellished the legend and tailored it to fit their own needs and desires. Such is the fate of charismatic leaders, whose aura lives on long after the leader's death but becomes decoupled from its point of origin and takes on a life of its own. Over time, however, the aura of charisma may fade, and the penumbra of inspiration can grow evanescent and eventually vanish. Despite the lively trade in representations of Herzl in our own era, he is slowly being forgotten. In a recent survey, only about half of Israeli youth knew who Theodor Herzl was. Many thought he was Israel's first president or first prime minister. Herzl's striking face, with its Assyrian beard and jet-black, deep-set eyes, remains a popular meme. Yet it is increasingly disconnected from that remarkable, singular man, as gifted as he was troubled, a quintessential product of fin-de-siècle Europe's faith in humanity and belief that the world can and must be changed for good.

All translations are my own unless otherwise identified.

Abbreviations

BT	*Theodor Herzl: Briefe und Tagebücher,* ed. Alex Bein, Hermann Greive, Moshe Shaerf, and Julius Schoeps (Frankfurt a. M.: Propyläen, 1983–96), 7 vols. Used with permission.
CD	*The Complete Diaries of Theodor Herzl,* ed. Raphael Patai, trans. Harry Zohn (New York: Herzl Press, 1960)
CZA	Central Zionist Archive, Jerusalem
Feuilletons	Theodor Herzl, *Feuilletons,* ed. Raoul Auernheimer, 2 vols. (Vienna, 1911)
JT	Jugendtagebuch, in *BT,* vol. 1
NFP	*Die Neue Freie Presse*
Rosenberger	Erwin Rosenberger, *Herzl as I Remember Him* (New York: Herzl Press, 1959)
RT	Reisetagebuch, in *BT,* vol. 1

| TH | Alex Bein, *Theodore Herzl* (German ed. Vienna, 1934; English ed. Philadelphia: Jewish Publication Society, 1941) |
| ZW | Theodor Herzl, *Zionist Writings: Essays and Addresses*, trans. Harry Zohn, 2 vols. (New York: Herzl Press, 1973–75) |

Introduction

1. Early biographies by Zionist activists who knew Herzl personally are palpably biased but are richly detailed, evocative, and colorful, e.g., Reuven Brainin, *Hayei Hertsel* (New York, 1919); and Jacob de Haas, *Theodor Herzl: A Biographical Study*, 2 vols. (Chicago: Leonard, 1927). Alex Bein, *Theodore Herzl* (German ed. Berlin, 1934; English ed. Philadelphia: Jewish Publication Society, 1941), was a pioneering work of scholarship, though it retained a reverential tone. Later biographies were increasingly critical, e.g., André Chouraqui, *A Man Alone: The Life of Theodor Herzl* (French ed. Paris, 1960; English ed. Jerusalem: Keter, 1970); Desmond Stewart, *Theodor Herzl: Artist and Politician* (New York: Doubleday, 1974); Amos Elon, *Herzl* (New York: Holt, Rinehart, and Winston, 1975); Ernst Pawel, *The Labyrinth of Exile: A Life of Theodor Herzl* (New York: Noonday, 1989); and Jacques Kornberg, *Theodor Herzl: From Assimilation to Zionism* (Bloomington: Indiana University Press, 1991). For assessments of Herzl's Zionist thought, see Joseph Adler, *The Herzl Paradox: Political, Social, and Economic Theories of a Realist* (New York: Hadrian, 1962); Steven Beller, *Herzl* (New York: Grove Weidenfeld, 1991); and Shlomo Avineri, *Herzl: Theodor Herzl and the Foundation of the Jewish State* (Hebrew ed. Jerusalem: Zalman Shazar Center, 2007; English ed. London: Weidenfeld and Nicolson, 2013).

2. Nassir Ghaemi, *A First-Rate Madness: Uncovering the Links Between Leadership and Mental Illness* (New York: Penguin, 2011), 19.

3. Anthony Storr, *Churchill's Black Dog and Other Phenomena of the Human Mind* (London: Collins, 1989), 5, 26.

4. Max Weber, *Economy and Society*, ed. Guenter Roth and

Claus Wittich (Berkeley: University of California Press, 1978), 1:241.

5. David Vital, *The Origins of Zionism* (Oxford: Oxford University Press, 1984), 277.

6. Samuel Bettelheim, "Wie hat Herzl ausgesehen?," in *Theodor Herzl Jahrbuch*, ed. Tulo Nussenblatt (Vienna: Heinrich Glanz Verlag, 1937), 337.

7. Ibid.

8. Quoted in Bettelheim, "Wie hat Herzl ausgesehen?," 331.

9. Georges Gusdorf, "Conditions and Limits of Autobiography," in *Autobiography: Essays Theoretical and Critical*, ed. James Olney (Princeton, N.J.: Princeton University Press, 1980), 39 and 43.

Chapter 1. Becoming Theodor Herzl

1. "Dr. Güdemann's *National-Judentum*," in *ZW*, 1:65.

2. Cited in Raphael Patai, "Herzl's School Years," *Herzl Year Book* 3 (New York: Herzl Press, 1960), 61.

3. JT, 10 January 1886, *BT*, 1:640–41.

4. JT, 10 January 1886, *BT*, 1:640.

5. Reproduced in Ernst Pawel, *The Labyrinth of Exile: A Life of Theodor Herzl* (New York: Noonday, 1989), 36–37.

6. Many thanks to Zsófia Mészáros for our email correspondence on this subject.

7. Herzl to Heinrich Kana, 21 December 1881, *BT*, 1:100.

8. JT, no date, *BT*, 1:648.

9. See file "Th. H. Militär Dokumente," CZA, H/10.

10. Letter of 25 November 1885, *BT*, 1:212.

11. Herzl to Heinrich Kana, 4 September 1879, *BT*, 1:91.

12. JT, 27 November 1883, *BT*, 1:636.

13. Herzl to Kana, 4 July 1883, *BT*, 1:135.

14. 27 June 1885, *BT*, 1:182. See also Herzl's letters to his parents of 4 June 1884, 19 June 1885, and 7 December 1885.

15. 3 August 1888, *BT*, 1:298.

16. Herzl to Kana, 18 August 1882, *BT*, 1:116–17.

17. RT, 2 August 1883, *BT*, 1:658.

18. RT, 26 July 1883, *BT*, 1:657–58.

19. RT 1885, early August, *BT*, 1:663–64.

20. Reproduced in Amos Elon, *Herzl* (New York: Holt, Rinehart, and Winston, 1975), 81.

21. Herzl to Helmut Teweles, 5 March 1890; also Herzl to Franz Wallner, same day, *BT*, 1:344.

22. Letters of 21 and 22 May 1890, *BT*, 1:376–78.

23. Letter of 25 May 1890 and an undated one, but presumably written on the next day, *BT*, 1:379–85.

24. Herzl to Jacob Naschauer, 16 May 1891, *BT*, 1:441.

25. Herzl to Oswald Boxer, 13 June 1891, *BT*, 1:447.

26. 28 November 1891, *BT*, 1:481.

27. Herzl to Kana, 10 April 1890, *BT*, 1:369.

28. Reproduced in Desmond Stewart, *Theodor Herzl: Artist and Politician* (New York: Doubleday, 1974), 131.

29. Ibid., 136.

30. Reproduced in *TH*, 66.

31. Ibid., 55–56.

32. See Michael Stanislawski's brilliant analysis of the story in *Zionism and the Fin de Siècle: Cosmopolitanism and Nationalism from Nordau to Jabotinsky* (Berkeley: University of California Press, 2001), 1–6. The quotations from the story are taken from this work.

33. "Der Herr Bischoff von Meaux" (1891), in *Feuilletons*, 2:225.

34. Letter of 19 September 1891, *BT*, 1:471.

35. Letter of 23 September 1891, *BT*, 1:474.

Chapter 2. Our Man in Paris

1. Marc Flandreau, "The Logic of Compromise: Monetary Bargaining in Austria-Hungary, 1867–1913," *European Review of Economic History* 10, no. 1 (2006): 3–33.

2. Bacher to Herzl, 6 October 1891, reproduced in Theodor Herzl, *From Boulanger to Dreyfus* [in Hebrew], ed. Alex Bein (Jerusalem: The Zionist Library, 1974), 3:1119–21.

3. Bacher to Herzl, 20 January 1892, CZA, H VIII.

4. Bacher to Herzl, 16 February and 5 March 1892, CZA, H VIII.

5. Cited in Shalom Rosenfeld, "Theodor Herzl, Journalist" [in Hebrew], *Kesher* 21 (1997): 2–4.

6. Herzl to Schnitzler, 29 July 1892, *BT,* 1:499–500.

7. Herzl to Schnitzler, 16 November 1892, *BT,* 1:503.

8. Herzl to Schnitzler, 13 May 1893, *BT,* 1:527.

9. Herzl to Schnitzler, 9 January and 16 February 1895, *BT,* 1:569, 572. As close as Herzl and Schnitzler became, they consistently used the formal second-person singular—*Sie*—instead of *Du.* The same was true for Herzl and Nordau. (See Chapter 4.)

10. *CD,* 5. The first pages of the diary are not dated.

11. *NFP,* 3 September 1892.

12. Ibid.

13. *NFP,* 29 April 1892.

14. Reproduced in Jacques Kornberg, *Theodor Herzl: From Assimilation to Zionism* (Bloomington: Indiana University Press, 1991), 124.

15. The letter is undated, but the editors of Herzl's collected letters infer that it was composed in the second half of July. *BT,* 1:536.

16. Quoted in Leon Kellner, *Theodor Herzls Lehrjahre (1860–1895): Nach handschriftlichen Quellen* (Berlin: R. Löwit, 1920), 141.

17. Cited in *TH,* 88.

18. *CD,* 8.

19. Quoted in *TH,* 89.

20. *TH,* 90.

21. *TH,* 100.

22. *CD,* 12.

23. *NFP,* 17 October 1894, 3.

24. Kornberg, *From Assimilation to Zionism,* 146 and n32.

25. All quotations from *Das neue Ghetto* are from the 1903 Vienna edition (https://archive.org/stream/bub_gb_T5k5AAAAMAAJ /bub_gb_T5k5AAAAMAAJ_djvu.txt).

26. *CD,* 11.

27. Herzl to Schnitzler, 8 November 1894, *BT,* 1:553.

28. Quoted in Yaakov Rabi, "A Portrait of the 'Visionary of the State' as a Foreign Correspondent" [in Hebrew], *Kesher* 21 (1997): 40.

29. Theodor Herzl, "Zionism," in *ZW,* 2:112. The essay was written for the *North American Review* but was never published.

30. *CD,* 601 (24 November 1897).

31. *Le Matin, Le Petit Parisien, Le Petit Journal,* and the *New York Times* reported slight variations in the crowd's words, but none mentioned explicit references to Jews. Nor did the anti-Dreyfusard writer and politician Maurice Barrès in his account of the event. On Barrès, see Ruth Harris, *Dreyfus: Politics, Emotion, and the Scandal of the Century* (New York: Metropolitan, 2010), 35.

32. *CD,* 24 (16 April 1896). This entry was inserted into the diary's narrative after the fact.

33. *CD,* 12–13.

34. *CD,* 18.

35. *CD,* 21–22 (22 May 1895).

36. *CD,* 25–30 (3 June 1895).

37. *CD,* 201 (24 July 1895).

38. *CD,* 57, 66 (9 and 10 June 1895).

39. *CD,* 69–70 (11 June 1895) and 105 (16 June 1895).

40. *CD,* 28 (3 June 1895).

41. *CD,* 88 (12 June 1895).

42. *CD,* 101 (14 June 1895).

43. *CD,* 104–5 (16 June 1895).

44. *CD,* 114 (17 June 1895).

45. A year later, Herzl heard from a third party that Bismarck had dismissed Herzl's letter as a "melancholy fantasy." *CD,* 436 (22 July 1896).

46. *CD,* 128 (22 June 1895).

47. *CD,* 216 (25 June 1895).

48. "Ravachol!," *Feuilletons,* 2:64. Pierre Alexis Ponson du Terrail (1829–1871) was a popular French writer of tales of adventure and fantasy.

49. Herzl, "Leroy-Beaulieu on Antisemitism," *ZW,* 1:116.

50. *CD,* 96 (12 June 1895).

51. *CD,* 212 (24 July 1895).

52. *CD,* 105 (16 June 1895).

53. *CD,* 34, 155 (6 and 15 June 1895).

54. *CD*, 151, 155 (14 June 1895), 171 (15 June 1895).

55. *CD*, 196 (6 July 1895).

56. *CD*, 287 (21 November 1895).

57. See also my discussion of Herzl's 1900 feuilleton "The Beloved of Venus" in Chapter 4.

58. *CD*, 203 (16 July 1895).

59. *CD*, 196, 216, and 219 (5, 25, 27 July 1895).

Chapter 3. The Organizational Genius

1. Arthur Kamczyk, "Orientalism, Herzl, and His Beard," *Journal of Modern Jewish Studies* 12, no. 1 (2013): 90–116.

2. *CD*, 232 (18 August 1895).

3. *The Jewish State*, trans. Sylvie D'Avigdor (New York: American Zionist Emergency Council, 1946), 10, available at http://www.mideastweb.org/jewishstate.pdf. All quotations from the pamphlet are taken from this online edition. So as not to entangle the reader in a thicket of notes, I have not provided page numbers for brief quotes, but the text is easily searchable.

4. Ibid., 15.

5. *CD*, 298 (9 February 1896).

6. *CD*, 248 (20 October 1895).

7. Nordau to Herzl, 26 February 1896, CZA, VIII.

8. Quoted in Mordechai Friedman, *The Bush Burned, and It Was Consumed* [Hebrew] (Jerusalem: World Zionist Organization, 2015), 98. The rabbinic reference is from the Babylonian Talmud, tractate Sanhedrin, 99a.

9. *CD*, 282 (25 November 1895).

10. *CD*, 310–12 (10 and 16 March 1896).

11. *CD*, 412 (8 July 1896).

12. *CD*, 533–34 (29 March 1897).

13. *CD*, 551–52 (20 May 1897).

14. *CD*, 500 (1 December 1896).

15. *CD*, 463–64 (6 September 1896).

16. *CD*, 505 (6 January 1897); see also 489 and 496 (22 October 1896).

17. *CD*, 449 (3 August 1896).

18. *CD*, 418–19 (13 and 15 July 1896).

19. *CD*, 538–39 (25 April 1897).

20. *CD*, 677 (2 October 1898).

21. *CD*, 623 (26 March 1898).

22. "Judentum" (1896), in *ZW*, 1:51.

23. Rosenberger, 49.

24. Cited in Peter Lowenberg, "A Psychoanalytical Study in Charismatic Political Leadership," in *The Psychoanalytic Interpretation of History*, ed. Benjamin B. Wolmon (New York: Basic Books, 1971), 172–73.

25. *Die Welt* I, no. 1 (4 June 1897), 1.

26. Quoted in Rosenberger, 91.

27. Theodor Herzl, "Mauschel," in *ZW*, 2:167.

28. Nordau to Herzl, 14 December 1896, CZA, H VIII.

29. Quoted in Georges Yitzhak Weisz, *Theodor Herzl: A New Reading* (Jerusalem: Gefen and the World Zionist Organization, 2013), 7.

30. Quoted in Robert S. Wistrich, "In the Footsteps of the Messiah," in *Theodor Herzl: Visionary of the Jewish State*, ed. Gideon Shimoni and Robert S. Wistrich (Jerusalem: Magnes, 1999), 321.

31. Jacob de Haas, *Theodor Herzl: A Biographical Study* (Chicago: Leonard, 1927), 169.

32. Hillel Halkin, "What Ahad Ha'am Saw and Herzl Missed—and Vice Versa," *Mosaic*, 5 October 2016, 7–8, available at https://mosaicmagazine.com/essay/2016/10/what-ahad-haam-saw -and-herzl-missed-and-vice-versa/ (accessed 1 August 2018).

33. Ibid.

34. Quoted in Friedman, *The Bush Burned*, 37.

35. Zionist Congress: First Zionist Congress and Basel Program, August 1897, available at Jewish Virtual Library, https:// www.jewishvirtuallibrary.org/first-zionist-congress-and-basel-pro gram-1897.

36. Quoted from the succinct, and nearly contemporary, analysis of the Basel Program by Gotthard Deutsch in the 1906 *Jewish Encyclopedia*, available at http://www.jewishencyclopedia.com /articles/2612-basel-program.

37. Joseph Frankel, "The History of the Shekel" (1952, 1956), available at http://begedivri.com/ZionistShekel/History.htm (accessed 1 August 2018). See also Hayim Orlan, "The Participants in the First Zionist Congress," *Herzl Year Book* 6 (New York: Herzl Press, 1964–65), 135; and Alison Rose, *Jewish Women in Fin-de-Siècle Vienna* (Austin: University of Texas Press, 2008), 130–31.

38. *New York Times,* 11 August 1897.

39. Johannes Lepsius, "Der Zionisten-Congress," *Der Christliche Orient* 1, no. 10 (1897): 434.

40. *CD,* 581 (3 September 1897).

41. Nordau to Herzl, 19 April 1898, CZA, H VIII.

Chapter 4. Reaching for the Stars

1. *CD,* 950–51 (18 May 1900).

2. Herzl to Wolffsohn, 20 May 1900, *BT,* 5:437–38.

3. *CD,* 896 (12 December 1899).

4. "Maupassant's Posthumous Works" (1900), quoted in Theodor Herzl, *Journalistic Stories: Feuilletons,* ed. Henry Regensteiner (New York: Cornwall Books and Herzl Press, 2002), 41. The pearl metaphor shows up in a different light in Isaiah Berlin's 1975 lecture "The Achievement of Zionism": "The grit introduced into the oyster causes the disease which ultimately can produce a pearl. It might happen only with one case in a million. But if an oyster said 'I don't want to produce a pearl, I just wish to live a normal, healthy life,' this is forbidden because the oyster's mission is to suffer and produce these pearls" (http://berlin.wolf.ox.ac.uk/lists /nachlass/achiezio.pdf, p. 4 [accessed 15 August 2018]).

5. "Nauheim" (1899), quoted in Herzl, *Journalistic Stories,* 41.

6. Compare "The Tragedy of Fame" (1900) and "The Immortal City" (1901). Herzl, *Journalistic Stories,* 42.

7. In the German original, the title is "Epaphroditus," a Greek name deriving from Aphrodite, the Greek equivalent of Venus.

8. Letter of 2 April 1898, *BT,* 4:451.

9. Herzl to Nordau, 13 December 1897, *BT,* 4:393.

10. *CD,* 607 (11 December 1898). On this point, see Shlomo Avineri, *Herzl: Theodor Herzl and the Foundation of the Jewish State*

(Hebrew ed. Jerusalem: Zalman Shazar Center, 2007; English ed. London: Weidenfeld and Nicolson, 2013), 33.

11. Nordau to Herzl, 10 May and 5 June 1898, CZA, H VIII; Herzl to Nordau, 19 May and 11 June 1898, *BT*, 4:472–73, 495–96.

12. Herzl to Nordau, 25 January 1898, *BT*, 4:412–13.

13. Erwin Rosenberger, who attended the Congress, claims that a local orchestra played the "Fantasie" from *Tannhäuser*, and some Herzl biographers have repeated this statement, while others write that the orchestra played the opera's overture. There was, in fact, no "Fantasie" in the opera. Rosenberger may have been referring to a ballet sequence, the "Baccanale," that came just after the overture and was added to the opera for its 1861 Paris premiere, sixteen years after the opera's composition. Given the fame as well as stirring power of the overture, however, it is likely that the orchestra played music from both it and the "Baccanale." Many thanks to Peter Bergamin for his insights on this point.

14. *CD*, 961 (17 June 1899).

15. Whitman to Herzl, 8 September 1899, CZA, H12073–48.

16. "Who Fears a State?" (1898), in *ZW*, 1:211–15.

17. Ibid.; "Leroy-Beaulieu on Antisemitism," in *ZW*, 1:115; "Opening Address at the Second Zionist Congress," in *ZW*, 2:19–20.

18. *NFP*, 6 June 1897, 5–6.

19. "Das Bischari-Lager," *Neue Freie Presse*, 30 April 1899, 4–5.

20. From *Die Fackel*, April 1899, reproduced in Werner Michael Schwartz, *Anthropologische Spektakel: Zur Schaustellung "exotischer Menschen," Wien, 1870–1910* (Vienna: Turia and Kant, 2001), 138.

21. Quoted in David Vital, *Zionism: The Formative Years* (Oxford: Clarendon Press, 1982), 52–53, 58.

22. Quoted in Mim Kemal Oke, "The Ottoman Empire, Zionism, and the Question of Palestine (1880–1908)," *International Journal of Middle East Studies* 14, no. 3 (1982): 329–41.

23. *CD*, 644 (1 July 1898).

24. Quoted in Alex Bein, "Memoirs and Documents About Herzl's Meeting with the Kaiser," *Herzl Year Book* 6 (1964–65), 59–60.

25. *CD*, 671 (21 September 1898).

26. Reproduced in full in *TH*, 529–30.

27. *CD*, 687 (7 October 1898).

28. *CD*, 727 (19 October 1898). See also Herzl's letter to his parents, 20 October 1898, *BT*, 4:553–54; and Bein, "Herzl's Meeting with the Kaiser," 61. In his memoir, Wilhelm claimed that Herzl's account of their meeting in Istanbul was written "quite accurately and in a very loyal manner."

29. "When Herzl Saw Palestine," in *Theodor Herzl: A Memorial*, ed. Meyer Weisgal (New York: Zionist Organization of America, 1929), 76.

30. *CD*, 739 (27 October 1898).

31. *CD*, 744–45 (29 October 1898); Gol Kalev, "Following Herzl's Footsteps in Jerusalem," *Jerusalem Post*, 20 May 2017; https://www.jpost.com/In-Jerusalem/Following-in-Herzls-footsteps-in-Jerusalem-490489 (accessed 21 August 2018).

32. *CD*, 739, 742–44 (27 and 29 October 1898). In their memoirs, von Bülow and Eulenburg claim that Herzl never made it to Palestine. Wilhelm's memoir mentions the meeting at Mikveh Israel but not the one in Jerusalem. Bodenheimer, however, confirms that the Jerusalem encounter did take place and that Herzl's representation is accurate. Apparently, the matter was of such little importance to the kaiser and his advisers that they forgot all about it.

33. *CD*, 746–47 (31 October 1898).

34. *CD*, 2:756 (2 November 1898).

35. Herzl to Maximilian Harden, 26 July 1901, *BT*, 6:253.

36. *CD*, 1606 (27 January 1904).

37. *CD*, 1037 (10 January 1901).

38. *CD*, 880–81 (27 October 1899).

39. Quoted in Rosenberger, 98.

40. Herzl to Ussishkin, 22 August 1901, *BT*, 6:295.

41. "After the Basel Congress" (1897), in *ZW*, 1:158.

42. Quoted in Andrea Livnat, *Der Prophet des Staates: Theodor Herzl im kollektiven Gedächtnis Israels* (Frankfurt a. M.: Campus, 2011), 39–40.

43. *The Belfast News-Letter*, 14 August 1900.

44. Compare the *Birmingham Daily Post, Glasgow Herald, Huddersfield Daily Chronicle* (Yorkshire), *Leeds Mercury, Liverpool Mercury, London Daily News, Sheffield and Rotherham Independent, Yorkshire Herald*, and *Western Mail* (Cardiff), for 14 and 15 August 1900.

45. *CD*, 556 (6 June 1897).

46. *CD*, 1105 (13 May 1901), 1109 (15 May 1901), 1110–11 (19 May 1901). Although I usually adhere to the English version of the diaries, I differ from its rendering of the German original, "märchenhafte Wunschmoment," as "fabulous moment of my desire." I have offered what I believe is a more accurate translation.

47. *CD*, 1111–12 (19 May 1901).

48. *CD*, 1126–27, 1135 (21 May 1901).

49. *CD*, 1179 (23 September 1901).

50. *CD*, 1151 (1 June 1901).

51. *CD*, 1153 (5 June 1901).

52. Letter of 8 November 1901, *BT*, 6:354.

53. Erwin Rosenberger, *Herzl as I Remember Him* (New York: Herzl Press, 1959), 150.

54. *CD*, 869 (30 August 1899), 1062 (30 January 1901), 1071 (14 March 1901).

55. *CD*, 1282 (4 June 1902).

Chapter 5. If You Will, It Is Still a Dream

1. *CD*, 1202.

2. Herzl to Maximilian Harden, 16 March 1897, *BT*, 6:206; Herzl to Rathenau, 26 July 1901, *BT*, 6:253.

3. *CD*, 851–52 (21 June 1899).

4. "Opening Address at the Fifth Zionist Congress," in *ZW*, 2:174.

5. *CD*, 1203 (25 January 1902).

6. *CD*, 1286 (9 June 1902).

7. 10 and 13 September 1902, *BT*, 6:591–92.

8. *CD*, 1347 (22 August 1902).

9. All quotations are from the 1960 English translation, published by the Haifa Publishing Company.

10. Quoted in Steven J. Zipperstein, *Elusive Prophet: Ahad Ha'Am and the Origins of Zionism* (Berkeley: University of California Press, 1993), 196.

11. Quoted in Halkin, "What Ahad Ha'Am Saw and Herzl Missed—and Vice Versa," *Mosaic*, 5 October 2016, 13; https://mosaicmagazine.com/essay/2016/10/what-ahad-haam-saw-and-herzl-missed-and-vice-versa/ (accessed 12 September 2018).

12. 15 September 1903, *BT*, 7:294.

13. *CD*, 1206–7 (30 January 1902).

14. Quoted in Ernst Pawel, *The Labyrinth of Exile: A Life of Theodor Herzl* (New York: Noonday, 1989), 487.

15. Herzl to Wolffsohn, 22 October 1903, *BT*, 7:421.

16. 12 January 1904, *BT*, 7:508.

17. "Die Brille," in *Feuilletons*, 2:285–95.

18. *CD*, 1194–95 (11 January 1902).

19. *CD*, 1321 (28 July 1902).

20. All quotations in this paragraph and the next are from "The Tragedy of Jewish Immigration: Herzl's Testimony Before the Royal Commission on Alien Immigration, July 7, 1902," in *ZW*, 2:179–215.

21. *CD*, 1363–64 (23 October 1902). Emphasis and English wording in the original.

22. *CD*, 1372 (7 November 1902).

23. Quoted in David Vital, *Zionism: The Formative Years* (Oxford: Clarendon Press, 1982), 147.

24. *CD*, 1381 (22 December 1902).

25. "Eine Reise nach Ägypten," *Feuilletons*, 1:235.

26. Ibid., 1:244.

27. *CD*, 1449 (26 March 1903).

28. *CD*, 1454 (29 March 1903).

29. *CD*, 1446–47 (25 March 1903).

30. *CD*, 1491 (16 May 1903).

31. *CD*, 1535 (14 August 1903).

32. *CD*, 1532 (11 August 1903).

33. Quoted in Vital, *Zionism: The Formative Years*, 263.

34. Many thanks to Gur Alroey for providing me with a copy

of the original document and the Foreign Office response. The documents were reproduced in Oskar Rabinowicz, "New Light on the East Africa Scheme," in *The Rebirth of Israel*, ed. Israel Cohen (London: Goldstein, 1952), 81–91.

35. Quoted in Vital, *Zionism: The Formative Years*, 275.

36. Herzl to Nordau, 13 July 1903, *BT*, 7:207–9.

37. Quoted in David Green, "1903. 'Uganda Plan' Prompts Shooting of Zionist Leader," *Haaretz*, 19 December 2013; https://www.haaretz.com/jewish/.premium-1903-zionist-leader-gets-shot-at-1.5301541 (accessed 16 September 2018).

38. 23 December 1903, *BT*, 7:487.

39. Quoted in Vital, *Zionism: The Formative Years*, 343–44.

40. CZA, Z1/198, 759–60.

41. *CD*, 1605–6 (26 and 27 January 1904).

42. Herzl to Hans Herzl, 9 May 1904, *BT*, 7:581.

43. Herzl to Wolffsohn, 6 May 1904; Herzl to Julie Herzl, 8 May 1904; Herzl to Jeanette Herzl, 20 May 1904; *BT*, 7:578, 580–81, 588.

44. Herzl to Jeanette Herzl, 25 June 1904, *BT*, 7:591.

45. Rosenberger, 240–41.

46. Stefan Zweig, *The World of Yesterday* (Lincoln: University of Nebraska Press, 1964), 109.

47. Reproduced in Mordechai Friedman, *The Bush Burned, and It Was Consumed* [Hebrew] (Jerusalem: World Zionist Organization, 2015), 298.

48. Ibid., 336.

49. *NFP*, 4 July 1904, 7.

50. Quoted in Andrea Livnat, *Der Prophet des Staates: Theodor Herzl im kollektiven Gedächtnis Israels* (Frankfurt a. M.: Campus, 2011), 44–45.

Epilogue

1. Andrea Livnat, *Der Prophet des Staates: Theodor Herzl im kollektiven Gedächtnis Israels* (Frankfurt a. M.: Campus, 2011), 86.

2. Quoted in Georges Yitshak Weisz, *Theodor Herzl: A New*

Reading (Jerusalem: Gefen and the World Zionist Organization, 2013), 15.

3. See "Hadag Nachash Gabi veDebi," at http://www.youtube .com/watch?v=uU-n3LzuIPU, accessed September 6, 2019.

ACKNOWLEDGMENTS

I AM GRATEFUL to Anita Shapira and Steven Zipperstein for inviting me to write on Herzl for Yale University Press's Jewish Lives series. It has been a pleasure working with Linda Kurz, Heather Gold, Susan Laity, and Joyce Ippolito. My agent, Beverley Slopin, has been a constant source of support and sound editorial advice.

Kathrin Bachleitner, Juliane Beck, Marco Brandl, Nimrod Lin, and Ela Anna Naegele provided invaluable research assistance. The staff of the Central Zionist Archive in Jerusalem patiently helped me navigate the now-digitized Herzl archive, and I had the great pleasure of perusing the massive private collection of Herzliana acquired by David Matlow, an attorney in Toronto.

I have had the good fortune to benefit from illuminating comments and criticisms from colleagues in many countries: in the United Kingdom, Peter Bergamin, Michael Berkowitz, David Cesarani (z"l), Faisal Devji, David Feldman, Peter Ghosh, Abigail Green, Todd Hall, Ruth Harris, Sara Hirschhorn, Yaron Peleg, and David Rechter; in Germany, Johannes Becke and Michael

Brenner; in Hungary, Zsófia Mészáros and Michael Miller; in Israel, Gur Alroey, Motti Friedman, Daniel Gutwein, Amos Morris-Reich, Orit Rozin, Hizky Shoham, Dmitry Shumsky, Michael Silber, and Scott Ury; in Canada, Emanuel Adler, Doris Bergen, Eric Jennings, Ivan Kalmar, Jacques Kornberg, James Retallack, and Anna Shternshis; and in the United States, David Biale, Nina Caputo, Arie Dubnov, John Efron, Judith Gurwich, Alison Frank Johnson, Jonathan Gribetz, Liora Halperin, Mitchell Hart, Eran Kaplan, Pnina Lahav, Yehudah Mirsky, Eugene Sheppard, Kenneth Stern, and Yael Zerubavel. Readings of the manuscript by two medical doctors—an internist (Richard Kravitz) and a psychiatrist (Michael Rosenbluth)—corrected embarrassing errors and offered cogent observations on the challenges of retrospective diagnosis.

The subject of a biography becomes an invisible yet constant presence in the biographer's family. My wife Robin put up with our house guest's extended stay with patience and grace. Our elder child, Josh, who is training to be a pediatric cardiologist, read the manuscript with an eye to Herzl's heart problems, while his sibling Emmett, a gifted wordsmith, provided rigorous line editing. Josh's wife Marisa, who is a native speaker of German, helped with knotty translation problems. My gratitude and love go to them all.

A few weeks before I submitted the manuscript to the Press, our granddaughter Selma took her first steps. This book is dedicated to her.

INDEX

Abdul Hamid II (sultan), 100, 101, 125,
    141, 145, 156–57
Adler, Hermann, 107
agricultural cooperatives, 165–66,
    174–75, 181, 192, 195
Ahad Ha-Am, 96, 117, 158, 175–76
Ahmet Tevfik Pasha, 144
Akademische Lesehalle (Academic
    Reading Hall), 24–25
Albia (fraternity), 25, 26, 130
Algeria, antisemitism in, 88, 135
Alkalai, Yehuda, 15
Alliance Israélite Universelle, 86
Alroey, Gur, 223n34
anarchism, 48, 58, 77
Anglo-Palestine Bank, 195
anticlericalism, 14
antisemitism: in Algeria, 88, 135; in
    Austria, 59, 68, 81, 88; and
    capitalism, 7, 106; and Christian
    Social movement, 59–60; and
    Dreyfus trial, 68–69; emancipa-

tion provoking, 63; in European
    political atmosphere, 26; in
    France, 56–57, 88, 134; in Ger-
    many, 88; in Hungary, 21; Jewish
    state seen as remedy for, 87–88,
    94; and Panama Canal Company
    scandal, 56; Rathenau on, 165;
    in Romania, 87–88; in Russia,
    87–88, 151, 186
anxiety, Herzl's struggles with, 3, 29,
    43, 132
Arabs: Herzl's views on, 9, 146, 169,
    183, 204; Israeli-Palestinian
    reconciliation, 209
Arendt, Hannah, 66
Argentina, Jewish settlements in, 72,
    90
Artin Dadyan Pasha, 150
Ashkenazic Jews, 13–14
assimilation, 61–63, 66, 89, 114, 140,
    181, 194–95
Auersperg, Leopold, 128

*specific organizations and
individuals*
Zionist Organization, 118–19, 121, 125,
  133, 136, 151, 158, 193
Zion Union of Austrian Societies for

the Colonization of Palestine and
  Syria (Zion Society), 97
Zola, Émile, 52; "*J'Accuse . . . !,*" 69
Zvi, Shabbetai, 117, 176
Zweig, Stefan, 199

Jacob: Unexpected Patriarch, by Yair Zakovitch
Franz Kafka: The Poet of Shame and Guilt, by Saul Friedländer
Rav Kook: Mystic in a Time of Revolution, by Yehudah Mirsky
Stan Lee: A Life in Comics, by Liel Leibovitz
Primo Levi: The Matter of a Life, by Berel Lang
Groucho Marx: The Comedy of Existence, by Lee Siegel
Karl Marx: Philosophy and Revolution, by Shlomo Avineri
Menasseh ben Israel: Rabbi of Amsterdam, by Steven Nadler
Moses Mendelssohn: Sage of Modernity, by Shmuel Feiner
Harvey Milk: His Lives and Death, by Lillian Faderman
Moses: A Human Life, by Avivah Gottlieb Zornberg
Proust: The Search, by Benjamin Taylor
Yitzhak Rabin: Soldier, Leader, Statesman, by Itamar Rabinovich
Walther Rathenau: Weimar's Fallen Statesman, by Shulamit Volkov
Jerome Robbins: A Life in Dance, by Wendy Lesser
Julius Rosenwald: Repairing the World, by Hasia R. Diner
Mark Rothko: Toward the Light in the Chapel,
     by Annie Cohen-Solal
Gershom Scholem: Master of the Kabbalah, by David Biale
Solomon: The Lure of Wisdom, by Steven Weitzman
Steven Spielberg: A Life in Films, by Molly Haskell
Alfred Stieglitz: Taking Pictures, Making Painters, by Phyllis Rose
Barbra Streisand: Redefining Beauty, Femininity, and Power,
     by Neal Gabler
Leon Trotsky: A Revolutionary's Life, by Joshua Rubenstein
Warner Bros: The Making of an American Movie Studio,
     by David Thomson

FORTHCOMING TITLES INCLUDE:

Judah Benjamin, by James Traub
Franz Boas, by Noga Arikha